The
Whimsical Bakehouse
Collection

LITTLE CAKES and KIDS' CAKES

kaye hansen & liv hansen

PHOTOGRAPHS BY BEN FINK

Clarkson Potter/Publishers
New York

Published in the United States by Clarkson Potter/Publishers,
an imprint of the Crown Publishing Group, a division of Random House LLC,
a Penguin Random House Company, New York.

www.crownpublishing.com
www.clarksonpotter.com

CLARKSON POTTER is a trademark and POTTER with colophon is a
registered trademark of Random House LLC.

Little Cakes from the Whimsical Bakehouse and *Kids' Cakes from the Whimsical Bakehouse*
were originally published separately by Clarkson Potter/Publishers, an imprint of the Crown
Publishing Group, a division of Random House LLC, New York, in 2008 and 2010, respectively.

A Cataloging-in-Publication record has been established for *Little Cakes from the Whimsical
Bakehouse* under the ISBN 9780307382825 and for *Kids' Cakes from the Whimsical Bakehouse*
under the ISBN 9780307463845

ISBN: 978-0-385-36438-6

Printed in China

Cover design by Jeff Kenyon

Little Cakes from the Whimsical Bakehouse: Design by Laura Palese; Photographs by Ben Fink

Kids' Cakes from the Whimsical Bakehouse: Design by Amy Sly; Photographs by Ben Fink

First Omnibus Edition

LITTLE CAKES

·····from the·····

whimsical bakehouse

kaye hansen & liv hansen

PHOTOGRAPHS BY BEN FINK

Clarkson Potter/Publishers
New York

For KASE,
our best little one

a c k n o w l e d g m e n t s

Wow, round three. To everyone who found inspiration in our first two books, thank you. Without you our little cakes would not have been baked and decorated. Our home testers and Bakehouse members—Jaime Raucci, Mariana Cintron, Sara Romeo, Traci Sherman, and Jessica DiPaci—thank you for giving us peace of mind. Laura Palese, thank you for your spooky inspirations. And of course what would we do without the usual suspects, Carla Glasser, Ben Fink, Aliza Fogelson, and the Bakehouse staff and customers?

contents

introduction

What is the allure of little cakes? Are they reminiscent of the magical tea parties we delighted in when we were small and the world seemed so big? Like chocolate, do they comfort our soul? Whether or not it's the child inside us that creates the appetite for these diminutive cakes, let's hope it stays, because little cakes are fun to make and fun to eat. After all, we all need a bit, and a bite, of joy in our lives.

Since the beginning of my decorating career, I have been fascinated with all things small. Even though I have been assisting my mom, Kaye, making her buttercream roses since I was ten, I didn't start experimenting with icing and chocolate until she opened up the Riviera Bakehouse in 1994, and we started our collaboration. My first decorating efforts graced the tops of cupcakes, an easy place to start for the novice. I covered them with piped buttercream spirals, polka dots, and stars in a festive palette. The first holiday I worked at the bakery was Halloween, and when we tested these simple though colorful treats with the public, they were a hit. Now our Halloween cupcakes go far beyond their simple roots, and although we still make some of the "old-fashioned" kind, each year I create new designs to delight our customers.

These days you may have noticed that cupcakes are BIG. Not just in size, although the Bakehouse does make a large cake that is decorated to look like a giant cupcake, but big in that they are ubiquitous. And we can't help ourselves; we love them too, not just the classic vanilla but carrot, lemon poppy, and caramel. These little gems are versatile; you can add dimension by applying chocolate decorations or go for a bit of trompe l'oeil by making the top look like a blooming rose or a basket. The options seem endless.

But your exploration of baking and decorating small cakes does not have to begin and end with cupcakes. My first foray into the world of miniature delights was not a petit four, but a four-inch chocolate cake that I baked and iced in bright sorbet colors and decorated with colored polka dots. My mom and I named it the Spring Fling. Ten years later we still make it. You, too, can find inspiration in the wide range of small cake pans that are on the market today, from 6-inch round cake pans right down to 2-inch round pans, from standard to mini muffin tins, from miniature Bundt to individual cheesecake pans. And as for 3-D or shaped pans, wow, I have found hemispheres, squares, cones, roses, sunflowers, ghosts, eggs, ice cream cones, hearts, bears, trains, wedding cakes, and more. Most of the time, just baking in one of these specialty molds will yield a cake that is pleasing to the eye. Add a little color, a dab of buttercream, a drizzle of chocolate, or a dusting of confectioners' sugar and voilà! Of course, most of the time I let my whimsical side run rampant, and before I know it, what was once a simple cone has become a witch's hat, a Christmas tree, or a shark breaching the water's surface.

Although the recipes in this book were baked in small pans, they can be baked in standard round or sheet pans as well. In fact many of these recipes come from the stock cake collection at our bakery. Whenever we whip up a batch of cheesecakes we bake most of the batter in our standard 7-inch round pans but we also set some aside to bake in individual-size ramekins. In this book we bake our Red Velvet cake in a small cone pan and decorate it to look like a shark, but we also use this recipe at the bakery to make the classic Red Velvet cake iced with Kids' Buttercream. So don't feel limited by size or flavor. We encourage you to mix and match recipes and designs. If Caramel Cake is your favorite but you have your heart set on making Basket Cupcakes, just switch recipes, adjusting the amount of batter or icing accordingly. For the most part, all of the recipes are interchangeable, with the possible exception of the cheesecakes, meringues, cream puffs, and truffles, which don't lend themselves to being baked in shaped pans, or to being filled or sculpted.

Because little cakes are lighthearted, it is often hard to take them seriously. Without a doubt there will be a sense of whimsy, but we'll also show you how a few simple touches transform little cakes into delicate and beautiful desserts. Take the Bakehouse's signature Mini Birthday Cake as an example. It is decorated with six bright colors, piped swags, borders, and edible candles . . . to say the least, it is an eye catcher. But erase the neon palette and you could be looking at a tier of a traditional wedding cake. Instead of using vivid colors, choose a softer palette, tone on tone, or all white. Instead of overpowering the presentation with too much decoration, keep it simple. Long the staple of kids' birthday parties, cupcakes are breaking free from their bonds. Now brides and grooms clamor to get their hands on them, too. On page 131 we will show you how to tier your cupcakes on stacked cake pedestals—perfect for a wedding.

The decorating process does not have to be daunting; in fact, a simple but creative presentation will add panache to little cakes. Fortunately, my mom's wonderful recipes are tasty enough to satisfy anyone. By serving the Pistachio Ganache Truffles in a pool of Caramel Sauce on a beautiful plate, you can set a seductive mood. Or by arranging your cupcakes on stacked pedestal cake plates or a wire pastry tree you are creating a playful centerpiece. Throughout the book we will give decorating, plating, and arranging tips to help you create the aura you want.

The level of difficulty of the sweets and the decorations ranges from simple to advanced, and will be noted in the recipe title, from one star, indicating a recipe or design that is easy to make or decorate, up to three stars for a challenging cake. Whenever possible we will offer alternatives to simplify the designs (see Simple Decorating Tips, page 37). Most recipes can stand on their own without decoration, while others deserve to be over the top. Explore and see which recipes and designs bring a smile to your face and a grumble of anticipation to your belly, and then go for it. My mom and I both love the thrill of trying something new, whether it is a recipe or a decorating technique, and even more we love seeing the delighted reaction of our customers and coworkers. Or why not create just for your own fulfillment? After all, what is more whimsical than a miniature cake just for you—one you don't have to share. We hope you find inspiration within these pages to venture out into new territory.

—Liv Hansen

GETTING STARTED

If you are like me, you probably want to dive in and tackle a recipe or design.

I am known for decorating cakes on a whim with little planning and a lot of surprise results. Luckily I am often rewarded with beautiful or kooky cakes, but that's after a long road of trial and error, from which I learn from mistakes and, through experimentation, discover new ways of decorating. Even if you are a bit impatient to get started, I recommend reading through this chapter. It contains invaluable information on tools of the trade, helpful baking and decorating tips, tricks for assembling little cakes, icing recipes, and hints for working with chocolate and decorating techniques that appear throughout the book.

tools of the trade

Here is a list of the basic tools you need to bake and decorate little cakes. Included is a chart to help you sort through the multitude of baking pans we used in this book.

Tools for Baking and Decorating

- **Bases**—Every dessert, from the lowly cupcake right up to a tiered wedding cake, needs something to be served on. It may be a napkin or it may be fine china. At the Bakehouse we cover cardboard rounds with decorative foil or doilies. It is easy, inexpensive, transportable, and disposable. Just make sure the base you choose fits the cake you plan on making. Ideally the base, whether it is a cake plate, cardboard round, or dessert plate, is sturdy and flat and at least 2 inches larger than the cake itself.

  - **Cardboard**—Even little cakes need a stable base for assemblage and presentation. Cardboard rounds make it easier to handle the cakes and give a clean edge for icing. You can purchase precut rounds in a variety of sizes; or, if you can't get your hands on the shape or size you need, trace your cake pan (or cake) onto a sheet of corrugated cardboard and cut it out with scissors. Cover cardboard rounds with decorative foil and you have a perfect portable and disposable base for your decorated cake.

  - **Cellophane**—At the Bakehouse we like to make our small pastry cones out of cellophane instead of parchment paper because they maintain a clean, sharp point as you work. We get 1.25 ml thick cellophane in precut 10" x 10" squares from our paper supplier. If you don't want to search the web for this product, you can buy cellophane by the roll at craft stores. Cut the roll of cellophane into 10-inch squares, and then cut these squares in half diagonally. With the hypotenuse, or longest side, of the triangle facing up, hold each of the two acute-angled points separately between your thumb and fingers. First curl the top right point downward, wrapping under itself until it lines up with the left side of the right angle. Hold this in place while you wrap the top left point down and around the back of the pastry cone until it lines up with the right side of the right angle. Adjust the cellophane with your thumbs inside and your pointer fingers outside until a sharp point forms. Tape close to the base to maintain the cone shape. Cellophane is also a great surface on which to pipe out chocolate decorations. Parchment will work fine as a substitute for making pastry cones and as a design work surface.

- Cake pans—See chart on pages 16–17.

- Coupler and ring—See Pastry bag, below.

- Electric mixer—This modern convenience is very handy; at the bakery, it is essential. Any brand will do, but we recommend the reliable 5-quart KitchenAid. With some elbow grease, most cake recipes can be made without the aid of an electric mixer. Handheld mixers also get the job done.

- Metal spatula—Metal spatulas come in all shapes and sizes. The small offset spatula (4½ inches), which we refer to at the Bakehouse as a "baby bent," is great for spreading icing on cupcakes or for any other small and delicate task. This may be the only spatula you need, but I find the 10-inch offset spatula useful for icing some of the "larger" cakes.

- Muffin scoop—We use muffin scoops, much like an ice cream scoop, to scoop muffin and cake batter into their small pans. Scoops are neat, and they evenly divide the batter, which allows for a consistent result. There are many scoops on the market; we recommend buying one with a spring-action lever that cleans out the inner shell of the scoop.

- Paint brush—Soft sable or acrylic brushes are used to paint with melted chocolate. For detailed shading I recommend using a #0, 1, or 2 brush.

- Parchment paper—This versatile paper is similar to wax paper, but without the wax coating. Use it to line cake pans to prevent baked goods from sticking. Chocolate doesn't stick to it, either, so any chocolate design, no matter how delicate, can be piped onto it. See Cellophane, above, for instructions for making a cone.

- **Pastry bag**—These cone-shaped bags make piping decorations a breeze. We recommend 12-inch polyester bags, which can be washed and reused. Disposable ones are available, but they are not as strong. The coupler, a plastic insert, allows you to change tips with ease. The ring screws on the outside of the bag and coupler to secure the tip in place. As an alternative, you can place a tip directly inside a bag without a coupler. Just make sure the hole is not too big, or the tip will slip right out. If you do not have a pastry bag handy, you can always make a pastry cone with parchment paper or cellophane (see Cellophane, above).

- **Pastry cones**—See Cellophane or Parchment paper, above.

- **Rubber spatula**—Like bowls or knives, a spatula is one of those items we find essential at the Bakehouse. Spatulas are perfect for scraping down your mixing bowl and mixing colors into buttercream or white wafer chocolate.

- **Scraper**—To ice a cake to a smooth finish, we often use a flat-edged metal or plastic scraper instead of a metal spatula. A bench scraper with a rolled handle can do the job as well. One side of the scraper rests flat on a turntable while the other edge runs flush with the cake, making for a steadier hand and a smooth finish. They are difficult to find, but if you decorate cakes often, it is worth the search.

- **Straws**—For the small-tiered cakes featured in this book, drinking straws are used to support the tiers. Drinking straws can also be used to make chocolate candles (see Adventurous Alternative, page 94).

- **Tips**—There is a special tip for almost every piping application. For a good selection of tips, I recommend buying a starter set. Tips can also be purchased individually. Before starting any design, make sure you have the appropriate tips. When applicable, I have noted alternative tips that can be used to achieve similar piping results. Check the suppliers listed on page 174 to order individual tips or sets.

- Turntable—Similar to a lazy Susan, a turntable makes icing a cake more efficient and neat. I use a heavy-duty metal turntable made by Ateco. They are expensive, but they're worth the money if you decorate cakes often.

- Wire cooling rack—These wire racks are used to cool cakes. We often place the pan itself on the rack to cool, rather than removing the hot cakes from their pans right away. They are also indispensable when glazing cakes or making chocolate molds.

Special Ingredients for Decorating

- Food coloring—We depend on liquid gel colors (a professional product) for achieving our vivid icing hues. They are sold at most high-end baking supply stores or through mail order. However, paste colors, which are more readily available, work just as well. Liquid colors, available at most grocery stores, can be used, but the palette is limited and they are less concentrated. For coloring the wafer chocolate, we use candy colors. These oil-based colors are used by confectioners to tint white chocolate; find them at candy-making specialty stores, craft stores, or from mail-order sources.

- Sprinkles/nonpareils—These are perfect for making any little cake festive and fun. You can even mix them into some cake batters to create a colorful confetti surprise.

- Wafer chocolate—Wafer chocolate is actually not chocolate; it is a candy coating also known as confectioners' chocolate. It is easier to work with than chocolate because it does not need to be tempered (so it stays shiny after it resolidifies). It comes in dark chocolate, white chocolate, and a limited range of colors. For more information on decorating with chocolate see pages 39—43.

Nowadays, miniature cake pans come in all different "little" shapes. In addition to cupcake pans and small cake pans, we have found many fun pans with shaped molds, from hearts to trains and from miniature Bundts to pans specially made for cheesecakes. In addition to the classic metal pans, and non-stick pans, many of the mini cake forms are now made out of nonstick silicone. We still prefer the metal or nonstick kind, because we found that cakes baked in silicone tend to burn more easily. But I did find a use for some of the silicone molds: they were great as chocolate molds.

Cake Pans	Pan Size	Mold Size	Batter Capacity	No. of Molds
MINI MUFFFIN/ CUPCAKE	10" x 15"	1¾" across x 1" deep	1½ tablespoons	24
STANDARD MUFFIN/ CUPCAKE	7" x 11"	2¾" across x 1½" deep	¼ to ⅓ cup	6
	11" x 15"	2¾" across x 1½" deep	¼ to ⅓ cup	12
		2¾" across x 1½" deep	¼ to ⅓ cup	24
JUMBO (GIANT) MUFFIN	10" x 13½"	3¾" across x 1¾" deep	⅔ to ¾ cup	6
MINI ROSE PAN	12" round	2½" inch round	¼ cup	12
CONE PAN (MINI WONDER MOLD)	10" x 10"	3½" across x 3" deep	¾ cup	4
ICE CREAM CONE PAN	10" round	2¾" across x 3" deep	½ cup	6
MINI BOWL PAN	8" x 12"	3" across x 1½" deep	¼ to ⅓ cup	6
MINI TIERED PAN SET	4", 3", 2" round	2" deep	1 cup, ½ cup, ¼ cup	1 each
4-INCH ROUND	4" round	3" deep	1½ cups	1

Cake Pans	Pan Size	Mold Size	Batter Capacity	No. of Molds
6-INCH ROUND	6" round	3" deep	3 cups	1
SCALLOPED MINI HEART PAN	11½" x 15"	3¾" across x 3¾" deep	¾ cup	6
MINI SQUARE PAN	11" x 15"	2½" x 2½" x 1½" deep	½ cup	12
MINI CHEESECAKE PAN		2" across x 1½" deep	¼ cup	12
MINI HEART CHEESECAKE PAN	10½" x 14"	2" deep	¼ cup	12
PINEAPPLE UPSIDE DOWN	9½" x 12"	1½" deep	½ cup	6
MINI BUNDT PAN	9" x 13"	3¾" across x 1¾" deep	½ cup	6
TWINKIE PAN	9" x 13"	4½" across x 1½" deep	⅓ cup	8
SILICONE MUFFIN/ CUPCAKE LINERS	set of 6 or 12	2¾" across x 1½" deep	¼ to ⅓ cup	6 or 12
HALF-SHEET PAN	12" x 16"	12" x 16" x 1"	6 cups	1

baking tips

We hope these useful hints will help you bake even more delicious goodies.

- It probably goes without saying, but please make sure you have all of the ingredients and equipment you need before you start a recipe. We also recommend familiarizing yourself with a recipe by giving it a read through before you begin.

- Always remember to preheat your oven. This will help ensure that the cakes bake properly. Ideally have an oven thermometer to check the temperature. One of our cake testers was having difficulty getting the proper rising and baking times for some cakes when she discovered her oven was not the correct temperature.

- Carefully measure all of your ingredients because baking is a science; it requires accuracy.

- Unless otherwise noted, it is important to have your ingredients, especially your butter and eggs, at room temperature. This will facilitate the creaming and mixing process.

- Unless otherwise noted, use a paddle attachment for combining ingredients in an electric mixer.

- Always remember to scrape down your mixing bowl often with a spatula, being careful to get all the way to the bottom of the bowl where sometimes the paddle or whip does not reach. This will ensure that all of the ingredients are well combined.

- If you don't have enough pans to bake all of your little cakes at once, use just one pan and bake in batches. Since the baking times are so short, the batter can be left at room temperature. Meringues, however, cannot sit out; they must be baked immediately.

- Most cakes have a rather short shelf life: only 2 to 5 days in an airtight container in the refrigerator or from 2 to 3 days at room temperature. But most cakes can be frozen after baking. We always store our unassembled and undecorated cakes and cupcakes in the freezer. Keeping them chilled makes them less likely to crumble and fall apart during decorating. Once they have cooled, wrap in plastic wrap and, if sealed well, they can last up to 1 month in the freezer. To thaw, place the cake, still wrapped, in the refrigerator overnight. Remove from the refrigerator when you are ready to assemble or ice. Alternatively, take the cake out of the freezer, still wrapped, and let it sit for 5 minutes (approximate time for a cupcake) to 30 minutes (approximate time for a 6-inch round), depending on the size. So if you know you will be short on time later, bake your cakes now, freeze, and assemble or decorate them the day you need them, or even the day before.

- Bundt cakes and pound cakes can be made in advance. Simply pour the batter into the pregreased pan or pans you plan on baking in. Wrap in plastic wrap and store in the refrigerator for up to 2 days or in the freezer for up to a month (or more if the wrapping is airtight). Simply remove from the refrigerator or freezer and let come to room temperature before baking.

- If you plan on serving your cakes a day or more after they are baked/decorated, or if it is a very hot day, chill the cakes until 1 to 4 hours before serving. For the fullest flavor, we recommend serving our little cakes at room temperature. In warmer weather, it will take less time for your cake to reach room temperature, but cakes iced in buttercream, as long as they are not in direct sunlight, can still be taken out of the refrigerator hours before serving. In cold weather you can leave a cake out anywhere from 3 hours to all day. Once a cake has come to room temperature try not to move it, because the layers might shift, and the design might break.

- Most cake and muffin recipes can be baked in cupcake papers.

- Never over-mix muffin or quick bread batters.

- Muffin batter or quick bread batters can be made up to 1 week ahead and stored in the refrigerator in an airtight container. Just scoop and bake whenever you want the aroma of freshly baked muffins to fill the air.

- We recommend using a muffin scoop, one with a spring-action lever, for scooping muffin and cake batter into their small molds. Not only is it neater, but you can divide the batter evenly.

- It is helpful to have a small ounce scale in the kitchen. It facilitates the measuring of chocolate, nuts, and other ingredients that are sold in ounces.

Notes on Baking Ingredients

- **Butter**—In our opinion, for taste purposes, butter is always superior to shortening or oil. But some of our muffin and icing recipes do call for the substitutes. When baking, use unsalted butter and unless otherwise noted, work with your butter at room temperature.

- **Kosher salt**—We use kosher salt at the bakery but table salt can be substituted measure for measure.

- **Pure vanilla extract**—For me there is no substitute for pure vanilla extract. The artificial extracts often leave a perfumed taste in your mouth.

- **High-ratio shortening**—A specialty product for bakers, high-ratio shortening contains emulsifiers that allow it to remain stable at a wider range of temperatures and enable it to hold more air when beaten, making icings fluffier. It can also incorporate more sugar and liquid than regular shortening without breaking, and it accepts coloring agents better. You can purchase this product through baking wholesalers (under the name Quick Blend) and on the web, from suppliers like countrykitchensa.com and cookscakeandcandy.com. Home use brand names include Alpine Hi-Ratio shortening and Sweetex. If you cannot get this product, however, the results you'll get with regular shortening will be fine.

- **Chocolate**—Most of the chocolate we bake with is either semisweet chocolate or cocoa powder. We use Dutch processed cocoa powder at the bakery as opposed to regular (Hershey's) cocoa powder. *Hershey's cocoa powder is good for Red Velvet cake, because its acidity creates a redder final product versus the darker chocolaty color of Dutch cocoa.* You can buy semisweet chocolate at the grocery store. It is normally sold in a break-apart tablet that is calibrated in ounces. This makes it easy to measure out the chocolate for your recipes.

filling, crumbing, & icing
LITTLE CAKES & CUPCAKES

In our first book, we filled and iced all of our cakes in the same manner. We approached all the little cakes in this book differently. To address these variations we have broken down this section into three parts: Filling, Crumbing, and Icing. But first there are some things you should know before working with any of the cakes.

- Never work with a warm cake, because it will crumble easily and melt the icing. Chilling the cake in the refrigerator for a few hours or overnight makes it much easier to work with. More often than not, we work with our cupcakes directly from the freezer. They defrost so quickly that by the time it comes to decorating them they have already partially or totally thawed. You can also wrap a cooled cake tightly in plastic wrap and freeze it for up to 1 month, letting it thaw when ready to use.

- If you plan on filling your creation, to ensure stability, your fillings should be as stiff as possible.

- Buttercream is the most stable of our icings. It holds up well under most weather conditions, unlike whipped cream, and acts as a protective shell, keeping the cake and filling fresh.

- Most muffins and cupcakes are served in their own paper liners. Other cakes need a base from which to serve them. This base could be a plate, a cupcake tree, or a cardboard round. Whatever the base, make sure it is large enough and strong enough to support and complete your cake with the decorations you have envisioned.

FILLING

Filling a Cupcake

It is an unexpected delight when you bite into a cupcake and discover a filling, even if it is just a morsel of mousse. You can tackle the task of filling a cupcake a few different ways. For each technique listed below, first remove the cupcakes from the freezer or refrigerator and let them come to room temperature.

1. The easiest way to fill a cupcake is to slice the top off of any cake that rises above the paper liner, pipe a giant swirl of mousse on the bottom, and replace the top. It won't resemble a cupcake anymore but it will definitely be delicious. If you want to ice the cupcake, simply pipe more mousse or icing on top.

2. A more discreet way to fill a cupcake is to slice the top off of the cupcake and set it aside. With a melon baller, or a small paring knife, scoop out a 1-inch-deep by 1-inch-wide cavity from the center of the cupcake; discard or snack on this piece. Fill this cavity with whatever filling you desire and replace the top. Chill for 15 minutes to 1 hour before icing and/or decorating.

3. The final option is the most amazing, but it will only work with light cakes, not dense cakes such as pound cake. Place the filling in a pastry bag with a coupler. Attach a round tip (#8, 9, or 10). Insert the tip of the pastry bag into the top of the cupcake and squeeze.* Continue squeezing until the filling just begins to seep out around the tip's edge. You will actually feel the cupcake expand in your hands as it fills. If desired, insert the tip again into another spot, being sure to stay at least $1/2$ inch from the side of the cupcake.

* To fill Cream Puffs, Nostalgic Nibbles, and Devilish Delights, follow the directions from step 3, but instead of inserting the pastry tip into the top, invert the pastry and insert the tip into the underside. This will keep the top surface unblemished.

Filling a Cake

It is quite simple to fill a little cake. Because the layers of cake are so small and the filling layers are so thin, there is no need to "ring the cake" as we do with our large cakes.

1. Let the cakes cool completely; preferably chill them for a few hours.

2. Start by leveling the cakes. Most cakes form a rounded dome when they are baked, so you will need to level the tops. Use a serrated knife and, keeping the knife horizontal, use a sawing action to cut off the rounded portions.

3. Cut the cakes into 3 layers (we recommend anywhere from two to four layers from one cake). To cut even layers, place the cake on a turntable. Rotate the turntable, lightly scoring the cake with a serrated knife at the place where it is to be cut in halves or thirds. Make sure the cut line is level and divides the cake equally. With your hand lightly resting on the cake to hold it steady, rotate the turntable as you use a sawing action to cut the cake along the guideline.

4. Adhere the bottom layer of the cake to the center of a cardboard round (or a portable base) with a drop of buttercream if you like. If the cake protrudes over the cardboard, trim the sides; but it should be no more than ⅛ inch from the cardboard edge.

5. Carefully set aside the top two layers of the cake. Spread half of the filling evenly over the first layer. The filling should be thin, no thicker than ¼ inch, and within the bounds of the cake's edge. This will make it easier to crumb-coat the cake.

6. Place the second layer of cake on top of the first, making sure it is centered and level. Spread the remaining filling on top of this layer. Place the final layer of cake on top, pressing gently with your hand to level the cake.

CRUMBING

Crumbing is the process of sealing an entire cake with a thin coating of icing. This "crumb coat" traps any stray or excess crumbs, sealing them in, thus creating a smooth backdrop for piped, spread, and applied decorations. Once chilled, this layer will also prevent crumbs from appearing in your final coat of icing.

Cupcakes in general do not need to be crumbed because they are not sliced. Even the filled ones usually have at most a few crumbs because the tops are replaced, sealing in any potential mess. On the other hand, cakes that are sliced and/or filled will generally need to be crumbed.

Crumbing a Cake

In nearly every case, you should use the same icing to crumb the cake that you will use to finish it. If you are planning on finishing with a color, however, your cake should be crumbed with uncolored buttercream, so don't tint your buttercream until you are ready to apply the finishing touches.

1. Place the filled cake in the center of the turntable.

2. Place a small amount of icing on top of the cake. With a metal spatula, spread the icing evenly over the entire top of the cake, making it as smooth as possible. Use the excess icing that comes over the edge to cover the sides. If necessary add more icing to cover the sides of the cake with a smooth coat. If you have your cake on a cardboard round, do not let the icing extend over this board. If your cake is rounded, to smooth the icing, hold a 2 x 10-inch strip of cellophane at both ends and drag it over the cake, starting at the bottom. The cellophane will curve to the shape of the cake, unlike a metal spatula.

3. Chill the cake. Cakes crumbed in buttercream should be refrigerated for at least 15 minutes or until the buttercream has set. Cakes crumbed with Whipped Cream (see page 35) or Whipped Chocolate Ganache (see page 82) should be placed in the freezer just until set (30 minutes to 2 hours, depending on your freezer). (Do not remove cakes crumbed with Whipped Chocolate Ganache until just before glazing.)

ICING

For some of us it's all about the icing. Moms, dads, and children alike devour sweet and glorious icing with glee. Kids may be notorious for fighting over buttercream roses, but I've known some grown-ups who will polish off any icing other people leave on their plates. Whether it is my mom's rich and buttery Italian meringue buttercream (Kaye's Buttercream) or decadent Chocolate Glaze, you will find yourself enjoying icing more than ever, maybe even stealing a bite from a loved one, after trying our recipes.

Each type of icing lends itself to a different application. Buttercreams can be made textured or flat, whereas poured glazes have a smooth glow whether they ice a shaped or flat cake. See which style and flavor goes best with your dessert.

Old-Fashioned Icing on a Cake or Cupcake

Keep it simple. Envision the cake on the cover of a Betty Crocker box and you will know what I mean. Old-fashioned icings, like Kids' Buttercream and Matt's Fudge Icing, are a dream to work with. Not only are they easy to whip up, but their texture is fluffy and application to cakes is easy to master. A slight flourish of the spatula, and you are finished.

To achieve this look we recommend Kids' Buttercream, Peanut Butter Icing, Whipped Cream, or Matt's Fudge Icing (see pages 33–35).

1. To ice, simply place a nice-size dollop of frosting on top of your cupcake or little cake; for a standard cupcake we recommend 2 tablespoons of icing.

2. With a small metal spatula, spread the icing so that it covers all of the exposed cake. Then create a textured pattern on the cake by pushing into the icing with the spatula and then pulling straight up; or apply light pressure while moving the spatula randomly about the surface of the icing, then glide the spatula off at a 45-degree angle to end the pattern. Anyone can do this.

3. If you plan on adding sprinkles or chocolate shavings, do so right away because the old-fashioned icings tend to form a hard shell quickly.

Smooth (Flat) Icing on a Cupcake

Instead of going for the traditional icing on a cupcake, consider trying a more polished approach. The smooth icing makes a stylish backdrop for buttercream flowers or chocolate decorations.

To achieve this look we recommend Kaye's Buttercream or House Buttercream, although a less refined version can be done with Kids' Buttercream, Peanut Butter Icing, Whipped Cream, or Matt's Fudge Icing (see pages 33–35).

1. Place a nice-size dollop of icing on top of your cupcake; for a standard cupcake we recommend 2 tablespoons of icing.

2. With the full length of a small metal spatula, spread the icing up to, and slightly over, the edge of the cupcake; the blade of the spatula should face away from you as you push away and face toward you as you pull toward you. Keep the spatula level; do not be tempted to follow the curvature of the cupcake edge downward. The icing will be a little thicker on the edges as compared to the center.

3. Hold the blade of the spatula at a 30- to 45-degree angle to the edge of the cupcake, then, holding the cupcake at approximately eye level, with a downward motion of the spatula, scrape off the icing that runs over the edge of the cupcake. Rotate the cupcake and continue scraping off the excess icing. A nice beveled edge should form around the circumference of your cupcake.

4. If desired, roll this beveled edge in nonpareils or sprinkles.

Smooth (Flat) Icing on a Cake

It is very difficult to get icing smooth on a shaped cake, unless the sides and top are straight, as in our beach pail, or evenly curved like our shark; see below, Smooth (Flat) Icing on a Shaped Cake. Even with a standard round cake, mastering a smooth finish will take practice and patience, but the end results will be worth the effort.

To achieve this look we recommend Kaye's Buttercream or House Buttercream, although a less refined version can be done with Kids' Buttercream, Whipped Cream, Peanut Butter Icing, and Matt's Fudge Icing (see pages 33—35).

1. Prepare the icing for the final coat, coloring your buttercream as desired. Place the cake in the center of the turntable.

2. With a metal spatula, spread a small amount of icing evenly over the top of the cake.

3. Ice the sides of the cake. Load the spatula with icing and run the bottom edge of it along the contour of the cardboard or hover just above the crumb coat, being careful to keep the spatula upright. Hold the spatula perpendicular to and flush against the cardboard (or crumb coat) to ensure even distribution of the icing. Reload the spatula as needed until the sides are covered.

4. Smooth the sides by holding the spatula upright against the side of the cake. (Instead of a spatula we often use flat metal or stiff plastic scrapers to make our smooth finish. If you can get your hands on one, it makes the job of icing a lot easier.) Slowly spin the turntable without lifting the spatula from the cake's surface. Remove any excess icing with the spatula. This step is probably the most challenging to master. I find it helpful to have a container of hot water nearby to dip my spatula in before each pass across the cake (dry it off after each dip). The heat will melt the icing, giving it a smooth surface.

5. A lip of excess buttercream will have formed at the top edge of the cake. Use your spatula to gently sweep the excess buttercream toward the center around the entire circumference of the cake until the top is smooth and level.

6. Push the spatula under the cake (and cardboard) and use it as leverage to lift one side of the cake. Place your fingers under this area and drag the spatula to the opposite side of the cake. Carefully lift, with the spatula and fingers, and place the cake on its base. Remove your fingers first, then slide the spatula out; if there is a cardboard round under the cake use glue to adhere it to the base, otherwise a dab of icing will suffice.

Smooth (Flat) Icing on a Shaped Cake

- If your cake is rounded, to smooth the icing, hold a 2 x 10-inch strip of cellophane at both ends and drag the long edge of it over the cake, starting at the bottom. Continue around the circumference of the cake until it is smooth. The cellophane will curve to the shape of the cake, unlike a metal spatula.

- If your cake is square or has corners, first make sure there is enough icing on the top corners (level with the rest of the top). To smooth the sides, with a metal scraper or spatula flatten one side at a time. Work in one direction, using the excess icing that comes over the corner to help smooth the next side. For the last side, slice off the excess icing that comes over the corner. Use your spatula to gently sweep the lip of excess buttercream that forms on the top edge toward the center of the cake.

Simple Glaze on a Cake or Cupcake

To achieve this look we recommend using Simple Glaze (see page 36).

- While the cake or cupcake is still hot, with a rubber spatula or even a soup spoon, dollop the glaze on top (1 tablespoon for a cupcake or muffin and 2 to 3 tablespoons for a mini Bundt cake). Swish the spatula or spoon around until the glaze begins to run over the edge. Let the cake cool and the glaze will form a thin, hard crust as it sets.

- For a different look, drizzle the tops of cooled (un-iced) cakes. The glaze should not run and will hold a linear form. Just keep in mind that if you want the cake to stay fresher longer, it must be kept wrapped in an airtight container.

Chocolate Glaze on a Cupcake

Chocolate Glaze can raise the cupcake's standing to a sophisticated treat or allow the cupcake to bask in the glow of its own whimsy when encrusted with nonpareils or sprinkles. Prefreeze the cupcakes for at least an hour or overnight before glazing; this allows the glaze to chill faster, stay in place, and not drip off the cupcake's edge.

To achieve this look we recommend using Semisweet or Milk Chocolate Glaze or White Chocolate Glaze (see pages 34 and 36).

1. Prepare the glaze. Work with the chocolate glaze at body temperature (approximately 100°F). If you premade the glaze, gently reheat it in the top of a double boiler. Be careful not to overheat the glaze or it will lose its shine, or crack when dry.

2. Take the cupcakes out of the freezer—just a few at a time so they do not stand long enough to sweat. Hold the cupcake firmly by the paper liner and invert it into the pot or bowl of melted glaze. Submerge the cupcake up to the paper line and move it about to ensure the entire surface is covered. Pull the cupcake straight up and gently spin it above the bowl by rotating your wrist, to allow any excess glaze to drip off. Flip the cupcake and carefully place it on a wire rack to set.

3. Allow the glaze to set for 3 to 5 minutes at room temperature before adding sprinkles or chocolate shavings.

Chocolate Glaze on a Cake

Unlike buttercream, which takes practice to get smooth, chocolate glaze pours over the prepared cake surface, hiding most imperfections. Because it is easy to work with, delicious, and beautiful, this is my favorite choice for icing a cake.

Freeze your cakes for one hour before glazing.

To achieve this look we recommend using Semisweet or Milk Chocolate Glaze or White Chocolate Glaze (see pages 34 and 36).

1. Work with the chocolate glaze at body temperature (approximately 100°F). If you premade the glaze, gently reheat it in the top of a double boiler. Be careful not to overheat the glaze or it will lose its shine, crack when dry, or cause the crumb coat to melt.

2. Place a wire cooling rack on a sheet pan and place the filled, crumbed, or plain cakes on top separated by 1 to 2 inches.

3. Pour the glaze into a liquid cup measure to make glazing easier, or pour or ladle the glaze directly around the top edge of the cake, allowing the glaze to run down the sides. Pour the remaining glaze on top. Immediately run a metal spatula over the top of the glaze to push the excess over the sides, being careful not to touch the cake itself. Make sure the sides are covered completely. Shake the sheet pan lightly to help the glaze settle. Let set for 3 to 5 minutes at room temperature before plating.

4. If you like, press chocolate shavings or chocolate sprinkles onto the sides of the cake.

5. Place the cake on its base; if there is a cardboard round under the cake use glue to adhere it to the base, otherwise a dab of glaze will suffice.

Piped Icing on a Cupcake or Cake

Instead of spreading icing on a cupcake or cake, place the icing into a pastry bag with a coupler and tip and pipe it on. A simple spiral of buttercream, piped out of a star tip, will suffice or you can be inventive and cover the top with small stars, dots, or flowers (see Flower Power, page 131). Basket weave, a traditional covering for cakes, takes a fun twist when it tops our Basket Cupcakes and our Straw Hat. Just keep in mind that if you want the cake to stay fresher longer, you must make sure the piping completely covers the cake surface, or consider crumbing your cake first (see page 24). See page 38 for more piping tips.

To achieve this look we recommend using Kaye's Buttercream or House Buttercream, although a less refined version can be done with Kids' Buttercream or Peanut Butter Icing (see pages 31–34).

pan ease

If you bake often at home this recipe is indispensable. Like most bakeries, we use pan ease to grease our pans. It is very economical and convenient, with a long shelf life. Just brush it on the pans and you are good to go.

In the bowl of an electric mixer, mix with a paddle attachment until smooth:

- 2 cups shortening
- ½ cup all-purpose flour

Using a whisk attachment add:

- ½ cup plus 1 tablespoon vegetable oil

At high speed, beat until light and fluffy.

Store at room temperature in an airtight container.

house buttercream** YIELD: 4¾ CUPS

Unlike Kaye's Buttercream (see page 32), this icing contains some shortening. Not only does this ingredient create a lighter flavor, it also gives this buttercream its pure whiteness, making it ideal for mixing with colors. We use high-ratio shortening, which can be found at any good cake decorating supply store, or online; high-ratio shortening does not affect the taste, but it does increase the buttercream's ability to accept color. If you can't find high-ratio shortening, substitute regular vegetable shortening.

House Buttercream can be stored in an airtight container at room temperature for up to 3 days and in the refrigerator for up to 3 weeks. To use the chilled buttercream, bring it to room temperature and beat at medium speed in the bowl of an electric mixer until smooth and creamy. To speed up this process you can lightly reheat the buttercream, in its mixing bowl, over a hot-water bath, before beating.

In the bowl of an electric mixer at low speed, stir together:

- 3 cups confectioners' sugar
- ¼ teaspoon salt
- ½ teaspoon pure vanilla extract

With a whisk attachment, add and whip at low speed:

- ½ cup boiling water (⅓ cup on hot days)

Whip until smooth and cool.

Add and whip until smooth:

- 1½ cups high-ratio shortening
- 3 ounces (¾ stick) slightly chilled unsalted butter, cut into 1-inch pieces

Increase the mixer speed to medium-high. Whip until light, fluffy, and doubled in volume (10 to 20 minutes). If the buttercream still appears too soft, add butter 1 tablespoon at a time until it is a spreadable consistency.

There is no escaping the fact that this is buttercream at its purest. If you are among the naysayers that claim they don't like buttercream, hold off on your judgment until you try my mom's delicious buttercream atop your next cake.

Although this buttercream can be tinted, it is not ideal to use when you want to mix bright or rich colors, as the food coloring tends to bead up and does not combine fully with the buttercream. The high butter content also creates a subtle yellow tone to the buttercream which can mute some colors, making them less bright or pure.

Kaye's Buttercream can be stored in an airtight container at room temperature for up to 3 days and in the refrigerator for up to 3 weeks. To use the chilled buttercream, bring it to room temperature and beat at medium speed in the bowl of an electric mixer until smooth and creamy. To speed up this process you can lightly reheat the buttercream, in its mixing bowl, over a hot-water bath, before beating.

In a small saucepan, bring to a boil:

- ¼ cup water
- 1 cup plus 2 tablespoons sugar

Use a clean pastry brush and cold water to wash down any sugar crystals that form on the sides of the pan as the water heats. When the sugar comes to a boil, set a timer for 7 minutes, and let boil.

After 5 minutes, in the bowl of an electric mixer, begin to whip at high speed:

- ½ cup egg whites (about 6 large egg whites)

Whip until stiff. They should be done when the timer goes off.

With the mixer on high speed, slowly beat the sugar syrup into the egg whites, pouring the syrup to the side of the bowl to avoid the whip.

Continue to beat until the bowl is cool to the touch, about 10 minutes. Slowly add:

- ¾ pound (3 sticks) unsalted butter at room temperature, cut into 1-inch pieces

When the buttercream begins to jump out of the bowl, reduce the speed to low.

Mix in at low speed:

- 1 teaspoon pure vanilla extract

Beat until light and fluffy. At some points the mixture might look curdled. Just keep beating; it will become smooth again.

This is the kind of icing that grandmas across the country have been spreading on cakes for generations, probably because it is so easy to make: no eggs, no cooking, no worries. We call this ultrasweet frosting Kids' Buttercream, because most often it is found atop our cupcakes, which kids, and adults (secretly), devour. We also ice our Red Velvet cakes with this creamy concoction. Although this icing tints beautifully, we don't use it for delicate piping applications because it has a dense and slightly gritty texture that tends to break.

Kids' Buttercream can be stored in the refrigerator in an airtight container for 1 week. To use the chilled buttercream, bring it to room temperature and beat at medium speed in the bowl of an electric mixer until smooth and creamy. To speed up this process you can lightly reheat the buttercream, in its mixing bowl, over a hot-water bath, before beating.

Meringue powder can be found at baking supply stores and some supermarkets.

In the bowl of an electric mixer at medium-high speed, beat until creamy:

- 8 ounces (2 sticks) unsalted butter

Add all at once and beat at low speed until smooth:

- 4 cups (1-pound box) sifted confectioners' sugar
- 1 tablespoon meringue powder
- 1 teaspoon pure vanilla extract
- ¼ teaspoon salt

Add and beat until light and creamy:

- 2 tablespoons milk

FLAVORED BUTTERCREAM

chocolate buttercream: In a bowl, combine 2 to 3 ounces of melted, body temperature (100°F) semisweet chocolate per 1 cup of Kaye's Buttercream. Mix until smooth and completely blended, scraping down the sides of the bowl to prevent the chocolate from hardening and causing unmelted flecks in the buttercream.

praline buttercream: In a bowl, combine ⅓ cup of finely chopped praline (see page 167) per scant 1 cup of Kaye's Buttercream. Stir until combined.

coffee buttercream: In a bowl, dissolve 2½ teaspoons of instant espresso powder in 2½ teaspoons of hot water. Whisk in 1 cup of Kaye's Buttercream. Mix until smooth and completely blended.

dulce de leche buttercream: In a bowl, for every 1 cup of Kaye's Buttercream, mix in ¼ cup of Dulce de Leche (see page 101). Stir or whip until thoroughly combined and no lumps of dulce remain.

peanut butter icing *

For all of you peanut butter lovers out there, here is a scrumptious twist on our Cream Cheese Frosting (from our first book, The Whimsical Bakehouse). *It is good enough to eat right off the spoon.*

Peanut Butter Icing can be stored in the refrigerator in an airtight container for 1 week. To use the chilled icing, bring it to room temperature and beat at medium speed in the bowl of an electric mixer until smooth and creamy. To speed up this process you can lightly reheat the icing, in its mixing bowl, over a hot-water bath, before beating.

In the bowl of an electric mixer at medium-high speed, beat until creamy:

- 2 ounces (½ stick) unsalted butter

Add and beat until creamy:

- 4½ ounces (one and a half 3-ounce packages) cream cheese
- ½ cup smooth peanut butter

Add all at once and beat at low speed until smooth:

- 1 cup sifted confectioners' sugar

Continue to beat at medium speed until light and fluffy.

chocolate glaze *

For beginners and professionals alike this is the perfect icing. It covers cakes smoothly and beautifully and it is one of the richest, most refined, and most decadent chocolate icings you can make. This glaze adds an elegant aura to any cake no matter how big or small, but you can also make it whimsical with the addition of sprinkles or chocolate decorations. This recipe can be made with semisweet or milk chocolate; the semisweet has a darker, richer glow. The icing can be used immediately or cooled and stored in the refrigerator in an airtight container for up to 2 weeks. Reheat slowly in a double boiler before using if chilled.

In a double boiler or in a medium metal bowl placed over a hot-water bath, melt:

- 1½ pounds semisweet chocolate or milk chocolate, chopped into small pieces

In a small saucepan, heat over medium-high heat:

- 2 cups heavy cream
- 5 ounces (1 stick plus 2 tablespoons) unsalted butter
- ¼ cup light corn syrup

Stir until the butter melts, then continue to heat to just before the boiling point (bubbles will form around the pan's rim). Slowly pour the scalded liquid over the melted chocolate, whisking constantly until smooth. Strain the icing through a fine sieve.

matt's fudge icing*

What would life be like without fudge? My brother-in-law Doug certainly
would not find much pleasure in cake, brownies, or ice cream were it not for this creamy and sweet
chocolate classic. This recipe comes from my Uncle Matt (the other beloved baker in our family). This
fudge has iced his Triple-Layer Chocolate Cake at the Hudson House in Nyack, New York, for as long
as I can remember—a chocoholic's dream come true.

Matt's Fudge Icing can be stored in the refrigerator in an airtight container for 2 weeks. To use
the chilled icing, bring it to room temperature and beat at medium speed in the bowl of an electric
mixer until smooth and creamy. To speed up this process you can lightly reheat the icing in its mixing
bowl, over a hot-water bath, before beating.

In a small saucepan over low heat, mix together:

- ¼ cup sugar
- 2 large egg yolks
- ¾ cup heavy cream
- 1 teaspoon pure vanilla extract
- Pinch of salt

Whisk until the mixture is slightly thickened and coats the back of a wooden spoon (175–180°F on a candy thermometer).

Remove from the heat and whisk in until melted:

- 8 ounces finely chopped semisweet chocolate
- 3 ounces (¾ stick) unsalted butter, cut into pieces

Whisk in:

- ¼ cup light corn syrup
- 2 tablespoons sour cream

Transfer to a bowl, cover with plastic wrap, and chill for 1 hour to overnight.

whipped cream*

Ah, whipped cream. It's light enough that you don't feel too indulgent when it is
spread atop your cupcake, rich enough to give balance to your strawberry shortcake, and the perfect
accompaniment to practically anything sweet. For best results, we recommend preparing the whipped
cream right before serving or assembling your cakes. Any leftovers can be stored in an airtight con-
tainer in the refrigerator for up to 3 days. The whipped cream will break down as it sits in the refriger-
ator, so rewhip in the bowl of an electric mixer for 1 minute or until medium to stiff peaks form.

In the bowl of an electric mixer fitted with a whisk attachment, whip until stiff:

- 1½ cups heavy cream
- 2 tablespoons confectioners' sugar, sifted
- ½ teaspoon pure vanilla extract

white chocolate glaze *

White Chocolate Glaze can be tinted with food coloring to achieve a veritable rainbow of decorative effects. Little red ladybugs are brought to vibrant life with a coating of this glaze. For Halloween, tint the glaze orange and make a batch of jack-o'-lanterns. Without any food coloring, the icing is a rather elegant creamy yellow. The icing can be used immediately or cooled and stored in the refrigerator in an airtight container for up to 2 weeks. Reheat slowly in a double boiler before using if chilled.

In a double boiler or in a medium metal bowl placed over a hot-water bath, melt:

- 1½ pounds white chocolate (or white wafer chocolate), chopped into small pieces

In a small saucepan, heat over medium-high heat:

- 1 cup plus 2 tablespoons heavy cream
- 1 ounce (2 tablespoons) unsalted butter

Stir until the butter melts, then continue to heat to just before the boiling point (bubbles will form around the pan's rim). Slowly pour the scalded liquid over the melted chocolate, whisking constantly until smooth. Strain the icing through a fine sieve.

simple glaze *

When you are looking for an easy way to finish off a Bundt cake, pound cake, or even a cupcake, just whip up a batch of this glaze and you have yourself a dessert you'll proudly make your table's centerpiece. The icing is gooey and sweet, but let it sit and a thin, hard crust will form over the cake, sealing in moistness and adding an extra sweet kick to every bite.

We flavored the glaze with coffee, but there are myriad other flavors to choose from. Substitute lemon juice, orange juice, or milk, in the same proportions, for the hot coffee. This is really as simple as you can get.

Sift into a bowl:

- 1 cup confectioners' sugar, plus additional as needed

Slowly whisk in:

- 2 tablespoons hot coffee, plus additional as needed

If the icing is too thick, add more liquid; and if it is too thin, add more confectioners' sugar.

Use the glaze immediately or place plastic wrap directly on the surface of the glaze. It can be stored in the refrigerator for 1 week.

simple decorating tips

By adding hints of color or a simple chocolate decoration, you can turn a muffin into a cupcake or a plain Bundt cake into a birthday cake. The following list includes some quick and easy ideas for making a plain cake into a special cake without too much fuss.

- Sprinkles or nonpareils are the easiest way to add pizzazz to a little cake. All you need to get the little beads of color to adhere is a layer of icing (½ cup of nonpareils will cover up to 16 glazed cupcakes). You can even mix nonpareils or sprinkles into the Caramel Cake or Pound Cake, or replace the poppy seeds with nonpareils in the Lemon Poppy Cake before baking to create a colorful confetti cake.

- Drizzle dark chocolate or tinted white chocolate directly on the tops of your cooled cakes. This is a great and simple decoration for Bundt cakes. Release your inner Jackson Pollock and have a ball. To add an extra kick to your cake, drizzle the tops with chocolate and then, before the chocolate has hardened, add sprinkles or nonpareils.

- By baking your cake batter in shaped pans (such as hearts or stars) instead of just a cupcake or small cake pan, you can create a decorated treat without much effort. Just dust with confectioners' sugar or pour some delicious Chocolate Glaze (page 34) on top and call it a day.

- Use color! By simply tinting your icing, you are creating a decorated cake. Mix up a soft pastel buttercream or pump it up a few notches and go for screaming neon buttercream.

- If you don't want to be bothered making a more complex icing, try making our Simple Glaze (opposite page). It pours nicely over Bundt cakes and cupcakes to create a frosted treat.

- If you are making a design that calls for a small amount of buttercream and you don't feel like whipping up an entire batch just to use ¼ cup, you can buy a package of vanilla icing at the store. It won't taste as good, but it is a big time saver.

- If you are making cupcakes, find a paper cupcake liner that matches your theme.

- The presentation for your little cake can be just as much of a decoration as the cake itself. By choosing a fun serving dish, you can change your little cake into an eye-catching dessert. Add a moat of Raspberry Sauce (page 69) or Caramel Sauce (page 82) and your guests will be awed. When displaying many little cakes together, consider using a stack of pedestal cake plates or a wire pastry tree. Height has impact, especially when the star of the show is so small!

- To make a simple base for your baked creations, glue a doily to a cardboard round of the same size. Cardboard rounds can also be covered with decorative foil; double the cardboards for a stronger base.

piping tips

- Icing consistency, whether it is soft or hard, smooth or lumpy, affects the appearance of your piping applications. You can often firm up or soften the buttercream by chilling it in the refrigerator for a few minutes or by lightly melting it over a double boiler. To remove any lumps, whisk or stir the buttercream. Soft buttercream flows easily, making it ideal for lace or line work. Most other piping applications need icing of a medium consistency that is fluid yet holds its form. Flowers need a medium to firm icing to hold the petal's shape, but keep in mind that if the icing is too stiff it will break or crack while piping.

- Bag pressure is influenced by two factors: the twisting and the squeezing of the pastry bag. Use one hand to guide the bag while squeezing with the other, twisting the top of the bag occasionally to maintain pressure. By altering the pressure you squeeze with, you can control the flow of buttercream. Your goal is to apply consistent pressure while moving the tip or bag at a steady pace or rhythm. However, some piping applications, such as "popcorn," call for irregular bag pressure and irregular rhythm. At the end of a line or embellishment, stop applying pressure to the bag and quickly spiral the tip, pull the tip downward, or pull the tip to the side. These actions are referred to as tailing off, and they end piping applications with a clean stroke.

- Tip placement, unless otherwise noted, is usually at a 45-degree angle to the cake. Two common exceptions are dots and rosettes, for which the tip is perpendicular to the cake surface. To begin, touch the pastry tip to the surface of the cake where you want to start piping, allowing the icing to adhere to the surface. Lift up the tip as you begin to apply pressure. Do not drag the tip along the surface of the cake, as this will indent the surface; instead, lightly touch the surface of the cake or hover above it as you pipe.

chocolate

At the Bakehouse we use a wide variety of chocolates: unsweetened chocolate, semisweet chocolate, milk chocolate, white chocolate, baker's chocolate, confectioners' chocolate (also called wafer chocolate or candy coating), and cocoa powder, not to mention chocolate chips (regular, mini, and white). Each type is suited for different recipes and applications. With the exception of cocoa powder, there are a few tips that hold true for working with chocolate.

- Do not get any water in chocolate, as this will cause it to "seize." Seizing is when chocolate resolidifies and becomes lumpy. If you are working with confectioners' chocolate, to counter-act any seizing that may occur on humid days, try whisking in a few drops of vegetable oil.

- Store chocolate in a cool, dry place—not in the refrigerator.

- It is best to work with chocolate in a room at room temperature (68°–70°F).

- Each type of chocolate has a slightly different melting point (between 104°F and 113°F, and 115°F for confectioners' chocolate), but when melted they should all be at a fluid state with a temperature ranging from 95° to 120°F. When chocolate is overheated it will become solid and unworkable. Semisweet, bittersweet, milk, white, and confectioners' chocolate can all easily be melted over a double boiler or in a microwave (see below). Chocolate chips, however, are not recommended for melting unless combined with other ingredients such as butter, because they get lumpy.

- Never melt chocolate directly over a heat source; always use indirect heat.

- For melting chocolate in the microwave: If not using wafers, coarsely chop the chocolate. Place it in a glass or microwave-safe bowl. For 1 to 2 cups of chocolate, microwave in 30-second intervals, stirring in between to ensure the chocolate does not burn. It will take approximately 1½ minutes to melt, but times will vary based on the room temperature, the amount of chocolate you are melting, and the power of your microwave. Stirring chocolate vigorously will often melt any remaining small pieces.

- For melting chocolate over a double boiler: Find a metal bowl that fits snugly in a medium-size pot, or use a double boiler. Fill the pot one third full with water and bring to a light simmer (hot but not boiling). If not using wafers, coarsely chop the chocolate and place it in the bowl. Place the bowl onto the pot. Do not let the bottom of the bowl touch the water. Heat the chocolate, stirring often, until all of the chocolate has melted (approximately 15 minutes). Remove from the heat.

THE CHOCOLATE METHOD

In our first book, *The Whimsical Bakehouse: Fun-to-Make Cakes That Taste as Good as They Look,* I introduced the Chocolate Method. I often compare this decorative process to painting on glass because everything is done in reverse; details like highlights and shadows are applied first, followed by the background. Using a template as a guide, melted chocolate is piped or painted onto parchment paper. When the design is complete it is set aside to harden, and then it is carefully flipped to reveal the starfish, or ghost, or cheetah print.

The One-Color Chocolate Method, simply put, is much like a silhouette created out of chocolate or tinted white chocolate. The Multicolor Chocolate Method combines bold chocolate outlines and a multitude of colors to create cartoon-like designs. Taken a step farther, the Advanced Chocolate Method combines fine lines and painterly shadows and highlights to create realistic designs, from portraits to blooming flowers. Finally the Relief Chocolate Method takes elements of all of these techniques and adds dimension through over-piping or stacking segments.

Chocolate Method Tips

• At the Bakehouse we use wafer chocolate to make all of our playful "chocolate" designs. Wafer chocolate is also referred to as confectioners' chocolate or candy coating. Because wafer chocolate does not need to be tempered, it is easy to work with, so it is ideal for the novice or home cake decorator. Unfortunately if you are looking for the true taste of chocolate you will have to temper your own semisweet or milk chocolate because wafer chocolate is a bit of a misnomer. Although the dark wafer chocolate contains cocoa, it does not contain chocolate liquor or cocoa butter, both of which give real dark chocolate its depth and richness.

• Approximately 6 ounces of unmelted wafer chocolate is equivalent to approximately 1 cup unmelted wafer chocolate or ½ cup melted wafer chocolate. All the measurements listed in design directions are calibrated in unmelted cups but you can measure the wafer chocolate by the ounce or by the cup in the melted state.

- When making designs, it is always a good idea to melt extra chocolate, and make extra designs, just in case a design breaks or you make a mistake and need more.

- Keep in mind that any design can be simplified by eliminating detail work and/or reducing the number of colors.

- If you are doing a multicolor design with outlines, make sure all of the colors overlap. This will prevent the design from breaking along the seams.

- The final design should be anywhere from $\frac{1}{8}$ to $\frac{1}{4}$ inch thick. The larger the design, the thicker it should be to ensure stability and ease of handling.

- Don't worry if you go outside the lines a little; the initial outline will maintain the definition of the design. In the worst-case scenario, you can carefully carve off the excess chocolate with a sharp paring knife, or score along a straight line and crack the excess off along the score.

- Consider drawing the design's outline with a color instead of just dark chocolate.

- To keep chocolates warm in the pastry cones, we use standard heating pads found at pharmacies. The temperature is hot but doesn't scald the chocolate as a double boiler or portable stove might do if the temperature isn't perfectly regulated. However, placing your chocolate bags on a sheet pan set over barely simmering water will do.

- Have all of your colors melted and placed in pastry cones before you begin. This will facilitate the decorating process.

- At the Bakehouse we often use cellophane instead of parchment paper to create our designs. Not only is it easier to see the template through the clear surface, but it leaves the chocolate nice and glossy.

- To remelt any chocolate on the paint brush, use a sheet pan over a pan filled with barely simmering water as a palette. Pushing the bristles about on this surface will remelt the chocolate. You have to work quickly, because when you are painting with thin layers, the chocolate dries quickly.

- A chocolate design can take anywhere from 5 minutes to 1 hour to set completely, depending on the room temperature and the size of the design. Because the chocolate designs in this book are for little cakes, the time range will usually be between 5 minutes and 15 minutes.

I will illustrate how to make an acorn using the Advanced/Relief Chocolate Method. The acorn is made in two segments (shell and nut) and then assembled after hardening, giving it added dimension. (See page 99 for Mini Acorn Cupcakes, which use these decorations.)

Use these directions as a guide for all of the Chocolate Method decorations in this book. You might have to change the palette, remove or add details, or adjust the amount of chocolate being melted, but in essence it is the same process. For a more in-depth look at the Chocolate Method, refer to our first book, *The Whimsical Bakehouse*.

WHAT YOU WILL NEED:

(MAKES APPROXIMATELY 10 ACORNS)

1 half-sheet pan

Parchment paper or cellophane

½ cup white wafer chocolate and ¼ cup dark wafer chocolate

Yellow and orange candy colors

Pastry cones

Small glass bowls

Rubber spatulas

Acorn template (page 170)

HOW TO

1. Photocopy or trace the acorn template. If you are making more than one acorn, you can trace one template and attach a long parchment tab, or handle, to it so that you can more easily move the template under the parchment paper to pipe out multiples without disrupting those you have already made. The other option is to trace or make as many photocopies of the template as you need. This may become problematic, however, when you need 40 of one design. Whichever way you choose, begin by placing the template onto a sheet pan or a flat surface. Cover the template with parchment paper or cellophane, and lightly secure with one or two pieces of tape.

2. Melt the white wafer and dark wafer chocolates separately. Set aside 1 tablespoon of white chocolate for the highlights. Tint the remaining white chocolate as follows: mix together approximately ¼ cup white chocolate with 2 drops of melted dark chocolate and one drop of yellow candy color to make the light brown. To make the dark brown, mix approximately ¼ cup white chocolate with 1 teaspoon melted dark chocolate and one drop of orange candy color. Pour the rest of the dark chocolate, white chocolate, and colored chocolates into 4

separate pastry cones. Keep the chocolates warm on a barely simmering double boiler or on a heating pad.

3. Cut a very small hole in the dark chocolate pastry cone. With a fine line, trace the outline of the acorn, including any interior crosshatching and details.

4. Pipe additional chocolate lines on the left edge of the shell and nut. Before these lines set, use a paintbrush to gently feather the chocolate toward the right and in a downward motion. You should still be able to see the parchment through these semitransparent shadows. Although the shadows overlap the line-work, they should not be applied so roughly as to wipe these initial lines off.

5. Cut a small hole in the white chocolate pastry cone and pipe a line along the right edge of the shell and a few thin lines following the contour of the nut. Before the lines on the shell set, use a paintbrush to gently feather the chocolate toward the left. Do not feather the nut lines.

6. Now cut medium holes in the colored bags. Fill in the nut with the tan and the shell with the brown. Set aside to harden.

7. When hardened, carefully flip the design and gently peel off the parchment paper.

8. Attach the shell to the nut with a dot of melted chocolate, gently holding them in place until the chocolate has set.

COLOR MIXING CHART

The buttercream colors below are mixed from a palette of red, neon brite pink, sunset orange, lemon yellow, neon brite green, leaf green, teal, royal blue, sky blue, violet, black, and buckeye brown liquid gel colors. The chocolate colors are mixed from a palette of red, pink, orange, yellow, green, royal blue, sky blue, violet, and black candy colors. Candy color is not available in brown; for those formulas, use melted dark wafer chocolate in place of brown coloring. You might not be able to mix a true sky blue or teal, depending on the range of colors available in the brand you buy; if these colors are important for your designs, I recommend buying a bag of pretinted wafer chocolate, or a jar of paste color for buttercream. When mixing colors, whatever colorant you are using, always err on the side of too little color as opposed to too much. Add color drop by drop. If a color is too dark, and you want to make it lighter, adding white buttercream or white chocolate doesn't always solve the problem. More often than not you end up adding cups of buttercream before reaching the desired color. Instead, start over and use the food coloring cautiously.

If you don't need a wide range of colors, you can just use blue, yellow, and red food coloring. These primary colors, in varying amounts and when mixed together in different proportions, can give you pinks, greens, oranges, purples, and more.

If you cannot find liquid gel colors, paste colors work just as well. Liquid colors can be used but the palette is limited and they are less concentrated. Use this chart as an approximate guide for mixing colors. Your results may vary depending on the brand and type of coloring you use. These formulas are based on drops of liquid gel colors per ¼ cup of House Buttercream and drops of candy colors per ¼ cup of melted white wafer chocolate.

color	buttercream with liquid gel colors	wafer chocolate with candy colors
RED	5 red	10 red
PALE PINK	scant drop neon pink or 1 red	scant drop pink or 1 red
PINK	2 neon pink	1 pink
NEON PINK	5 neon pink	3 pink
ORANGE	3 orange	4 orange
PALE ORANGE/PEACH	scant drop orange	1 orange

color	buttercream with liquid gel colors	wafer chocolate with candy colors
RUST	3 orange + 3 red	4 orange + 5 red
TERRA COTTA	5 orange + 1 brown + 1 red	8 orange + 8 drops dark chocolate
CORAL	1 orange + 2 neon pink	2 orange + 1 pink
DARK CORAL	2 orange + 4 neon pink	4 orange + 2 pink
YELLOW	2 yellow	4 yellow
SOFT BUTTERY YELLOW	scant drop yellow	scant drop yellow
STRAW YELLOW	2 yellow + scant drop orange + scant drop brown	5 yellow + 1 orange + 1 drop dark chocolate
GREEN	3 green + 1 brown	4 green + 12 drops dark hocolate
LIGHT GREEN	scant drop green + scant drop brown (optional)	1 green + 2 drops dark chocolate
NEON GREEN	2 green + 4 yellow or 3 neon brite green	3 green + 5 yellow
PALE NEON GREEN	1 green + 1 yellow or 1 neon brite green	1 green + 1 yellow
TEAL GREEN	4 teal or 1 green + 2 sky blue	2 sky blue + 1 green
LIGHT BLUE	1 royal or sky blue	1 royal or sky blue
SKY BLUE	3 sky blue	2 sky blue
ROYAL BLUE	5 royal blue	6 royal blue
PERIWINKLE	1 royal blue + 1 violet	1 royal blue + 1 violet
VIOLET / PURPLE	3 violet	3 violet
BRIGHT PURPLE	1 violet + 4 neon pink	1 violet + 2 pink
PALE VIOLET / LAVENDER	1 violet	scant drop violet or 1 pink + 4 chocolate
LIGHT BROWN	1 brown	15 drops dark chocolate + 1 orange (optional)
DARK BROWN	5 brown	45 drops dark chocolate + 2 orange (optional)
GRAY	1 black	1 black

ANYTIME LITTLE CAKES & MUFFINS

You don't need a special occasion to mix up a batch of these little cakes. For breakfast, as a treat with tea, or as a midnight snack, these recipes are perfect anytime.

Hidden within these pages is a little surprise for you: a collection of our best muffin recipes. We know; you are probably thinking: this is a cake book, why include muffins? Well, the way we see it, muffins may have become a breakfast staple, but even when occasionally packed with a bit more nutritional value, they are really just little cakes. Another added bonus: most muffin recipes are so easy to make you don't even need an electric mixer. Unless otherwise noted, all you need is a bowl and a wooden spoon.

Muffin batter can be made up to a week ahead and stored in an airtight container in the refrigerator. Just scoop and bake whenever you are craving a fresh and warm treat. Once baked, however, muffins are best eaten within the day. Wrap them in an airtight container and they will last a couple days longer, and if frozen they can last up to a month. When you are ready to eat your baked goodies, let them come to room temperature in their airtight container. To bring them back to full flavorful and textural life, just pop them in a 350°F oven for 5 minutes.

You will also find a variety of little cakes like Almond Coffee Cakes and Coffee Pecan Pound Cakes in this chapter. Like muffins, many of these cakes are traditionally associated with breakfast, but don't let that stop you from eating them whenever you like. We love Plum Kuchens for dessert and Blueberry Crumb Cakes as an after-school snack.

If you are looking for a wonderful way to save time when you are planning a party, consider making the anytime cakes in advance. They can be made and assembled in their pans, wrapped well in plastic wrap, and frozen (unbaked) for up to 2 weeks. Let the cakes thaw in the refrigerator overnight, then bring to room temperature (approximately 30 minutes) and bake as directed.

Some of the recipes in this chapter call for two or more pans to be used. This doesn't mean you have to run to the store. If you don't have enough pans to bake all of your little cakes at once, use just one pan and bake in batches. Since the baking times are so short, the batter can be left at room temperature.

corn muffins*

Corn muffins are believed to be the first manifestation of a muffin ever made in America. Whoever baked the first one, thank you! That corn muffin evolved into countless other delicious muffins. This is our version of the classic. We love to slice them, spread them with butter, and then fry them on a griddle until they are golden brown and crispy. Scrumptious.

Grease the top of a 12-mold muffin pan and line it with paper liners. Preheat the oven to 350°F. Have all ingredients at room temperature.

In a large bowl, stir to blend:
- ¾ cup sugar
- ½ cup vegetable oil

Mix in:
- 2 large eggs

On a piece of wax paper, sift together:
- 1½ cups all-purpose flour
- 1 tablespoon baking powder
- ½ teaspoon salt

Transfer the dry ingredients to a medium bowl and add:
- 1½ cups cornmeal

Add the dry ingredients to the sugar and egg mixture alternately with:
- 1 cup milk

Mix just to combine.

Scoop the batter into the prepared molds, filling each to the top of the paper liner. Bake for 20 to 25 minutes, or until a cake tester inserted into the center of a muffin comes out clean. Cool on a wire rack for 5 to 10 minutes before removing the muffins from their pan.

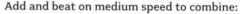

blueberry muffins *

Imagine waking up on a buzzing summer morning to the aroma of freshly baked blueberry muffins. That is better than any alarm clock! Add this light and sweet classic to your repertoire and make someone's morning unforgettable. You can use fresh or frozen blueberries, so you can enjoy these muffins year-round.

Grease and flour the top of a 12-mold muffin pan and line it with paper liners. Preheat the oven to 350°F. Have all ingredients at room temperature.

In the bowl of an electric mixer, beat at high speed until light and fluffy:

- 4 ounces (1 stick) unsalted butter
- 1⅓ cups sugar

Add and beat on medium speed to combine:

- 2 large eggs
- ¾ teaspoon pure vanilla extract

On a piece of wax paper, sift together:

- 2 cups all-purpose flour
- 2 teaspoons baking powder
- ½ teaspoon salt

Mix the dry ingredients into the butter and egg mixture at low speed just until combined.

Add and mix until combined:

- 1 cup buttermilk

Fold in:

- 9 ounces (2 cups) fresh or thawed frozen blueberries

Scoop the batter into the prepared molds, filling each to the top of the paper liner. Bake for 25 to 30 minutes, or until a cake tester inserted into the center of a muffin comes out clean. Cool on a wire rack for 5 to 10 minutes before removing the muffins from their pan.

zucchini muffins *

YIELD: 12 MUFFINS

Don't let the idea of using a vegetable in your morning treat turn you off, because these muffins are delicious, moist, and sweet. At my mom's first bakery, the Runcible Spoon, she had a customer we nicknamed "Zucchini Man" because, without fail, he would come in every morning for his zucchini muffin. Perhaps you should make this muffin your morning ritual, too. And if you are a chocoholic, believe it or not, these muffins are great with some chocolate chips thrown into the batter.

Grease the top of a 12-mold muffin pan and line it with paper liners. Preheat the oven to 350°F. Have all ingredients at room temperature.

In a medium bowl, mix well:
- 2 cups sugar
- 1⅓ cups vegetable oil
- 4 large eggs
- 1 teaspoon pure vanilla extract

On a piece of wax paper, sift together:
- 3 cups all-purpose flour
- 1 teaspoon baking powder
- 1½ teaspoons baking soda
- 1 teaspoon salt
- 1 tablespoon ground cinnamon
- ¼ teaspoon ground cloves

Add the dry ingredients to the wet ingredients and mix to combine.

Add and mix just to combine:
- 1 cup chopped walnuts
- ¾ cup raisins
- 14 ounces (3 cups) grated zucchini (approximately 3 medium zucchini)

Scoop the batter into the prepared molds, filling each to the top of the paper liner. Bake for 20 to 25 minutes, or until a cake tester inserted into the center of a muffin comes out clean. Cool on a wire rack for 5 to 10 minutes before removing the muffins from their pan.

• 51 •

banana muffins *

My mom has to try the banana muffins at every bakery, deli, or restaurant she visits, and, in her "unbiased opinion," she says hers (the recipe below) are the best she has ever eaten. They are unbelievably moist and banana-y. The richness of the muffin may be attributed to the butter. Nuts are optional, but as any Hudson will tell you (Hudson is my mom's maiden name), nuts make anything better.

Grease the top of a 12-mold muffin pan and line it with paper liners. Preheat the oven to 350°F. Have all ingredients at room temperature.

In a medium bowl, mix well:
- 1 cup sugar
- 4 ounces (1 stick) unsalted butter, melted
- 2 large eggs

On a piece of wax paper, sift together:
- 2 cups all-purpose flour
- 1½ teaspoons baking soda
- ¾ teaspoon salt

Add the dry ingredients to the wet ingredients and mix to combine.

Add and mix just to combine:
- 1 cup mashed bananas (approximately 2 bananas)
- ½ cup chopped walnuts
- 2 tablespoons hot water

Scoop the batter into the prepared molds, filling each to the top of the paper liner. (Optional: Before baking, sprinkle ½ cup chopped walnuts over the tops of the muffins.) Bake for 20 to 25 minutes, or until a cake tester inserted into the center of a muffin comes out clean. Cool on a wire rack for 5 to 10 minutes before removing the muffins from their pan.

whole wheat blackberry muffins *

YIELD: 16 MUFFINS

This is my favorite muffin at the Bakehouse, partly because I can delude myself into thinking it is good for me (whole-wheat flour, blackberries). Bursts of blackberry tartness punctuate the subtle sweetness. How do you make a great muffin even better? Top it off with a sprinkling of buttery streusel.

Prepare one batch of Streusel Topping (page 59) and set aside. Any remaining streusel can be stored in a sealed container in the refrigerator.

Grease and flour the tops of three 6-mold muffin pans and line 16 of the molds with paper liners. Preheat the oven to 350°F. Have all ingredients at room temperature.

In a small bowl, whisk together just to combine:

- 6 ounces (1½ sticks) unsalted butter, melted
- 2 large eggs
- 2 cups buttermilk

In another medium bowl, stir together:

- 1¾ cups all-purpose flour
- 1¾ cups whole-wheat flour
- 1 cup sugar
- 2½ teaspoons baking powder
- 1½ teaspoons baking soda
- 1 teaspoon salt

Stir the egg and butter mixture into the dry ingredients, just until combined.

Add and stir just to combine:

- 2½ cups blackberries (fresh or frozen)

Scoop the batter into the prepared molds, filling each to the top of the paper liner. Sprinkle approximately 2 tablespoons of streusel over the top of each muffin. Bake for 20 to 25 minutes, or until a cake tester inserted into the center of a muffin comes out clean. Cool on a wire rack for 5 to 10 minutes before removing the muffins from their pans.

oatmeal muffins*

Instead of starting your day with a granola bar or a bowl of oatmeal, we recommend baking a batch of these muffins. Filled with all of the goodness of oats, a sprinkling of golden raisins for sweetness, and buttermilk for that luscious bite, these tasty little numbers are sure to make you love breakfast again.

And if you are looking for a recipe that is not overly sweet, look no farther.

Grease the tops of three 6-mold muffin pans and line 16 of the molds with paper liners. Preheat the oven to 350°F. Have all ingredients at room temperature.

In a medium bowl, stir to blend:

- 1½ cups old-fashioned oats
- 1½ cups buttermilk
- ¾ cup golden raisins

Soak for one hour at room temperature.

Add and mix to combine:

- 6 ounces (1½ sticks) unsalted butter, melted
- 3 large eggs, lightly beaten
- 1½ cups light brown sugar, packed

On a piece of wax paper, sift together:

- 2¼ cups all-purpose flour
- 1 tablespoon baking powder
- 1¼ teaspoons baking soda
- 1½ teaspoons salt

Add the dry ingredients to the wet ingredients and mix to combine.

Scoop the batter into the prepared molds, filling each to the top of the paper liner. Bake for 25 to 30 minutes, or until a cake tester inserted into the center of a muffin comes out clean. Cool on a wire rack for 5 to 10 minutes before removing the muffins from their pans.

pumpkin muffins*

YIELD: 24 MUFFINS

Our customers ask for this delicious muffin year-round, but when the leaves start to fall in October we really begin to crave it. It is subtly spicy with an overtone of pumpkin warmth, just perfect for a crisp autumn morning. Save the top for last since it is encrusted with our delicious butter streusel.

Prepare one recipe of Streusel Topping (page 59). Set aside.

Grease the tops of two 12-mold muffin pans and line them with paper liners. Preheat the oven to 350°F. Have all ingredients at room temperature.

In a large bowl, mix to combine:

- 3 cups sugar
- ¾ cup plus 2 tablespoons vegetable oil
- 3 extra-large eggs
- 1 15-ounce can of plain pumpkin purée

On a piece of wax paper, sift together:

- 3¼ cups all-purpose flour
- 2½ teaspoons baking soda
- 2 teaspoons salt
- 2 tablespoons plus 1 teaspoon ground cinnamon
- 2 teaspoons ground nutmeg
- 1 teaspoon ground cloves
- Pinch of allspice

Add the dry ingredients to the wet ingredients and mix to combine.

Add and stir just to combine:

- 1 cup chopped walnuts
- ¾ cup golden raisins

Scoop the batter into the prepared molds, filling each to the top of the paper liner. Sprinkle approximately 2 tablespoons of streusel over the top of each muffin. Bake for 25 to 30 min-utes, or until a cake tester inserted into the center of a muffin comes out clean. Cool on a wire rack for 5 to 10 minutes before removing the muffins from their pans.

coffee chocolate chip muffins*

You won't believe you are eating a muffin when you bite into these flavorful gems packed with rich coffee flavor and overflowing with chocolate chips. Our recipe comes from one of our favorite former employees, Monica Lender. It was her favorite and it is beloved by family and customers alike. My mom still brings two of these home every weekend to enjoy on the days she is being "bad," and sometimes she brings three, including one for my husband, Luiz.

Grease the tops of three 6-mold muffin pans and line them with paper liners. Preheat the oven to 350°F. Have all ingredients at room temperature.

In the bowl of an electric mixer, beat at high speed until light and fluffy:

- 12 ounces (3 sticks) unsalted butter
- 1 cup granulated sugar
- ½ cup light brown sugar, packed
- 2 large eggs
- 5 tablespoons instant espresso powder

On a piece of wax paper, sift together:

- 4 cups all-purpose flour
- 2 tablespoons baking powder
- ¼ teaspoon salt

At low speed, add the dry ingredients to the butter mixture and mix until just combined.

Still at low speed, add and mix until just combined:

- 1 cup milk
- 6 ounces (1 cup) chocolate chips

Scoop the batter into the prepared molds, filling each to the top of the paper liner. Bake for 20 to 25 minutes, or until a cake tester inserted into the center of a muffin comes out clean. Cool on a wire rack for 5 to 10 minutes before removing the muffins from the pans.

almond coffee cakes*

During the writing of our first book, we wooed our publisher with sweet treats. One of the cakes we took them was our Almond Coffee Cake, and it was a hit. After much begging for the recipe, finally, here it is. Enjoy.

CRUMBED ALMONDS

Pulse in a food processor until finely chopped:

- ⅓ cup granulated sugar
- 1 cup almonds
- 1½ teaspoons ground cinnamon

Set aside.

BATTER

Grease and flour 10 molds of a 12-mold mini square pan. Preheat the oven to 350°F. Have all ingredients at room temperature.

In the bowl of an electric mixer, beat at high speed until light and fluffy:

- 4 ounces (1 stick) unsalted butter
- ½ cup granulated sugar
- ½ cup light brown sugar, packed

Continue beating at medium speed and add:

- 1 large egg

Add and beat on medium speed to combine:

- 1 cup sour cream
- 1 teaspoon pure vanilla extract

In a small bowl, stir together:

- 1 cup all-purpose flour
- 1½ teaspoons baking powder
- Pinch of salt

Mix the dry ingredients into the butter and egg mixture at low speed just until combined.

Scoop 2 generous tablespoons of batter into each prepared mold. Spread 1 tablespoon of the crumbed almonds on top, followed by 2 generous tablespoons of batter. Finish with a sprinkling of crumbed almonds. Bake for 25 to 30 minutes, or until a cake tester inserted into the center of a cake comes out clean. Cool on a wire rack for 10 to 20 minutes before turning the cakes out of their pans. Once turned over, invert immediately to keep the crumbed almonds on top.

blueberry crumb cakes*

YIELD: 12 CRUMB CAKES

Our crumb cakes practically melt in your mouth. Unlike some crumb cakes that use a shortening-based crumb topping that can be sandy or dry, our crumb topping is made with—you guessed it—butter, so it is moist to the last bite. We add blueberries in the summer and apples in the fall. Try your favorite seasonal fruit.

We found the crumb-cake paper liners online (www.kingarthurflour.com). If you can't find them, grease and flour a jumbo muffin pan.

STREUSEL TOPPING

In the bowl of an electric mixer, using a paddle attachment, mix:

- 1 cup all-purpose flour
- ¼ cup light brown sugar, packed
- ⅓ cup granulated sugar
- 4 ounces (1 stick) cold unsalted butter, cut into ½-inch cubes
- 2 teaspoons ground cinnamon
- Pinch of salt

Continue mixing until pea-size bits of streusel form.

Set aside.

BATTER

Place twelve 3 x 1-inch crumb cake paper liners on a cookie sheet or half-sheet pan. Preheat the oven to 350°F. Have all ingredients at room temperature.

In the bowl of an electric mixer, beat at high speed until light and fluffy:

- 5 ounces (1 stick plus 2 tablespoons) unsalted butter
- 1½ cups granulated sugar
- ½ teaspoon pure vanilla extract

Add and beat on medium speed to combine:

- 2 large eggs

On a piece of wax paper, sift together:

- 2 cups all-purpose flour
- 2 teaspoons baking powder
- 1 teaspoon salt

Mix the dry ingredients into the butter and egg mixture at low speed just until combined.

Add and mix until combined:

- ¾ cup milk

Fold in:

- 2 cups (1 pint) fresh or thawed frozen blueberries

Divide the batter evenly among the paper liners. Spread ¼ cup of streusel on top of each. Bake for 22 to 28 minutes, or until a cake tester inserted into the center of a cake comes out clean. Cool on a wire rack for 5 to 10 minutes.

coffee pecan pound cakes*

YIELD: 10 MINI BUNDT CAKES

Initially our Coffee Pound Cake was paired with the usual suspect: chocolate chips. But while experimenting with other add-ins we sampled one cake baked with pecans. We liked the way the pecans' sweet warmth brought out, instead of overwhelmed, the robust coffee flavor. Of course, you can still throw a handful of chocolate chips in for good measure.

We also smothered the little Bundts with a coffee-flavored Simple Glaze. It adds an attractive shine and a delicious jolt of flavor.

Grease and flour 10 molds of two 6-mold mini Bundt pans. Preheat the oven to 350°F. Have all ingredients at room temperature.

In the bowl of an electric mixer, beat at high speed until light and fluffy:
- 10 ounces (2½ sticks) unsalted butter

Add and beat well at high speed:
- 6 ounces (2 3-ounce packages) cream cheese
- 2 tablespoons instant espresso powder

Add and cream at high speed until light and fluffy:
- 1½ cups sugar

Add and mix well at medium speed:
- 2 tablespoons sour cream
- 1 teaspoon pure vanilla extract

Add one at a time, mixing well after each addition:
- 4 large eggs

On a piece of wax paper, sift together:
- 2¼ cups cake flour
- 2 teaspoons baking powder
- ¼ teaspoon salt

Add the dry ingredients to the butter and egg mixture and mix on low speed until smooth.

Stir in by hand:
- 1 cup chopped toasted pecans (see Note)

Place the batter into a pastry bag. Pipe it so that each prepared mold is three-quarters full. If you don't have a pastry bag, carefully spoon the batter into the molds. Bake for 20 to 25 minutes, or until a cake tester inserted into the center of a cake comes out clean. While the cakes are baking, prepare a Simple Glaze (page 36) and set aside. Cool the cakes on a wire rack for 15 to 20 minutes before turning them out of their pans. While the cakes are still warm to hot, spread the Simple Glaze on top (see page 28).

NOTE:

To toast pecans, place the nuts on an ungreased sheet pan. Bake at 350°F for 12 to 15 minutes or until fragrant. Let cool.

plum kuchens*

YIELD: 14 KUCHENS

*Our testers, coworkers, and family agree, hands down, this is the best recipe.
Envision a late summer brunch replete with a squash and onion frittata, sweet potato home fries,
and these delicious plum mini kuchens. But the nutty streusel, plum, and cake aren't just perfect for
brunch; they also make a wonderful light dessert or sweet bite to go with your coffee.*

*At the Bakehouse we make kuchens (Kuchen is German for "cake") year-round. We replace plums
with other seasonal fruits such as apples, pears, peaches, or mangos.*

TOPPING

Pulse in a food processor until finely chopped:

- 1½ tablespoons all-purpose flour
- ¾ cup light brown sugar, packed
- 1½ cups pecans
- 1½ teaspoons ground cinnamon

Add and process until pea-size bits of dough form:

- 3 ounces (¾ stick) cold unsalted butter, cut into ½-inch cubes

Set aside.

BATTER

Grease the tops of three jumbo muffin pans and line 14 molds with large foil or paper liners. Preheat the oven to 350°F. Have all ingredients at room temperature.

In a small bowl, combine:

- 1½ pounds pitted and finely cubed plums
- 2 tablespoons granulated sugar
- 1 teaspoon ground cinnamon

Set aside.

In the bowl of an electric mixer, beat at high speed until light and fluffy:

- 8 ounces (2 sticks) unsalted butter
- 1 cup granulated sugar
- ¾ cup light brown sugar, packed

Add and beat on medium speed to combine:

- ¾ cup sour cream

Continue beating at medium speed and add, one at a time:

- 3 large eggs

At low speed, add and mix just to combine:

- ¾ teaspoon pure vanilla extract
- 1 teaspoon fresh lemon juice

The batter may look curdled.

In a medium bowl, stir together:

- 2¾ cups all-purpose flour
- 1½ teaspoons baking powder
- 1½ teaspoons baking soda
- 1 teaspoon salt

Mix the dry ingredients into the butter and egg mixture at low speed just until combined.

Fold in the plum mixture.

Fill each lined mold three-quarters full. Divide the topping evenly over the kuchens. Bake for 25 to 30 minutes, or until a cake tester inserted into the center of a cake comes out clean. Cool on a wire rack for 10 to 20 minutes before turning the kuchens out of their pans. Once turned over, invert to keep the nut topping on top.

SPECIAL OCCASION LITTLE CAKES

Now it is time to combine my mom's wonderful recipes with some of my fun decorations.

Whether it is Carrot Cake baskets for Easter, classic vanilla Make a Wish Cupcakes for—you guessed it—your birthday, or Big Bang Pistachio Truffles when you just can't survive another night without chocolate, this chapter has a little cake for almost every special occasion.

All you really need to start the decorating process is a fun baking pan. Take the Rose Is a Rose cakes. The individual molds are shaped like small roses, so you don't need to do anything to these lovely delights; just bake and serve. While the Nostalgic Nibbles are decorated simply with a dusting of confectioners' sugar, other little cakes, such as the 3-D beach pail, are complex. But, if you are up for the challenge of creating a mini masterpiece, you will be rewarded with oohs and aahs from your family and friends. Keep in mind that these more difficult designs can be simplified by reducing the number of colors, or by making fewer and simpler chocolate decorations.

When my mom and I plan events, we try to match the flavors of the cake with the design or the season. Although it can be enjoyed year-round, apple cake is an edible representation of autumn. Pineapple upside-down cake combines a tangy and tropical sweetness with a rich, buttery cake, making it perfect after a summer barbecue or as a midwinter reminder that somewhere the sun is shining brightly. And chocolate ganache, cookie crumbs, and Chocolate Butter Cake bring the Flower Pots to life, hinting at the rich dark soil beneath the buttercream violets.

To create a visual delight, display your little cakes on interesting plates or pastry trees. The Raspberry Cheesecakes are plated with a tart and sassy raspberry sauce. Not only is the sauce a delicious accompaniment, but the red color beautifully accents the single berry nestled in the cheesecake. Our Flower Power cupcakes become a gorgeous bouquet when they are arranged on stacked cake pedestals, ideal for a wedding reception or a party centerpiece.

strawberry shortcakes*

YIELD: 8 STARS

You can make a fresh fruit filling for just about any cake, but nothing comes close to the real deal: shortcake. This slightly sweet biscuit is cut in half and filled with fresh strawberries, blueberries, and a generous dollop of whipped cream. Instead of a berry medley, take advantage of the delicious August peach crop, or for an exotic twist try mangos with fresh ginger (see Variation).

We cut out our shortcakes with a star cookie cutter, and they always dazzle on the Fourth of July. Experiment with other simple cookie cutters, such as hearts for Valentine's Day or flowers for a garden party.

SHORTCAKE

Preheat the oven to 350°F. Line a cookie sheet or half-sheet pan with parchment paper.

Pulse in a food processor just to combine:
- 2½ cups all-purpose flour
- 4 teaspoons baking powder
- ½ teaspoon salt
- ¼ cup brown sugar, firmly packed

Add and pulse until pea-size bits of dough form:
- 5 ounces (1¼ sticks) cold unsalted butter

Transfer the butter-flour mixture to a medium bowl. Add and mix until just combined:
- ¾ cup cold milk

If the batter appears too dry, add cold milk 1 tablespoon at a time until the dough just comes together.

Transfer the dough from the bowl to a lightly floured work surface, knead briefly, and then roll out to ½ to ¾ inch thick. Cut out the dough using a 4-inch star cookie cutter. Place the 8 stars 2 inches apart on the prepared pan. Lightly brush the tops of the stars with milk (you will need approximately 2 tablespoons), then sprinkle with granulated sugar.

Bake for 20 to 25 minutes or until golden. Place the pan on a wire rack to cool completely.

FRUIT FILLING

In a bowl combine:
- 2 pints sliced strawberries
- 1 pint blueberries
- 2 tablespoons granulated sugar

Set aside at room temperature for 30 minutes to 2 hours, to let the juices form.

VARIATION

Mango filling: Follow the directions above for fruit filling, replacing the strawberries and blueberries with 2 chopped mangos. To add a bit more zing, add the juice of half a lime and finely grated fresh ginger to taste.

SHORTCAKE ASSEMBLY

Prepare one recipe of Whipped Cream (page 35).

With a serrated knife slice the stars in half horizontally. Place the shortcake bottoms on their serving plates. Scoop approximately ½ cup of fruit on top of each bottom. Dollop whipped cream on top of the fruit. Gently replace the shortcake top. Do not press down. Serve immediately.

raspberry cheesecakes**

As July rolls around and the raspberries are ripe for the picking, make a batch of these tiny delights to celebrate the summer's bounty, or spread the love on Valentine's Day by boxing up a heart-shaped cheesecake for everyone important in your life.

The raspberry sauce is delicious plated beneath these cheesecakes or on a scoop of vanilla ice cream.

RASPBERRY SAUCE (YIELD: ²/₃ TO ³/₄ CUP)

In a food processor, combine and mix until puréed:
- 1 six-ounce container fresh raspberries, gently washed and picked over
- 1 to 2 tablespoons sugar
- 1 tablespoon fresh lemon juice or Framboise liqueur

Strain into a bowl to remove the seeds. Set aside.

Store in the refrigerator in an airtight container.

GRAHAM CRACKER CRUST

Grease 15 molds of two 12-mold mini heart cheesecake pans and wrap the bottom of the pans with aluminum foil.

In a small bowl, mix:
- ³/₄ cup finely crushed graham crackers
- 1 tablespoon sugar

Stir in:
- 2 tablespoons plus 1 teaspoon melted unsalted butter

Divide the crumb crust evenly among the prepared molds (about 1 tablespoon per mold). Press firmly onto the bottom.

FILLING

Preheat the oven to 350°F. Have all ingredients at room temperature.

In the bowl of an electric mixer, beat at medium speed until smooth:
- 12 ounces (one and a half 8-ounce packages) cream cheese

Scrape the bowl down often while beating.

Gradually beat in:
- ¹/₂ cup sugar
- 1 tablespoon all-purpose flour

When the sugar and flour are combined and the batter is smooth, scrape the bowl again. Add and mix at low speed until combined:
- 2 teaspoons grated lemon zest
- 2 tablespoons fresh lemon juice

Add and mix just until smooth:
- 2 large eggs

Pour the filling into the crust.

Insert into the center of each cheesecake:
- 1 large raspberry (15 raspberries in total)

Place the pans in a larger pan and fill the larger pan with ¹/₂ inch of hot water. Bake for 18 to 22 minutes or until set. Let the cheesecakes sit at room temperature for 20 minutes before unmolding. To remove the cheesecakes from the pan, push a wooden spoon through the pan opening under each cheesecake. With a metal spatula remove the metal bottom from each cheesecake. Serve the cheesecakes warm or at room temperature. Alternatively, store the cheesecakes in the refrigerator in an airtight container for up to 2 days. Remove the cheesecakes from the refrigerator 2 hours before serving. Plate with the raspberry sauce.

falling leaves *

Thanksgiving at the Bakehouse is wildly busy, but I always take time to roam the streets looking for saplings with green leaves that have not yet fallen to the ground in a flurry of yellow and orange. It is like a treasure hunt. When I do find the perfect tree, I pluck the leaves off and scurry back to the bakery. These maple and oak leaves are given a gentle bath, patted dry, and then painted with chocolate. This is a classic technique among decorators and chocolatiers, who often use rose leaves. Instead of using dark chocolate, I pay homage to autumn's vibrant colors and paint my leaves yellow, orange, and rust. Because leaves have a thin layer of wax, chocolate doesn't stick to them. So when the leaf is peeled away you are left with a strikingly realistic chocolate leaf, embossed with all of the veins and intricacies of the real leaf.

WHAT YOU WILL NEED:

Cake
12 Pumpkin Spice Cheesecakes (page 72)

Decoration
1 cup white wafer chocolate to make 12 leaves

Colors
yellow, red, and orange candy color

Miscellaneous
1 mini cheesecake pan, a small sable or acrylic paint brush, 1 half-sheet pan, parchment paper, 12 freshly picked small green leaves

HOW TO

1. Pick 12 leaves from nonpoisonous trees; we used small maple and oak leaves, taking care to leave some of the stem intact. Rose leaves work well if you do not have access to the deciduous trees. Gently clean the leaves in mild soapy water. Rinse well and place the leaves between paper towels. Pat dry.

2. Melt the white wafer chocolate (see page 39). Divide the chocolate evenly among three small bowls. Using the Color Mixing Chart on pages 44–45, tint one bowl rust, one orange, and one yellow.

3. Hold a leaf by the stem and gently rest the leaf over your cupped fingers or palm. With a paintbrush, paint the chocolate on the top of the leaf, dragging the chocolate up to the edge but not over it. The leaf can be one color or multicolored (lightly swirl the colors together). The chocolate should be at least ⅛ inch thick. Set the leaf on a parchment-lined sheet pan to harden. To make the leaf look like it is fluttering in the wind, drape part of the leaf over a wooden spoon and let it harden.

4. When hardened, carefully peel the leaf off the chocolate. If you let the chocolate set overnight the leaves are easier to remove.

5. Place one leaf on top of or adjacent to each cheesecake.

pumpkin spice cheesecakes**

YIELD: 12 MINI CHEESECAKES

When I was in college, my mom would send me care packages filled with chocolate chip cookies for my friends and gingersnap cookies all for me. So I was hooked when she told me these autumn cheesecakes combine the snap of our ginger cookie crust with the warmth of pumpkin and fall spices. You might find yourself saying bye-bye to pumpkin pie and hello to pumpkin cheesecake at your next Thanksgiving dinner.

GINGERSNAP CRUST

This recipe makes a lot of cookies, so we recommend baking only what is needed for this recipe. On a lightly floured board roll any leftover dough into logs. Wrap the logs in plastic wrap and freeze for up to 2 months. Remove the logs from the freezer and slice and bake whenever you want gingersnaps.

Line a cookie sheet or half-sheet pan with parchment paper. Grease one 12-mold mini cheesecake pan (the molds should be 2 inches in diameter; see the Cake Pan Chart on pages 16–17). Wrap the bottom of the cheesecake pan with aluminum foil. Preheat the oven to 350°F. Have all ingredients at room temperature.

In the bowl of an electric mixer at medium speed, cream until fluffy:

- 8 ounces (2 sticks) unsalted butter
- 1¼ cups sugar

Add and mix until smooth:

- 1 large egg
- ¼ cup molasses
- 1½ teaspoons vinegar

On a piece of wax paper, sift together:

- 2½ cups all-purpose flour
- 1 teaspoon baking soda
- 1 tablespoon plus 1 teaspoon ground ginger
- ½ teaspoon ground cinnamon
- ¼ teaspoon ground cloves
- Pinch of salt

Add to the butter mixture and mix at low speed until well combined.

Chill the dough, while it is still in the mixing bowl, for 10 minutes. Shape a portion of the dough into 12 ¾-inch balls. (Freeze the remaining dough; see headnote.) Arrange the balls 2 inches apart on the prepared cookie sheet. Bake the cookies for 8 to 10 minutes or until lightly colored. Let the cookies cool on the pan for 5 minutes, then, using a 2-inch round cookie cutter, cut out circles from the center of each cookie. Save the leftover edges for a snack. Place one cookie round in the bottom of each prepared cheesecake cup.

PUMPKIN FILLING

Preheat the oven to 350°F. Have all ingredients at room temperature.

In the bowl of an electric mixer, beat at medium speed until smooth:

- 12 ounces (one and a half 8-ounce packages) cream cheese

Scrape down the bowl often while beating.

Gradually beat in at medium speed:

- ⅓ cup brown sugar, packed
- 2 tablespoons all-purpose flour
- 2 tablespoons heavy cream

Add and stir to combine:

- ¼ cup canned pumpkin purée
- ½ teaspoon ground cinnamon
- ¼ teaspoon ground ginger
- ⅛ teaspoon allspice
- ⅛ teaspoon ground nutmeg
- 2 tablespoons finely chopped crystallized ginger (optional)

Add one at a time at low speed:

- 2 large eggs

Beat only until the eggs are fully incorporated. Pour the filling over the gingersnap crust in the prepared molds.

Place the pan in a larger pan and fill the larger pan with ½ inch of hot water. Bake for 20 to 25 minutes or until set. Let the cheesecakes sit at room temperature for 20 minutes before unmolding. To remove the cheesecakes from the pan, push a wooden spoon through the pan opening under each cheesecake. With a metal spatula remove the metal bottom from each cheesecake. Serve the cheesecakes warm or at room temperature. Alternatively, store the cheesecakes in the refrigerator in an airtight container for up to 1 week. Remove the cheesecakes from the refrigerator 2 hours before serving.

matt's
upside-down cakes*

YIELD: 12 CAKES

My mom isn't the only amazing baker in her family. My uncle Matt Hudson is also known for his amazing dessert creations. Every time I go to his restaurant, the Hudson House in Nyack, New York, I can't resist getting one of his upside-down cakes. They change seasonally from pear to plum. When we found these mini upside-down baking molds at Williams-Sonoma, we knew we had to try pineapple. We thank Matt for his recipe, and I think you'll be thanking him, too, once you mix up a batch.

Lightly butter two 6-mold mini pineapple upside-down pans, or two 6-mold cupcake pans if making pear or plum upside-down cakes (see Note). Preheat the oven to 350°F. Have all ingredients at room temperature.

In a saucepan, melt:
- 3 ounces (¾ stick) unsalted butter

Add and whisk until combined:
- 1 cup firmly packed light brown sugar

Pour 1½ tablespoons of the butter-sugar mixture into each mold.

In the center of each mold place one slice of peeled and cored fresh or canned pineapple and one candied or canned cherry (12 pineapple slices and 12 cherries in total), or one slice of plum or pear (12 slices in total).

In the bowl of an electric mixer, combine:
- 2¼ cups all-purpose flour
- 2¼ cups granulated sugar
- 1 tablespoon cardamom
- 1¾ teaspoons baking soda
- ¾ teaspoon salt

Add and mix to combine:
- ¾ cup vegetable oil
- 3 large eggs

Mix in:
- ¾ cup (6 slices) coarsely grated pineapple with accumulated juice
- 1 tablespoon grated peeled fresh ginger

Divide the batter among the prepared pans.

Bake for 20 to 25 minutes or until a cake tester inserted into the center of a cake comes out clean. The tops should spring back when lightly pressed. Let the pan cool on a wire rack for no longer than 5 minutes, then place a sheet pan or large plate on top of the upside-down pan and invert. The pineapple cakes should unmold easily. They are best served warm, or refrigerate in an airtight container for up to 2 days, and reheat for 10 minutes at 350°F.

NOTE:

Substitute ¾ cup grated pear or plum (approximately 1 to 2 pears or 3 to 4 plums) for the grated pineapple when making pear or plum upside-down cakes.

nostalgic nibbles and devilish delights*

Here are some snacks that will have you skipping down memory lane.
Our renditions of the classic Twinkie and Devil Dog are even better than the originals since they are home-baked and fresh. Kids will adore them, and they will make you feel like a kid again.

We fill these treats with light whipped cream or Dulce de Leche—whatever strikes your fancy. Milk Chocolate Glaze is optional, but it adds another dimension of flavor. Serve with a cup of chilled milk and you are set.

WHAT YOU WILL NEED:

Cake

16 Caramel Cake Twinkies minus the chips (page 79), or 18 Devil's Food Cake Twinkies (page 78), cooled

Filling

Whipped Cream (page 35) or 1½ cups Dulce de Leche (page 101)

Icing

¼ cup confectioners' sugar or 1 recipe Milk Chocolate Glaze (see page 34)

Tip

12 round tip or comparable

Miscellaneous

pastry bag, coupler, sifter for confectioners' sugar, or wire rack and half-sheet pan if glazing (optional 2 tablespoons melted chocolate for decorative drizzling)

HOW TO

1 Prepare the Dulce de Leche, if needed.

2 Bake the cakes and let them cool completely.

3 Prepare the Milk Chocolate Glaze, if needed. Prepare the Whipped Cream, if needed.

4 Place the Whipped Cream or Dulce de Leche into a pastry bag with a coupler and a #12 round tip. Insert the tip of the pastry bag into the center bottom of the cake and squeeze. Continue squeezing until the cake begins to swell in your hands or until the filling just begins to seep out around the tip's edge. Insert the tip again to the left and right of the center, being sure to stay at least ½ inch from the ends.

5 If you are keeping it simple, place the confectioners' sugar in a sifter and dust the tops of the filled cakes.

6 If glazing, freeze the filled cakes for 30 minutes. Once chilled, arrange the cakes 1 inch apart on the wire rack placed over the sheet pan. Ladle or pour the glaze over the tops. Remove the cakes from the rack with a metal spatula and plate.

7 Drizzle the tops with melted chocolate for added effect, if using.

8 For fullest flavor, serve the cakes at room temperature.

devil's food cake*

YIELD: 18 CUPCAKES OR 18 DEVILISH DELIGHTS

This versatile Devil's Food Cake is great baked in cupcake liners, Twinkie pans, or standard round cake pans. Smother it in Matt's Fudge Icing (page 35) or make it more angelic with a coating of Whipped Cream (page 35). Some recipes call for additional red dye; instead, the extra baking soda gives this recipe a red tint.

If you are making Devilish Delights (page 76), grease 18 molds of three Twinkie pans. If you are making cupcakes, grease the tops of three 6-mold muffin pans and line them with paper liners. Preheat the oven to 350°F. Have all ingredients at room temperature.

In the bowl of an electric mixer, beat at high speed until light and fluffy:

- 6 ounces (1½ sticks) unsalted butter
- 1 cup granulated sugar
- ¾ cup light brown sugar, packed
- ½ cup cocoa powder

Add one at a time and beat on medium speed until well creamed:

- 3 extra-large eggs
- 1 teaspoon pure vanilla extract

On a piece of wax paper, sift together:

- 2¾ cups cake flour
- 2 teaspoons baking soda
- 1½ teaspoons salt

At low speed, add the dry ingredients to the butter mixture alternately with:

- 1½ cups buttermilk

Pour the batter into the prepared molds, filling each mold three-quarters full. Bake for 20 to 25 minutes, or until a cake tester inserted into the center of a cake comes out clean. Cool on a wire rack for 15 to 20 minutes before turning the cakes out of the pans or 5 to 10 minutes before removing the cupcakes from their pans.

caramel cake*

I am a sucker for caramel or anything in the caramel family: Dulce de Leche,
butterscotch, caramel apples, caramel popcorn. So, whether caramel is drizzled all over ice cream,
plated with a dessert, piped into a truffle, or made into a cake, I'll try it. And this cake is amaz-
ing. We added some butterscotch chips for even more yummy-ness. Now, if you happen to be a
chocoholic, simply substitute mini chocolate chips for the butterscotch chips.

If you are making Nostalgic Nibbles (page 76), grease and flour 16 molds of three Twinkie pans. If you are making cupcakes, grease and flour the tops of three 6-mold muffin pans and line 16 of the molds with paper liners. If you are making the beach pail (see A Day at the Beach, page 128), grease and flour four 4-inch round cake pans. Preheat the oven to 350°F. Have all ingredients at room temperature.

In the bowl of an electric mixer, beat at high speed until light and fluffy:
- 6 ounces (1½ sticks) unsalted butter
- 1¼ cups light brown sugar, packed

Add slowly and beat on medium speed until fluffy:
- 3 extra-large eggs
- 1 teaspoon pure vanilla extract

On a piece of wax paper, sift together:
- 2½ cups cake flour
- 2 teaspoons baking powder
- ¼ teaspoon baking soda
- ½ teaspoon salt

At low speed, add the dry ingredients to the butter and egg mixture alternately with:
- 6 ounces (¾ cup) milk

Fold in:
- 3 ounces (¾ cup) butterscotch chips or mini chocolate chips

Fill each mold or liner three-quarters full. Bake for 18 to 20 minutes, or until golden, or 30 minutes for the 4-inch round cakes. The tops should spring back when lightly pressed. Cool on a wire rack for 5 to 10 minutes before removing the cupcakes from their pans or before turning the cakes out of their pans.

the big bang*

I first heard the term "Big Bang" during my high school biology class. The only way I was able to translate this immense and unfathomable happening was to capture it with paper and pencil. Years later I am still trying to visually encapsulate it. This is my edible glimpse of our galaxy. A rich chocolate truffle echoes the molten center of our planet while a crunchy exterior of encrusted pistachios will have you digging in for more. To top it all off, chaotic swirls of chocolate explode from the truffle.

Cake
12 Pistachio Ganache Truffles (page 82)

Plating
Caramel Sauce (page 82)

Decoration
1 cup dark wafer chocolate, ½ cup white wafer chocolate, and two tablespoons ground pistachios to make 12 explosions of chocolate

Colors
yellow and orange candy color

Miscellaneous
one mini cheesecake pan, pastry cones, 1 half-sheet pan, parchment paper

HOW TO

1 Melt the dark wafer and white wafer chocolates separately. Using the Color Mixing Chart on pages 44—45, tint the white chocolate caramel. Pour the dark and caramel-colored chocolate into two separate pastry cones.

2 Line the half-sheet pan with parchment paper. Cut a medium hole in the dark chocolate pastry cone and pipe overlapping, random elliptical lines onto the parchment, keeping the design no more than 2 inches wide and 3 inches high. It is best if one end of the design is narrower to facilitate insertion into the truffle. Cut a medium hole in the caramel chocolate pastry cone and pipe it over the dark chocolate with a few sporadic elliptical lines. Before the chocolate sets sprinkle ground pistachios on top. Make 12 swirls in total. Set the designs aside to harden.

3 If desired, flip the designs and over-pipe additional caramel lines and sprinkle with pistachios.

4 Prepare the truffles and caramel sauce.

5 Before the ganache has completely set, press the chocolate designs ½ inch deep into the center of each truffle.

6 Plate the truffles on a bed of caramel sauce.

7 For fullest flavor, serve the cakes at room temperature.

pistachio
ganache truffles*

YIELD: 12 TRUFFLES

This is one of the tastiest desserts the Bakehouse offers for Passover, a
decadent treat from the rich ganache to the sea of caramel the truffle rests on. You would be
hard-pressed to find a more perfect finale. Enjoy every bite.

You'll need one ungreased 12-mold mini cheesecake pan. Preheat the oven to 350°F.

CARAMEL SAUCE

This sauce is great paired not only with these truffles, but with ice cream, too. It keeps well in the refrigerator for at least a month.

In a heavy saucepan, melt:
- 4 ounces (1 stick) unsalted butter

Add and cook until amber colored, stirring occasionally:
- 1 cup sugar

Meanwhile, in a separate saucepan, over medium heat, scald:
- 1 cup heavy cream

When the sugar mixture is caramelized, slowly whisk in the heavy cream; be careful, because the sugar mixture will bubble up as the cream is added. Stir until smooth. Remove from the heat. Set aside.

CRUST

In a small bowl, combine:
- 1 cup finely ground pistachios
- ⅓ cup sugar
- 2 tablespoons plus 1 teaspoon melted unsalted butter

Place 2 tablespoons of crust into the bottom of each cheesecake mold. Press firmly onto the bottom and one third of the way up the sides. Bake for 5 to 10 minutes or until lightly browned. Set aside.

GANACHE

In a small bowl placed over a hot-water bath, melt:
- 6 ounces finely chopped semisweet chocolate

In a saucepan over medium heat, bring to a boil:
- ¾ cup heavy cream

Add the heavy cream to the chocolate and let sit for 3 minutes. Then whisk until the chocolate is melted and the ganache is smooth.

Pour the ganache into the crust molds. Chill until firm (approximately 2 hours). If you plan on making the Big Bang (page 80), before the ganache has completely set, press the chocolate designs ½ inch deep into the center of each truffle.

To unmold, push a wooden spoon through the pan openings under each mold. With a metal spatula, remove the metal bottom from each truffle. Store the ganache truffles in the refrigerator in an airtight container for up to 1 week. Remove the truffles from the refrigerator 2 hours before serving. Plate with the caramel sauce.

cream puff nests*

Whenever I mention cream puffs, my mom steps back in time to recount how her mother often served them with chocolate sauce; it was a family favorite. All of my mom's nine brothers and sisters delighted in the feast. I'm sure it wasn't easy to bake for a brood of ten, but Pâte à Choux is a simple recipe that makes it seem feasible.

I transformed the pâte à choux into little eggs sitting in birds' nests. Perfect for a baby shower or Easter, the nests are simply decorated with chocolate grass, a sprinkling of sliced almonds, and a dusting of confectioners' sugar.

Take care not to eat all of the cream-puff eggs before your guests arrive!

Cake
6 to 8 Pâte à Choux nests and 18 to 24 Pâte à Choux eggs (page 85)

Filling
3 cups French Custard made from Pastry Cream (page 86)

Decoration
½ cup dark wafer chocolate to make grass, ¼ cup sliced almonds

Tips
choose a star tip between #26 and #30, and a #6 or #7 round tip

Miscellaneous
pastry cones, 1 half-sheet pan, parchment paper, six to eight 5-inch (or larger) bases, confectioners' sugar

HOW TO

1. Prepare the Pastry Cream.

2. Prepare the Pâte à Choux nests and eggs.

3. Line the half-sheet pan with parchment paper. Melt the dark wafer chocolate and pour it into a pastry cone. Cut a medium hole in the cone and pipe semi-parallel lines, by moving the cone back and forth across the length of the sheet pan. Set aside to harden.

4. Prepare the French Custard.

5. With a small serrated knife, carefully trim off the over-piped portion of the nest and set aside. Adhere the bottom portion of the nest to its base with a dollop of French Custard.

6. Place the rest of the French Custard into a pastry bag with a coupler, and with the tip between #26 and #30, pipe a spiral to cover the bottom of the nest. Pipe extra French Custard on the outer edge. Place the trimmed edge back on top of the custard. Repeat with the remaining nests.

7. Change the tip to a #6 round tip. To fill the eggs, insert the pastry tip into the underside of each cream puff. Squeeze until the cream seeps out around the tip's edge or you feel the egg swell in your hand. Repeat with the remaining eggs.

8. Place 3 eggs in each nest. Finely dust with confectioners' sugar.

9. Break apart the chocolate into 3- to 4-inch strips and randomly place the segments into each nest. Sprinkle almonds over the tops of the nests.

10. Serve right away.

pâte à choux nests*

YIELD: 6 TO 8 NESTS AND 18 TO 24 EGGS

This classic French recipe is versatile enough to be used for sweet éclairs and cream puffs or as a shell for savory appetizers. Don't be intimidated by its French origins; it is so easy to make that all you need is a saucepan and a wooden spoon.

Trace six to eight 3½-inch circles onto a piece of parchment paper. Invert the parchment paper onto a sheet pan. Line an additional sheet pan with parchment paper. Preheat the oven to 350°F. Have all ingredients at room temperature.

In a saucepan over medium heat, bring to a boil:

- 1 cup milk
- 4 ounces (1 stick) unsalted butter, cut into slices
- Pinch of salt
- 1 teaspoon sugar

Turn the heat to medium and add:

- 1 cup all-purpose flour, sifted

Beat with a wooden spoon until the batter pulls away from the side of the pan and forms a ball.

Remove from the heat.

Beat in one at a time:

- 4 large eggs

Beat until glossy.

Place the dough, while it is still warm, into a pastry bag with a coupler and a #12 round tip. Using firm pressure and staying within the border of the template you traced, pipe out a 3½-inch circle and fill it in with a continuous spiral. The dough should be approximately ½-inch high. Pipe an additional circle on top of the first 3½-inch circle; it should be about ½ inch higher than the center spiral. Do not pipe an overlapping additional spiral. Make 6 to 8 nests in total. On a separate sheet pan, pipe 3 nickel-size balls (the eggs) per nest.

Bake the eggs for 20 to 25 minutes and the nests for 28 to 35 minutes, or until puffed and browned.

p a s t r y   c r e a m **

YIELD: 1¹/₂ CUPS

Pastry cream is basically vanilla custard. Use it to fill cream puffs, éclairs, or lighten the texture by folding in whipped cream—thus making French Custard (see below). It holds up well when being piped, so it is perfect for our Cream Puff Nests. Prepare the Pastry Cream in advance, but do not fold in the whipped cream until you are ready to assemble the nests. Any leftover Pastry Cream can be made into a crème anglaise by thinning it out with cream.

In a saucepan over high heat, bring to a boil:

- 1 cup milk
- ¼ vanilla bean, sliced down one side (see Note)

In the bowl of an electric mixer on medium speed, beat until light and fluffy:

- 3 large egg yolks
- ⅓ cup sugar
- Pinch of salt

Add and mix to combine:

- 2 tablespoons cornstarch

Remove the vanilla bean from the milk. Scrape the seeds out with a small paring knife and put them back in the milk, discarding the bean. Slowly beat the hot milk into the yolk mixture and return the mixture to the saucepan. Bring it to a boil over medium-low heat, stirring constantly. Reduce the heat to low and continue boiling for 1 minute, stirring constantly.

Pour the pastry cream into a medium stainless-steel bowl, cover it with plastic wrap, and refrigerate until cold.

NOTE:

You can substitute ¾ teaspoon pure vanilla extract for the vanilla bean. Add the vanilla extract right at the end when the pastry cream is removed from the heat.

FRENCH CUSTARD

YIELD: 4¹/₂ CUPS FRENCH CUSTARD

For best results, we recommend preparing the French Custard right before serving or assembling your cakes.

Prepare the Pastry Cream as directed above.

In the bowl of an electric mixer fitted with a whisk attachment, whip until stiff:

- 1½ cups heavy cream
- 2 tablespoons confectioners' sugar
- ½ teaspoon pure vanilla extract

Stir the pastry cream until smooth. Fold in one quarter of the whipped cream and mix just until combined. Fold in the remaining whipped cream.

i scream,
you scream...*

We all scream for ice cream! While browsing through our local Williams-Sonoma, I found these great ice-cream-cone pans, and I knew I would have to include them in the book. Even though I make cakes for a living, ice cream remains one of my favorite desserts, and mint chocolate chip is my favorite flavor. We topped our classic Pound Cake with a soft-serve spiral of mint chocolate chip cream. Feel free to create an ode to your favorite. How about a Pecan Pound Cake cone with a Whipped Chocolate Ganache (page 105) topping? Now that is very adult.

Dip the "ice cream" in sprinkles or try our hard Chocolate Shell. What fun.

Cake
12 Pound Cake ice cream cones (page 89)

Topping
Mint Chocolate Chip Cream (page 90)

Optional Topping
colored sprinkles (½ cup of sprinkles covers approximately 6 cones) or Chocolate Shell (page 91)

Tip
large #848 star

Miscellaneous
2 ice-cream-cone pans, pastry bag

HOW TO

1. Bake the cakes and let them cool completely. Trim the domes off and trim the bottoms to make sure the ice cream cones will not wobble when standing on their own.

2. Prepare the cream and other optional toppings.

3. Place the cream in the pastry bag with the star tip. Make sure the star tip's rays are as open as possible to allow the mini chips to pass through without clogging the tip.

4. Pipe a large circle on top of each cone, being careful to stay within the confines of the cone's top edge. Continue spiraling upward, getting narrower with each pass until tailing off with a flourish to create a point. Chill in the refrigerator or freezer for 1 to 2 hours or overnight in an airtight container. Remove 1 hour before serving. If adding additional toppings, see steps 5 to 7.

5. Freeze the filled cones until the mousse is hard to the touch, 1 to 2 hours.

6. Sprinkles: Place the colored sprinkles in a bowl large enough to accommodate a cone rolling in it. Roll each soft-serve portion of the frozen cone in the sprinkles, pressing the mousse firmly to adhere the sprinkles.

7. Glaze: Pour the Chocolate Shell into a tall, narrow container. Submerge one inverted cone at a time up to the cake line. Pull up and out while lightly spinning the cone to allow any excess glaze to drip off. Place right side up on a sheet pan to set. If necessary, dip the cone again once the first layer of Chocolate Shell has dried.

8. For the fullest flavor, serve the cakes at room temperature.

pound cake*

YIELD: 12 ICE CREAM CONES OR 3 MINI TIERED CAKES

Most of my mom's pound cakes have sour cream added in, but this classic comes from my sweet-toothed husband, Luiz. Since we reduced the recipe, we are just shy of the traditional "pound of sugar, pound of butter, pound of flour" pound cake. But, true to its name, it is dense, moist, and delicious.

If you are making I Scream, You Scream . . . (page 87), grease two 6-mold ice-cream-cone pans or mini tiered cake pans.

If you are making mini tiered cakes, grease two 2-inch, two 3-inch, and two 4-inch round cake pans.

Preheat the oven to 350°F. Have all ingredients at room temperature.

In the bowl of an electric mixer, cream well:
- 12 ounces (3 sticks) unsalted butter
- 1¾ cups sugar

Add and cream at high speed until light and fluffy:
- 7 extra-large egg yolks
- 1 teaspoon pure vanilla extract

On a piece of wax paper, sift together:
- 2½ cups all-purpose flour
- ½ teaspoon baking powder

Add the dry ingredients to the butter and egg mixture and mix on low speed just until combined.

In a clean bowl of an electric mixer with a whip attachment, whip until stiff but not dry:
- 5 extra-large egg whites

Fold one quarter of the egg whites into the batter until combined. Then gently fold in the remaining egg whites.

Pour the batter into the prepared pans, filling each three-quarters full. Bake for 28 to 30 minutes, or until a cake tester inserted into the center of a cake comes out clean. Cool on a wire rack for 15 to 20 minutes. Turn the cakes out of their pans. Invert to cool, so they are right side up. Slice off the dome that formed when baking.

mint chocolate chip cream*

YIELD: 6 CUPS

I still feel a bit childish going into an ice cream shop asking for my usual:
"I'll have the mint on a sugar cone with"—spoken very quietly—"colored sprinkles." Now I can
make my own version at home.

For best results we recommend preparing the Mint Chocolate Chip Cream right before serving
or assembling your cakes.

In the bowl of an electric mixer fitted with a whisk attachment, whip until stiff:
- 3 cups heavy cream
- 5 tablespoons confectioners' sugar, sifted
- ½ teaspoon mint extract

Fold in:
- ¼ cup plus 1 tablespoon mini chocolate chips

CHOCOLATE SHELL*

Inspired by the Brown Bonnet served at the Carvel ice cream shops, and by all of the other old-fashioned ice cream dips, we made our soft-serve wafer cone complete with a dunk into our Chocolate Shell. Choose between milk chocolate or tinted white chocolate—both are sure to please.

This glaze is meant to cover frozen desserts. If the cream or cake is at room temperature or not cold enough, the glaze will drip off, melt the cream, or turn out semi-transparent. The glaze is meant to be used in a warm to hot liquid state, 98° to 105°F.

Any leftovers can be stored in an airtight container, at room temperature, for up to 1 month.

MILK CHOCOLATE SHELL

The ingredients can alternatively be melted in a double boiler.

YIELD: 1³/₄ CUPS
LIQUID GLAZE

In a glass bowl, combine and microwave at 30-second intervals, stirring in between, until melted (it should take approximately four passes in the microwave):
- 9⅓ ounces chopped milk chocolate
- 7 ounces (1 cup) vegetable shortening

If necessary, whisk to combine.

WHITE CHOCOLATE SHELL

The ingredients can alternatively be melted in a double boiler.

YIELD: 1³/₄ CUPS
LIQUID GLAZE

In a glass bowl, combine and microwave at 30-second intervals, stirring in between, until melted (it should take approximately four passes in the microwave):
- 10½ ounces chopped white chocolate
- 5¼ ounces (¾ cup) vegetable shortening

To tint the glaze, stir in:
- 6 drops red candy color

If necessary, whisk to combine.

The Bakehouse's signature cake is our Mini Birthday Cake, and although we taught everyone how to make it in our first book, I was sad not to see it represented in our Little Cakes book, since it was one of the first little cakes I ever made. A batch of fifteen 4-inch cakes brightened up our storefront way back in 1996, and everything began to change. This time around I am offering a variation on the original, which I designed on a whim: Make a Wish Cupcakes. These cupcakes use some of the same piping techniques as the original, and they too have edible chocolate candles, and a colorful palette.

The directions below illustrate how to make a cupcake with purple icing, green and teal piping, and a pink candle. Substitute whatever colors match your party.

Cake
12 Classic Vanilla Cupcakes (page 95)

Icing
House Buttercream (page 31) or Kaye's Buttercream (with a pastel palette) (page 32) or Kids' Buttercream (page 33)

Optional filling
Goodies and Cream made with shaved chocolate (page 98)

Decoration
1 cup white wafer chocolate to make 12 candles

Colors
Choose three liquid gel colors from the following list: purple, teal, green, yellow, blue, violet, neon pink, and orange. Choose one candy color plus yellow from the following list: neon bright pink, green, blue, or violet

Tips
#16 Ateco and/or #27 P&H star tip

Miscellaneous
one 12-mold muffin pan, 2 pastry bags, 2 couplers, pastry cones, 1 half-sheet pan, parchment paper or cellophane

1   Bake the cupcakes and let them cool completely. Freeze for 1 hour to overnight.

2   Prepare the icing and optional filling.

3   Fill the cupcakes as directed in Filling a Cupcake, number 2 or number 3, on page 22. Chill for at least 30 minutes or overnight.

4   Melt the white wafer chocolate. Using the Color Mixing Chart on pages 44—45, tint ⅛ cup yellow and ⅜ cup neon pink. Pour the chocolates into two separate pastry cones and cut a medium-size hole in each. On the sheet pan lined with parchment paper pipe out twelve 3-inch candles (see Adventurous Alternative). They should be at least ¼ inch wide and ⅛ inch thick. Set aside to harden.

5   When the chocolate has set, pipe yellow flames on the top of each candle. Set aside to harden. When the flames have set, flip the candles over and pipe flames on the opposite side. This way the flame can be seen from both sides of the candle.

6   Prepare the colored buttercream: approximately 1½ cups purple for the base, 1 cup neon green for the shell borders, and ½ cup teal for the rosettes.

7   Ice the cupcakes with a smooth finish as directed on page 26.

8   Place the neon green buttercream into a pastry bag with a coupler, and with a star tip pipe a shell border around the top edge of each cupcake. See the piping techniques below.

9   Place the teal buttercream in a pastry bag with a coupler, and with a star tip pipe a rosette in the center of each cupcake.

10 Stick the candles into the rosettes, pressing them halfway down into each cupcake.

11 For fullest flavor, serve the cakes at room temperature.

ADVENTUROUS ALTERNATIVE

Cut 6 drinking straws down one side. Pipe melted and tinted chocolate into the straws, gently tapping them to release any air bubbles as you go, until the straws are full. Set aside to harden. When the chocolate has set, carefully remove the plastic straws to reveal solid chocolate cylinders. With a paring knife, score the cylinders every 3 inches. Break the cylinders along these score marks. Pipe a yellow flame on the top of each cylinder and set aside to harden.

PIPING TECHNIQUES

Shell Border
  • Star tip (#16)

Hold the bag at a 45-degree angle to the cake surface. Rest the tip where you are going to begin piping the shell. Without moving the pastry bag, apply a heavy, consistent pressure, allowing the tip to rise as the icing builds. Once the shell has formed, decrease the pressure while dragging the tip downward, forming a tail. Begin the next shell overlapping the preceding tail.

Rosettes
  • Star Tip (# 27)

Hold the bag perpendicular to the surface of the cake. Using consistent pressure, pipe a tight circle. Without releasing the pressure, continue the spiral over the first circle, releasing the pressure as you tail it off.

classic vanilla cupcakes*

Our Classic Vanilla Cupcake has a nostalgic flavor and is wonderful paired with vanilla buttercream or fudge. It is also delicious glazed, left plain, or even cut in half and served with fresh fruit and a dollop of whipped cream.

Grease the top of a 12-mold muffin pan and line it with paper liners. Preheat the oven to 350°F. Have all ingredients at room temperature.

Sift into a mixing bowl:
- 1¾ cups plus 2 tablespoons cake flour
- ¾ teaspoon salt

Add and mix to combine:
- 1 cup sugar

Add:
- ½ cup plus 2½ teaspoons warmed milk (110°F)
- 2 large eggs
- 4 ounces (1 stick) very soft unsalted butter
- ½ teaspoon pure vanilla extract

Beat at low speed with a whisk attachment for 1 minute. Scrape down the bowl. Raise the speed to medium-low and beat for 1½ minutes.

Add:
- 1½ teaspoons baking powder

Mix at low speed for 30 seconds.

Scoop the batter into the prepared molds, filling each three-quarters full. Bake for 18 to 20 minutes, or until golden.

The tops should spring back when lightly pressed. Cool on a wire rack for 5 to 10 minutes before removing the cupcakes from the pan.

halloween cupcakes **

Halloween is my favorite holiday, perhaps because it is so visual—from the costumes to the treats. I also love the fact that the chance to be creative and daring is welcomed.

We sell more than a thousand of these spooky cupcakes every Halloween. With twenty designs to choose from including ghosts, skeletons, gravestones, and mummies, you won't know which to make—so why not try them all? The cupcakes are devil's food (how appropriate) and all of the decorations are made with chocolate. A simple decorating alternative that most kids will love is to encrust the top of these cupcakes with small candies such as M&Ms or Sno Caps. Any leftover candy can be handed out to the trick-or-treaters.

When your favorite holiday rolls around, use the same Chocolate Method techniques to decorate your cupcakes: for Christmas make chocolate reindeer, Santa hats, stockings, and candy canes and for Easter make chocolate Easter baskets, bunnies, and eggs.

. . . .

WHAT YOU WILL NEED:
. . . .

Cake
18 Devil's Food cupcakes (page 78)

Icing
Kids' Buttercream (page 33) or Matt's Fudge Icing (page 35)

Optional Filling
Goodies and Cream made with crushed Butterfingers or Heath bars (page 98)

Decoration
The amounts of chocolate may differ depending on your chosen design. To be on the safe side, have approximately 2 cups of dark and 3 cups of white wafer chocolate on hand, along with sprinkles or nonpareils for cupcake edging.

Colors
blue, orange, yellow, green, and purple liquid gel colors and orange, red, blue, green, yellow, and purple candy color. Choose colors according to what's appropriate for your design.

Miscellaneous
three 6-mold muffin pans, pastry cones, Halloween templates (pages 171–172), 1 half-sheet pan, parchment paper or cellophane

1. Bake the cupcakes and let them cool completely. Freeze for 1 hour to overnight.

2. Prepare the icing of your choice.

3. Melt the dark wafer and white wafer chocolates separately. Using the templates provided, make 18 Halloween designs as illustrated in The Chocolate Method (pages 40–43). Here are sample chocolate amounts: to make 18 jack-o'-lanterns melt 2⅔ cups white wafer chocolate and ¼ cup dark wafer chocolate. Tint the white chocolate: tint approximately 1 cup of it orange, 3 tablespoons yellow, and 3 tablespoons green. To make 18 ghosts, melt 1½ cups of white wafer chocolate and ⅛ cup of dark wafer chocolate. To make the hand in a pool of blood, melt 5 cups of white wafer chocolate and ¼ cup of dark wafer chocolate. Tint half the white chocolate red and the other half neon green. Set aside the completed designs to harden. For all other designs, use the photograph as a color guide and melt and tint chocolate accordingly. The base colors will need the most chocolate, while the details will need less.

4. Fill the cupcakes as directed in Filling a Cupcake, number 2 or number 3, on page 22. Chill for at least 30 minutes.

5. Ice the cupcakes with an old-fashioned or flat icing as directed on pages 25 and 26.

6. Put a dollop of icing on the underside of each design and place it right side up on the cupcake. If the design is freestanding, press it halfway into the cupcake.

7. Add any over-piping such as dots, grass, stars, or dirt with the remaining chocolate.

8. For fullest flavor, serve the cakes at room temperature.

goodies and cream filling*

YIELD: 2½ CUPS

Originally we added crushed Oreos to a whipped-cream base to create one of the simplest and best-tasting fillings around. Since then we have found many goodies that can be crushed and added to create a variety of flavors. At Halloween we make an awesome candy bar mousse by crushing Heath bars and Butterfingers and folding them into our whipped-cream base. Add graham crackers for a touch of s'mores flavor, or for a more refined palate simply take your favorite chocolate (chilled) and grate it into the whipped cream. This provides a bit of crunch and a lot of flavor!

For best results, we recommend preparing the Goodies and Cream right before serving or assembling your cupcakes.

NOTE:

If you plan on piping this filling, make sure the add-ins are finely ground so they do not get clogged in the pastry bag.

In the bowl of an electric mixer fitted with a whisk attachment, whip until stiff:
- 1¼ cups heavy cream
- 2 tablespoons confectioners' sugar
- ¼ teaspoon pure vanilla extract

Gently fold in:
- ½ cup of your favorite crushed goody

mini acorn cupcakes**

Fun for children and adults alike, these bite-size cupcakes are a twist on their larger cousin. If you have embraced little plates and tasting menus, consider having dessert tapas. Make three or more different cakes in these bite-size portions; then plate, serve, and watch your guests swoon. On a similar note, if you are planning a brunch, fill a basket with a variety of mini muffins.

Here we ice our Chocolate Coconut Cupcakes with a dollop of German Chocolate Icing—sinfully delicious. If the mood strikes you, top the icing with a chocolate acorn.

WHAT YOU WILL NEED:

Cake
40 miniature Chocolate Coconut Cupcakes (page 100)

Icing
German Chocolate Icing (page 101)

Decoration
2 cups white wafer chocolate and ½ cup dark wafer chocolate to make 40 acorns

Colors
Yellow and orange candy color

Miscellaneous
2 mini muffin pans, pastry cones, acorn templates (page 170), 1 half-sheet pan, parchment paper or cellophane

HOW TO

1. Prepare the German Chocolate Icing.

2. Bake the cupcakes and let them cool completely. Freeze for 1 hour or overnight.

3. Melt the dark wafer and white wafer chocolates separately. Set aside 2 tablespoons white chocolate for highlights. Tint the remaining white chocolate light brown and dark brown. To make the light brown, mix together approximately ½ cup white chocolate, ½ teaspoon dark chocolate, and 1 drop each of yellow and orange candy color. To make dark brown, mix together approximately ½ cup white chocolate, 1 tablespoon dark chocolate, and 2 drops of orange candy color. Using the templates provided, make 40 acorn tops and 40 acorn bottoms as illustrated in The Chocolate Method (pages 40–43).

4. When the chocolate has set, adhere the top of the acorn to the bottom with a dot of melted chocolate (any leftover chocolate will do, as this dot will not be seen). Hold in place for 10 seconds until set.

5. Ice the cupcakes as directed in Old-Fashioned Icing on a Cupcake, page 25.

6. Place one acorn on the top of each cupcake.

7. For fullest flavor, serve the cakes at room temperature.

chocolate coconut cupcakes with german chocolate icing *

YIELD: 40 MINI CUPCAKES

Instead of the classic milk chocolate cake usually paired with German chocolate icing, we went over the top and made a chocolate coconut cake. In addition, unlike the traditional icing, which has unpredictable results, our simple and irresistible icing is made with sweetened condensed milk, toasted coconut, and pecans.

Grease the tops of two 24-mold mini muffin pans and line 40 molds with mini paper liners (optional). If not using paper liners, grease the molds as well. Preheat the oven to 350°F. Have all ingredients at room temperature.

In the bowl of an electric mixer, beat at high speed until light and fluffy:

- 6 ounces (1½ sticks) unsalted butter
- 1 cup sugar

Add, one at a time, and beat on medium speed until fluffy:

- 3 large eggs

Add and beat just to combine:

- 1 teaspoon pure vanilla extract

On a piece of wax paper, sift together:

- 1 cup all-purpose flour
- ½ cup cocoa powder
- ½ teaspoon baking soda
- ¼ teaspoon salt

At low speed, add the dry ingredients to the butter and egg mixture alternately with:

- ½ cup buttermilk

Fold in:

- 1 cup toasted sweetened coconut

Fill each liner or mold three-quarters full. Bake 15 to 17 minutes, or until a cake tester inserted into the center of a cupcake comes out clean. The tops should spring back when lightly touched. Cool on a wire rack for 5 to 10 minutes before removing the cupcakes from the pans.

Spread with German Chocolate Icing (see opposite).

DULCE DE LECHE *

My Brazilian husband, Luiz, was the first to introduce me to this sweeter-than-sweet delicacy. Now I see it everywhere: in ice cream, as a filling for churros, or in cheesecake. Personally, I like it best out of the can.

The classic, and Brazilian, way of preparing this delicacy is to boil a can of sweetened condensed milk. There are rumors that the can can explode, although I have never heard of a case firsthand. But please take care and follow the directions carefully. As an alternative, you can buy cans of dulce de leche that have already been cooked. They aren't as easy to find, but we recommend looking in the Latin section of your grocery store. In addition, we are giving stovetop and oven directions.

Boiling directions:

Place one 14-ounce unopened can of sweetened condensed milk in a deep saucepan. Cover with water. Bring to a boil. **You must make sure that the can is always totally covered with water.** Reduce the heat to low and simmer, adding more water as necessary to keep the can covered. Simmer for 2 hours.

Using tongs, carefully remove the can from the water or let it sit in the water bath until it reaches room temperature. Once it has reached room temperature, the can can be refrigerated to speed up the cooling process. The can must be permitted to **cool down completely before opening** to avoid any danger of explosion and/or burn injuries.

Stovetop directions:

Pour one 14-ounce can sweetened condensed milk into the top of a double boiler. Over low heat, simmer for 1 to 1½ hours or until thick and caramel-colored, stirring occasionally.

Oven directions:

Pour one 14-ounce can sweetened condensed milk into a 9-inch pie plate. Cover the plate with aluminum foil. Place the pie plate in a larger shallow pan. Fill the larger pan with hot water. Bake at 425°F for 1 hour or until thick and caramel-colored. With a whisk or in the bowl of an electric mixer, beat until smooth.

GERMAN CHOCOLATE ICING *

Like candy, this thick and gooey icing is so sweet and good you just can't stop devouring it.

Mix together:
- 1 recipe Dulce de Leche (above)
- ¾ cup chopped toasted pecans (see Note)
- ¾ cup toasted sweetened coconut (see Note)

NOTE:

To toast pecans and coconut, place on an ungreased sheet pan. Bake at 350°F for 12 to 15 minutes, or until fragrant. Let cool.

The rather serious meringue cake takes a wild turn when it is decorated with *faux animal prints. The leopard spots and zebra and tiger stripes are made with chocolate. Vary the base color according to which animal print you want to make: coffee for the leopard, white for the zebra, and orange for the tiger.*

WHAT YOU WILL NEED:

Cake
sixteen 3½-inch Crisp Meringues to make 4 Wild Meringue cakes (page 104)

Filling
1 cup Whipped Chocolate Ganache (page 105) and 1 cup Whipped Cream (page 35)

Icing
Kaye's Buttercream (page 32)

Decoration
for 4 cakes decorated with zebra or tiger stripes, 1 cup dark wafer chocolate; for 4 cakes decorated with leopard spots, ⅔ cup white wafer chocolate and 1 cup dark wafer chocolate

Colors
yellow and orange candy color, yellow and orange liquid gel color

Miscellaneous
3 half-sheet pans, four 3¾-inch cardboard or thick grease-proof paper rounds, pastry cones, parchment paper, turntable, four 6-inch (or larger) bases

1. Prepare the chocolate ganache and buttercream. Refrigerate the ganache until you are ready to assemble the meringues. The buttercream can be stored in an airtight container at room temperature for up to 3 days. If making the zebra, reserve 1½ cups buttercream. Flavor the remaining buttercream with coffee (see page 33). Flavor all of the buttercream with coffee if making leopard or tiger cakes.

2. Prepare the meringues. Let cool (once cool, assemble the meringue cakes right away or they will lose their crispness).

3. Meanwhile, melt the dark wafer and/or white wafer chocolates separately. If making tiger or zebra stripes, draw a guide: on a piece of parchment paper draw 2 parallel lines 4 inches apart. Pour the chocolate into a pastry cone and cut a medium-size hole in the tip. On a sheet pan lined with parchment paper, with the guide underneath, pipe out tiger/zebra stripes running between the two lines, staying within the guidelines. They should be at least ⅛ inch thick and between 2 and 4 inches long. If making leopard spots, tint the white chocolate light brown (see the Color Mixing Chart on pages 44—45). Pour the chocolates into separate pastry cones and first pipe out dark chocolate irregular outlines, then fill in with caramel (refer to the photograph). Set aside to harden.

4. Prepare 1 cup of Whipped Cream. Whip 1 generous cup of the chocolate ganache. Remix the buttercream to get out any air and lumps.

5. To fill the meringues: There are 16 meringues in total. Place 4 of the meringues, flat side down, onto four 3¾-inch cardboard rounds, adhering them with a dot of coffee buttercream. Spread a thin layer of buttercream on top of each of these meringues. Divide the whipped cream evenly among the four meringues, spreading to make level. Next, spread a thin layer of coffee buttercream on the tops of the remaining 12 meringues. Place one layer of meringue (from the 12), flat and un-iced side up, on top of the whipped cream layers. Spread a thin layer of coffee buttercream on the flat and un-iced side and stack another meringue flat side down. Divide the whipped chocolate ganache evenly among the 4 cakes, spreading to make level. Top off with a final layer of meringue, flat side up. Place in the freezer for 30 minutes to firm up.

6. Crumb-coat the cakes with coffee buttercream as directed on page 24. Chill.

7. Prepare the final coat of buttercream: coffee buttercream with 1 drop each of orange and yellow liquid gel for the leopard fur, reserved untinted Kaye's Buttercream for the zebra, or coffee buttercream with 3 drops of orange liquid gel for the tiger fur.

8. Adhere the cardboard round supporting the cakes to their bases.

9. Score the chocolate zebra and tiger stripes accordingly, cutting some to the height of the cake, some shorter. Stick the chocolate designs randomly around the cakes.

10. Place any remaining buttercream into a pastry cone. Cut a large hole in the tip and pipe a wavy line border around the bottom edge of the cakes.

11. Serve the cakes at room temperature, chilled, or frozen.

crisp meringues**

YIELD: SIXTEEN 3½-INCH ROUNDS

Before my husband studied computers and business, he worked at a French bakery. A rather sedate version of our Wild Meringues was one of their best sellers (their cake was simply encrusted with toasted almonds), and the Bakehouse has embraced it, selling out every Passover. The meringues are delicious served at room temperature or as a frozen dessert in the summer; both melt in your mouth.

Trace eight 3½-inch circles onto two pieces of parchment paper. Invert the parchment papers onto two separate sheet pans. Preheat the oven to 250°F. Have all ingredients at room temperature.

In a food processor, finely grind:
- 1¼ cups sliced almonds
- 1 tablespoon cornstarch
- 2 tablespoons sugar

In the bowl of an electric mixer, whip until frothy:
- 6 large egg whites

Gradually add, and beat until very stiff:
- ¾ cup sugar
- ¼ teaspoon cream of tartar

Fold the nut mixture into the egg mixture with:
- ⅛ teaspoon almond extract
- 1 teaspoon pure vanilla extract

Gently place the meringue into a pastry bag with a #805 tip. Pipe out sixteen 3½-inch circles, filling in each circle with a spiral into the center. Bake for 2½ hours, or until totally crisp. Fill and assemble the meringues immediately so they do not lose their crispness (see directions on page 103).

whipped chocolate ganache*

YIELD: 4 3/4 CUPS OF FILLING WHEN WHIPPED

If you are looking for a filling or topping for your cake but don't want to be overwhelmed by sweetness, try this ganache. No sugar is added to the semisweet chocolate, so the true chocolate essence comes through. The recipe is simple to make, whips up easily, and tastes delicious. Unwhipped, it will stay fresh for 2 weeks in your refrigerator.

In a double boiler or in a medium metal bowl placed over a hot-water bath, melt:

- 8 ounces chopped semisweet chocolate

In a small saucepan, heat over medium-high heat:

- 1 quart heavy cream

Whisk one third of the cream into the chocolate until smooth. Slowly whisk in the remaining cream.

Refrigerate overnight or freeze for a few hours.

Whip until stiff.

little gifts**

These little gifts are subdued yet playful. A rich and elegant chocolate glaze unexpectedly tops a Peanut Butter Brownie. To add an extra punch of flavor, we first crumbed the brownies with a thin layer of Peanut Butter Icing.

The bows adorning the gifts are made with white chocolate "plastic." Top your precious gifts with a classic bow, Jorge's birthday bow, or a rosebud (see below).

WHAT YOU WILL NEED:

Cake
9 square Peanut Butter Brownie Cakes
(page 108)

Icing
Peanut Butter Icing (page 34) and Chocolate
Glaze (page 34)

Decoration
white Chocolate Plastic (page 109) ribbons and
¼ cup buttercream for piping patterns
(optional)

Miscellaneous
one 12-mold square mini cake pan, ½ cup cornstarch for dusting, rolling pin, pastry cones
(optional), wire rack for glazing, nine 4-inch (or
larger) serving plates or bases

1. Prepare the white Chocolate Plastic. Bake the cakes and let them cool completely. Freeze for 1 hour to overnight.

2. Prepare the Peanut Butter Icing and Chocolate Glaze.

3. Crumb-coat the cakes with a thin layer of Peanut Butter Icing. Freeze for 30 minutes.

4. Glaze the cakes as directed on page 29. With an offset metal spatula, carefully place each cake onto its serving plate or base. Chill for 15 minutes.

5. Optional: Place $\frac{1}{4}$ cup of buttercream in a pastry cone and pipe out a delicate pattern of your choice onto the glaze or use the photographs as a guide.

6. Dust a clean, flat surface with cornstarch. With a rolling pin, roll out half of the white Chocolate Plastic to $\frac{1}{16}$ inch thick (keep the remaining chocolate wrapped tightly in plastic wrap to prevent it from drying out). Cut it into $\frac{1}{3}$ x 5-inch strips. Starting at the base of one side, place a strip down on the cake, carefully draping it over the top and then down the opposite side. Cut off any extra plastic by pressing a knife into the base of the cake. Repeat the process with another strip on the adjacent side so the ribbons cross in the center.

7. To make a classic bow (opposite, at right): Roll out the remaining chocolate plastic to $\frac{1}{16}$ inch thick. Cut a $\frac{1}{3}$ x 4-inch strip. Mark the center point. Gently curl the outer ends so they meet at the center. Press them together at the center and form two loops. Cut a $1\frac{1}{4}$-inch strip and wrap it around the center of the bow, so that the seam is on the underside. Cut two $1\frac{1}{2}$-inch ribbon tails, trimming their ends at an angle, and place them down at a diagonal to the crossed ribbons. Place the bow on top.

8. To make Jorge's birthday bow (opposite, at left): Roll out the remaining chocolate plastic to $\frac{1}{16}$ inch thick. Cut nineteen $\frac{1}{3}$ x 2-inch strips. Curl each strip so their ends meet. Press the ends together and form a loop. Arrange 8 loops in a circle so that the ends meet in the center. Press together. Arrange 6 loops in a tight circle within the first circle, pressing gently to adhere at the center. For the next row, arrange 4 loops close together in the center of the bow. Lastly, place one loop on top. Carefully place the bow on top of the cake.

9. To make a rosebud (opposite, center): Roll out the remaining chocolate plastic to $\frac{1}{16}$ inch thick. Cut a $2\frac{1}{2}$ x $\frac{3}{4}$-inch strip. From this strip, cut out an arc along one length with the apex remaining $\frac{3}{4}$ inch. Starting at one point, roll the plastic tightly into a coil along the straight edge. When complete, flare some of the petals outward. Cut out two small leaves. Place the bud in the center of the cake with one leaf on each side.

10. For fullest flavor, serve the cakes at room temperature.

peanut butter brownie cakes*

YIELD: 9 MINI SQUARE CAKES

Don't let the name fool you; these Peanut Butter Brownie Cakes are a serious dessert. Our little gifts to you are so dense, rich, and moist you will think you are feasting on chocolate truffles.

Grease and flour 9 molds of a 12-mold mini square pan. Preheat the oven to 350°F. Have all ingredients at room temperature.

In a saucepan over low heat, melt, whisking often:

- 3 ounces chopped unsweetened chocolate
- 8 ounces chopped semisweet chocolate
- 3 ounces (³/₄ stick) unsalted butter
- ½ cup crunchy peanut butter

Remove from the heat and set aside.

In the bowl of an electric mixer, beat at high speed until light and fluffy:

- 3 large eggs
- 1 cup sugar
- 2 teaspoons pure vanilla extract

Fold the chocolate mixture into the egg mixture, mixing only until combined.

On a piece of wax paper, sift together:

- ½ cup all-purpose flour
- ½ teaspoon baking powder
- ½ teaspoon salt

On low speed, add the dry ingredients to the batter and beat until combined.

Stir in by hand:

- 1 cup semisweet chocolate chips

Pour the batter into the prepared molds, filling the molds three-quarters full. Bake for 17 to 20 minutes, or until almost set. Cool on a wire rack for 15 to 20 minutes before turning the cakes out of the pans.

chocolate plastic*

Chocolate Plastic is a versatile and fun medium to work with. We made the bows that top our Little Gifts with it (page 106) but you can also make sculpted flowers from it much like you can with gum paste. You can even cover a cake with Chocolate Plastic, and it tastes much better than fondant. We used white chocolate, but in this recipe you can substitute dark, milk, or even wafer chocolate.

In a glass bowl, place in a microwave:
- 7 ounces chopped white chocolate

Melt the chocolate at 30-second intervals (approximately 3 passes in the microwave), stirring in between.

Add, stirring quickly just to combine:
- ¼ cup light corn syrup

Remove the chocolate plastic from the bowl and wrap it tightly in plastic wrap. Let the chocolate plastic set for a few hours or overnight at room temperature, or for 1 hour in the freezer.

When ready to roll out the plastic, dust a clean, flat surface with cornstarch. Knead the dough with your hands to make it smooth and malleable. If the dough is too hard to work, soften it in the microwave for 4 to 5 seconds and knead again. Roll the dough out to ¼ to ¹⁄₁₆ inch, depending on the design. Do not let the plastic sit out unwrapped because it will harden and become unworkable. When working with plastic, if necessary use dabs of water to adhere one piece to another.

Do you have a hot date for Valentine's Day? Well, try this cake as a gift to warm up the atmosphere. Or maybe for Mother's Day give one to Mom, one to your mother-in-law, and one to any mother important in your life. Even for a little girl's birthday, these cakes would be a giggly hit—just omit the spices and change the palette to light pinks and purples instead of the flaming reds and neons. Or go for that red-hot look and glaze the hearts with red-tinted white chocolate glaze.

Cake
12 spicy chocolate heart cakes (see page 112)

Filling
Cinnamon Chocolate Whipped Cream (page 113)

Icing
Chocolate Glaze (page 34)

Decoration
2½ cups white wafer chocolate to make 12 hearts and for drizzling, ¾ cup chocolate shavings or sprinkles (optional)

Colors
red and pink candy color

Miscellaneous
one scalloped mini heart pan, pastry cones, heart templates (page 169), 1 half-sheet pan, parchment paper or cellophane, wire rack for glazing

HOW TO

1. Bake the heart cakes and let them cool completely. Freeze for 1 hour or overnight.

2. Prepare the glaze.

3. Melt the white wafer chocolate and divide it equally among 3 bowls. Using the Color Mixing Chart on pages 44–45, tint one bowl pale pink, one bowl red, and one bowl neon pink. Pour the colored chocolates into 3 separate pastry cones. Cut small to medium holes in each.

4. Using the templates provided, make 12 hearts as illustrated in The Chocolate Method (pages 40–43). Set aside to harden. Save the remaining chocolate for drizzling. When needed, remelt the chocolate in a microwave or on the sheet pan over a hot-water bath.

5. Prepare the filling. Scoop approximately 1 tablespoon of filling into the indentation in each heart. With a small metal spatula, spread the filling so it's flat and flush with the top surface of the cake. Freeze for 30 minutes or until the filling has set.

6. Glaze the cakes as directed on page 29.

7. Drizzle colored chocolate over the top of each cake until you are satisfied with the spattering effect.

8. Place a chocolate heart on the top of each heart cake; if it doesn't stick, squeeze a drop of melted chocolate under the heart to adhere it.

9. If desired, press chocolate shavings or sprinkles around the bottom of each cake before plating.

10. For fullest flavor, serve the cakes at room temperature.

spicy chocolate cakes*

YIELD: 12 MINI HEART CAKES

I was trying to think of a new flavor for a cake and I knew my mom had long been trying to combine cinnamon and chocolate. Ding! I had an idea: not just cinnamon, but something fiery. Think Red-Hots meet chocolate: daring, spicy, and unexpectedly tempting.

Grease two 6-mold scalloped mini heart pans. Preheat the oven to 350°F. Have all ingredients at room temperature.

In a medium bowl, combine and whisk until smooth:
- 1 cup cocoa powder
- 1 cup hot water

Add and whisk until melted:
- 2 ounces chopped semisweet chocolate

Add and mix until smooth:
- ⅓ cup sour cream
- ½ teaspoon pure vanilla extract

In the bowl of an electric mixer, beat at high speed until light and fluffy:
- 8 ounces (2 sticks) unsalted butter
- 1 cup granulated sugar
- ⅓ cup light brown sugar, packed

Add one at a time and beat on medium speed until well creamed:
- 3 large eggs

On a piece of wax paper, sift together:
- 1¾ cups cake flour
- 1½ teaspoons baking soda
- ¼ teaspoon salt
- 2½ teaspoons ground cinnamon
- ¾ teaspoon cayenne pepper

At low speed, add the dry ingredients to the butter mixture alternately with the chocolate mixture, mixing until smooth.

Fill each heart three-quarters full with batter. Bake for 28 to 32 minutes, or until a cake tester inserted into the center of a cake comes out clean. Cool on a wire rack for 15 to 20 minutes before turning the cakes out of the pans.

cinnamon chocolate whipped cream *

Our Cinnamon Chocolate Whipped Cream can fill and ice the Spicy Chocolate Cake, opposite, but it is also delicious spooned onto pumpkin pie.

For best results we recommend preparing the whipped cream right before serving or assembling your cakes. Any leftovers can be stored in an airtight container in the refrigerator for up to 2 days. The whipped cream will break down as it sits in the refrigerator, so rewhip it in the bowl of an electric mixer for 1 minute or until medium to stiff peaks form.

In a glass bowl, melt in a microwave:
- 2 tablespoons finely chopped semisweet chocolate

Let the chocolate come to body temperature.

Meanwhile, in the bowl of an electric mixer fitted with a whisk attachment, whip until slightly thickened:
- ½ cup heavy cream
- 1 tablespoon confectioners' sugar
- Pinch of ground cinnamon

Add the chocolate and continue whipping at high speed until stiff.

caramel popcorn
cupcakes***

Are you having a sleepover birthday party? An Oscar bash? Or just a movie
marathon? Why not serve these little popcorn cupcakes.

Wanting to imitate an old-fashioned popcorn box, I searched for red and white striped cup-
cake papers to no avail. So, I decided to make a striped chocolate shell to hold the cupcake instead.
I piped buttercream "popcorn"—definitely more filling than the real thing, but very fun. An extra
sweet surprise awaits you at the bottom of the shell (if you get that far): dulce de leche.

Cake
14 caramel cupcakes (see page 79)

Icing
Kaye's Buttercream (page 32) or House Buttercream (page 31)

Filling
Dulce de Leche (page 101)

Decoration
3½ cups white wafer chocolate to make 14 chocolate boxes

Colors
yellow liquid gel color and red candy color

Tip
#8 or #10 round

Miscellaneous
three 6-mold muffin pans, pastry bag, coupler, pastry cones, 6 to 12 silicone cupcake liners

HOW TO

1. Bake the cakes and let them cool completely. Freeze for 1 hour to overnight. Prepare the filling and icing.

2. Rest the silicone cupcake liners in a cupcake pan so that they are slightly flared at the top and do not touch the bottom.

3. Melt the white wafer chocolate. Pour one third of the chocolate into a bowl and tint it red. Pour the white and red chocolate into separate pastry cones and cut medium holes in the tip of each. Pipe alternating red and white stripes up the inside of each liner, using the ridges of the liner as a guide. Do not pipe any chocolate in the bottom of the liner until the chocolate has set on the sides; it may get filled as the chocolate settles. Let the chocolate set for a few minutes. Pipe an additional line of white chocolate around the top inner edge to give support, and fill in any areas where the cupcake liner is still visible. Set aside to harden (approximately 1 hour).

4. Carefully peel the silicone liner off the popcorn bucket.

5. Remove the cupcakes from the freezer.

6. Place 1½ tablespoons of dulce de leche in the bottom of each bucket. Place one cupcake, with the paper liner removed, into each bucket, trimming the bottom of the cupcake at an angle if necessary.

7. Prepare the tinted and flavored buttercream: approximately 2 tablespoons soft buttery yellow and 2 tablespoons dulce de leche buttercream (see page 33).

8. Place a coupler inside a pastry bag. With a metal spatula, spread a very small amount of the dulce de leche buttercream up one side of a pastry bag. Spread a very small amount of yellow adjacent to the dulce de leche. Fill the rest of the bag with the untinted buttercream. With a #8 or #10 round tip, pipe popcorn all over the top of the cupcake by squeezing and holding in place until a ball forms. Tail off. Then squeeze with fluctuating pressure as you move the tip up and down along half to three quarters of the ball's circumference.

9. For fullest flavor, serve the cakes at room temperature.

constructed cupcakes**

I never noticed the vast array of trucks, cars, and construction vehicles on the road until my son, Kase, was born. Anything with wheels calls for his attention. When he saw this construction site he wanted to dig in—not just eat, but play, too.

What makes these cupcakes unique is how they are assembled and decorated to look like a cake. Your guests can just reach for a cupcake and pull it apart from the rest—easier than slicing a cake!

Cake
18 Classic Chocolate Cupcakes to make 1 pull-apart cake (page 118)

Icing
one and a half recipes of Matt's Fudge Icing (page 35)

Decoration
⅛ cup dark wafer chocolate and 1½ cups white wafer chocolate to make 5 construction vehicles; cookie crumbs and candy

Tip
#12 round tip

Colors
orange, blue, yellow, and black candy color

Miscellaneous
three 6-mold muffin pans, pastry cones, vehicle templates (page 173), 1 half-sheet pan, parchment paper or cellophane, 16-inch square base (or larger)

HOW TO

1 Bake the cupcakes and let them cool completely. Freeze for 1 hour to overnight.

2 Prepare the fudge icing.

3 Melt the dark wafer and white wafer chocolates separately. Set aside 2 tablespoons of white chocolate. Using the Color Mixing Chart on pages 44—45, tint the white chocolate: approximately 2 tablespoons each of yellow, orange, royal blue, light blue, and gray. Using the templates provided, make 5 construction vehicles as illustrated in The Chocolate Method (pages 40—43). Extend the wheels of each vehicle with a ¼-inch-thick chocolate line at least 1 inch down. The vehicles will look as if they are standing on stilts. Set aside to harden.

4 With scissors trim the sides of each cupcake so that it looks like a square from the top. On a flat base arrange the cupcakes, touching one another, in four rows of 5, 4, 5, and 4.

5 Place the fudge icing into a pastry bag with a coupler and a #12 round tip. Pipe the fudge icing so that it covers all of the cupcakes. Once the surface is completely covered, with a metal spatula spread the icing randomly, then carve a shallow indentation for a road.

6 Cover the top of the cupcakes with cookie crumbs, candy, or any other items that will add to the feel of a construction site. Carefully press the vehicles into the cake up to the wheel line. Add any over-piping accents, such as rocks, with the extra chocolate.

7 For fullest flavor, serve the cakes at room temperature.

classic
chocolate cupcakes*

Here is another must-have for your recipe file. This classic will delight a gaggle of kids or a gathering of your most mature friends. We love them smothered in Matt's Fudge Icing or iced with soft peaks of Kids' Buttercream.

NOTE:

This recipe must be baked in paper cupcake liners, because even if the pan is greased, the batter might stick.

Grease the tops of three 6-mold muffin pans and line them with paper liners. Preheat the oven to 350°F. Have all ingredients at room temperature.

In a saucepan over low heat, melt, whisking often:

- ½ cup milk
- 1 cup brown sugar, packed
- 3 ounces chopped unsweetened chocolate

When chocolate is melted, whisk in:

- 1 large egg yolk

Remove from the heat and set aside.

In the bowl of an electric mixer at medium-high speed, cream:

- 4 ounces (1 stick) unsalted butter

Add and cream until light and fluffy:

- 1 cup granulated sugar

Add slowly, beating well and scraping down after each addition:

- 2 large eggs
- 1 large egg white

On a piece of wax paper, sift together:

- 2 cups cake flour
- 1 teaspoon baking soda
- ½ teaspoon salt

On low speed, add the dry ingredients alternately to the butter and egg mixture with:

- ¾ cup milk
- 1 teaspoon pure vanilla extract

Stir the chocolate mixture into the batter by hand, mixing only until combined.

Pour the batter into the cupcake liners, filling each ⅞ full. Bake for 18 to 20 minutes, or until the tops spring back when lightly pressed.

yummy yummy bumblebee cupcakes*

There is no sting here, but definitely a delicious bite. Our cute and chubby bumblebees take flight from their cupcakes in a blur of yellow nonpareils and edible chocolate wings. Easy to make and fun to eat.

Cake
12 Lemon Poppy Cupcakes (opposite)

Icing
½ recipe of Chocolate Glaze (page 34)

Decoration
2 cups white wafer chocolate and ½ cup dark wafer chocolate to make eyes, stripes, and wings; 1½ cups of yellow nonpareils (online at wilton.com and kitchenkrafts.com)

Colors
blue candy color

Miscellaneous
one 12-mold muffin pan, pastry cones, wing templates (page 173), 1 half-sheet pan, parchment paper or cellophane

HOW TO

1. Bake the cupcakes and let them cool completely. Freeze for 1 hour to overnight.

2. Prepare the glaze.

3. Melt the dark wafer and white wafer chocolates separately. Set aside ⅛ cup of white chocolate for the eyes and highlights. Using the Color Mixing Chart on pages 44–45, tint the remaining white chocolate sky blue. Pour the white, blue, and dark chocolates into separate pastry cones. Keep the chocolates warm on a heating pad or a pan placed over a hot-water bath, since they will be needed in various steps throughout the directions.

4. Using the templates provided, make 12 pairs of wings and 12 stingers. Set aside to harden.

5. Glaze the cupcakes as directed on page 29.

6. Pour the nonpareils into a small bowl. Carefully dip three quarters of the cupcake into the nonpareils; try to create a straight edge where the glaze and nonpareils meet. The glaze will act as the bug's black head.

7. Pipe two white eyes on each head. Pipe chocolate dots on top of the whites to give the effect of googly eyes.

8. At a point ½ inch from the cupcake's edge and perpendicular to the head, press the wings halfway into each cupcake at a 45-degree angle. If necessary, score these points first with a small, sharp knife. Opposite the head, attach the stinger to the cupcake with a dot of chocolate.

9. With the remaining dark chocolate in the pastry cone, pipe 3 to 4 chocolate stripes on the bee's body, parallel to the head's line.

10. For fullest flavor, serve the cakes at room temperature.

lemon poppy cupcakes*

I love desserts that combine textures. One of my favorite accents for any cake is a thin layer of melted chocolate. Once set, every bite has a crispness to balance the airiness or moistness of the cake. So I was happy to unite the light lemony flavor with the crunch of poppy seeds. We enjoy this recipe not just for dessert but as a morning muffin, too.

Grease the top of a 12-mold muffin pan and line it with paper liners. Preheat the oven to 350°F. Have all ingredients at room temperature.

In the bowl of an electric mixer, beat at high speed until light and fluffy:

- 6 ounces (1½ sticks) unsalted butter
- ½ cup granulated sugar
- ¼ cup light brown sugar, packed
- 1 large egg
- ½ teaspoon pure vanilla extract
- 3 tablespoons lemon zest (from 2 lemons)

On a piece of wax paper, sift together:

- 2 cups all-purpose flour
- 1 tablespoon baking powder
- Pinch of salt

At low speed, add the dry ingredients to the butter mixture and mix until just combined.

At low speed, add:

- ½ cup milk
- 2 tablespoons fresh lemon juice
- 1½ tablespoons poppy seeds

Scoop the batter into the prepared molds, filling to the paper liner. Bake for 20 to 25 minutes, or until a cake tester inserted into the center of a cake comes out clean. Cool on a wire rack for 5 to 10 minutes before removing the cupcakes from the pan.

Our creepy spiders and friendly ladybugs come alive in three dimensions. *Chocolate legs, fangs, and antennae sprout from their rotund bodies. We glazed the ladybugs in brilliant red but we also make them in green, orange, and yellow at the Bakehouse; apparently, outside of New York, these beetles come in all different colors. As for the spiders, they can be sleek in just chocolate glaze, or add chocolate sprinkles to make a furry arachnid.*

We bake both critters in the very versatile bowl pan, which we also use to make sunflowers, eyeballs, jack-o'-lanterns, the planet Earth, floating balloons, or any number of sports balls. See what other designs you can create from it.

In a pinch you can substitute the fudge icing with chilled chocolate glaze to pipe out the spider and ladybug heads.

WHAT YOU WILL NEED:

Cake
12 white chocolate raspberry bowl cakes (see page 124)

Icing
Chocolate Glaze (page 34) for the spiders or White Chocolate Glaze (page 36) for the ladybugs; Matt's Fudge Icing (page 35) (2 cups for spiders, 1½ cups for ladybugs)

Decoration
2 cups dark wafer chocolate and ¼ cup white wafer chocolate to make eyes, smiles, fangs or antennae, legs, and dots; approximately 1½ tablespoons chocolate sprinkles per spider (optional)

Tip
#12 round

Colors
green and yellow candy color for the spider and red liquid gel color for the ladybug

Miscellaneous
two mini bowl pans; pastry cones; leg, antennae, eye, smile, and fang templates (page 169); 1 half-sheet pan; parchment paper or cellophane; wire rack for glazing; twelve 6-inch (or larger) bases

1. Bake the cakes and let them cool completely. Freeze for 1 hour to overnight.

2. Prepare the glaze of your choice. If making the ladybugs, tint the white chocolate glaze red with liquid gel, paste, or liquid colors.

3. Melt the dark wafer and white wafer chocolates separately. If making the spiders, set aside ⅛ cup of the white chocolate. Using the Color Mixing Chart on pages 44—45, tint the remaining white chocolate neon green.

4. Using the templates provided, make 12 sets of legs and 12 spider fangs, or 12 sets of ladybug antennae, dots, eyes, and smiles as illustrated in The Chocolate Method (pages 40—43). Set aside to harden.

5. Glaze the cakes as directed on page 29. You may have to glaze the ladybugs twice—in which case, freeze the cakes in between coats for best results. If desired, make the spiders hairy by encrusting them with chocolate sprinkles before plating.

6. With an offset metal spatula, carefully place each cake onto its serving plate or base.

7. Place the fudge icing into a pastry bag with a coupler, and with a #12 tip pipe a 1-inch-diameter dot in the front of each cake for the critter's head. For spiders, pipe four ½-inch dots on each side of the body starting at least ½ inch from the head.

8. For the spiders, press the fangs into the base of the head. Pipe eight neon green eyes on each head. Pipe chocolate dots on top of each eye to give the effect of googly eyes. For the ladybugs, stick the eyes and smile to the fudge head.

9. For the spider, press the legs into the small fudge dots and if possible a little into the edge of the cake for stability, resting the bottom edge of the legs on the base. For the ladybug, press the legs into the abdomen, about ½ inch up from the base, resting the feet on the base.

10. For the ladybug, pour 1 tablespoon of melted chocolate into a pastry cone. Cut a medium-size hole and pipe a line running from the base of the head to the back of the abdomen. Place 3 chocolate dots on each side of this line.

11. For fullest flavor, serve the cakes at room temperature.

white chocolate raspberry cakes*

YIELD: 12 MINI BOWLS

While writing our Christmas cookie book, we developed a recipe for our spritz machine that used raspberry extract. We liked the flavor so much we decided to add it to our white chocolate cake; after all, raspberry and chocolate are a match made in heaven, and it's no different with white chocolate.

Grease two 6-mold mini bowl pans. Preheat the oven to 350°F. Have all ingredients at room temperature.

In a double boiler or in a medium metal bowl placed over a hot-water bath, melt:
- 4½ ounces chopped white chocolate

If not at body temperature, set aside and let cool to body temperature.

In the bowl of an electric mixer, beat at high speed until light and fluffy:
- 6 ounces (1½ sticks) unsalted butter
- ¾ cup sugar

Add the melted chocolate and mix until combined.

On a piece of wax paper, sift together:
- 2¼ cups cake flour
- 1 tablespoon baking powder
- ¼ teaspoon salt

Add the dry ingredients to the butter mixture alternately with:
- ¾ cup milk
- ¾ teaspoon pure vanilla extract
- 1½ teaspoons raspberry extract

In a separate small bowl, beat until foamy:
- 3 large egg whites

Continue beating the whites at high speed while gradually adding:
- 2¼ tablespoons sugar

When stiff (but not dry) peaks form, fold the whites into the cake batter with a rubber spatula. Blend just until the whites are evenly distributed.

Pour the batter into the prepared molds. Bake for 20 to 25 minutes, or until a cake tester inserted into the center of a cake comes out clean. Cool the cakes on a wire rack for 15 to 20 minutes before turning them out of their pans.

shark cakes**

Years ago, one of our former cake decorators, Rob Berner, made a batch of these shark cakes for the storefront. I loved them immediately because they are goofy, morbid, and fun all at once, and I have been making them ever since. To make them even more gory, I used a Red Velvet cake filled with Chopped Cherry Whipped Cream. What was this shark's last meal?

WHAT YOU WILL NEED:

Cake
8 Red Velvet cone cakes (see page 127)

Icing
one and a quarter recipes of Kaye's Buttercream (page 32) or one recipe House Buttercream (page 31)

Filling
Chopped Cherry Whipped Cream (page 127)

Decoration
¼ cup dark wafer chocolate and 1½ cups white wafer chocolate to make eyes and fins

Colors
red, royal blue, teal, and (optional) orange liquid gel colors, and blue candy color

Miscellaneous
two mini cone pans, pastry bag, coupler, pastry cones, eye and fin templates (page 170), 1 half-sheet pan, parchment paper or cellophane, turntable, eight 6-inch (or larger) bases

1. Bake the cakes and let them cool completely. Prepare the buttercream.

2. Prepare the filling. To fill the cake, cut each cone in half horizontally and, with a small paring knife, cut out a 2-inch-long x ¾-inch-deep cone from the bottom of the cake and a 1-inch-long x ¾-inch-deep cone from the top. Fill the holes with a generous amount of Chopped Cherry Whipped Cream and replace the top on the cone. Scrape off any Chopped Cherry Whipped Cream that may have come through the seam. Chill for 30 minutes.

3. Melt the dark wafer and white wafer chocolates separately. Set aside ⅛ cup white chocolate for the eyes. Using the Color Mixing Chart on pages 44—45, tint the remaining white chocolate royal blue. Using the templates provided, make 8 sets of tail fins, 8 dorsal fins, and 8 pairs of eyes as illustrated in The Chocolate Method (pages 40—43). Set aside to harden.

4. Set aside 1¼ cups of uncolored buttercream. Prepare the colored buttercream: approximately 2 cups royal blue, ⅛ cup red, 1 cup teal, and (optional) 2 tablespoons pale peach.

5. Remove the cakes from the refrigerator. Place a cake in the center of a turntable. Cover the shark four fifths with blue and one fifth with white. Make sure there is extra buttercream at the top of the cake to create the point of the shark's head. Finish icing the cone as directed in Smooth Icing on a Shaped Cake (page 28) with one exception: pull the cellophane up from the base, but do not curve it over the top of the dome; instead just continue pulling up at the same angle. Continue around the cake in the same manner until a point forms.

6. Using an offset spatula, carefully place the cake onto its base.

7. With a small offset spatula, spread the teal buttercream around the base of the shark, pulling some up onto the shark's head. Spread some white buttercream randomly on top, pulling the spatula straight up to create the look of white caps.

8. Place the remaining red buttercream into a pastry cone and cut a medium hole in the tip. Free-hand pipe the mouth.

9. Place the remaining white buttercream into a pastry cone and cut a small to medium hole in the tip. To pipe teeth on the edge of the mouth, squeeze while holding the tip in place until you have the size base you desire, then pull down or up (depending on whether you are piping the upper or lower teeth) as you release the pressure, ending with a sharp point.

10. Press the wide-set eyes into the shark's head above the mouth. Pipe two nostrils at the top of the head with chocolate.

11. Press the back fin into the shark's back near the base and the dorsal fins at its side. With an offset spatula, gently carve gills on both sides of the shark above the fins.

12. If you wish, place the pale peach buttercream into a pastry cone with a medium tip. For those with a love of the grotesque, free-hand pipe a human body in the water, using the photograph on page 28 as a guide. Repeat with the remaining 7 cones.

13. For fullest flavor, serve the cakes at room temperature.

red velvet*

YIELD: 8 CONES OR 18 CUPCAKES

Red velvet cake is all the rage these days, and I understand why. Its nostalgic look and simple flavors appeal to just about anyone. During the holidays we like to mix it up a little and make red and blue velvet for the Fourth of July or orange and green velvet for St. Patty's Day.

If you are making Shark Cakes, grease two mini (4-mold) cone pans.

If you are making cupcakes, grease the top of three 6-mold muffin pans and line them with paper liners. Preheat the oven to 350°F. Have all ingredients at room temperature.

In the bowl of an electric mixer, beat at high speed until light and fluffy:
- 8 ounces (2 sticks) unsalted butter
- 1½ cups sugar

Add and beat on medium speed until well creamed:
- 2 large eggs
- 1 tablespoon red liquid gel color or 3 tablespoons McCormick's red food-coloring

On a piece of wax paper, sift together:
- 2½ cups cake flour
- 2 tablespoons cocoa powder
- 1 teaspoon baking soda
- 1 teaspoon salt

At low speed, add the dry ingredients to the butter mixture alternately with:
- 1 cup buttermilk
- 1 teaspoon pure vanilla extract
- 1 teaspoon vinegar

Pour the batter into the prepared molds, filling each three-quarters full. Bake for 20 to 25 minutes, or until a cake tester inserted into the center of a cake comes out clean. Cool on a wire rack for 10 to 15 minutes before turning the cone-shaped cakes out of the pans or removing the cupcakes from the pans.

CHOPPED CHERRY WHIPPED CREAM*

YIELD: 3 CUPS

In the bowl of an electric mixer fitted with a whisk attachment, whip until stiff:
- 1⅓ cups heavy cream
- ¼ cup confectioners' sugar
- 1 teaspoon pure vanilla extract

Fold in:
- ¾ cup chopped cherries (fresh, frozen, or canned) with up to 3 tablespoons of their juice

To celebrate the start of summer, to throw a festive beach party, or to say to the hot weather when Labor Day rolls around, these little beach pails will have you wanting to run down to the water's edge to build one more sand castle. To echo the sandy colors, we filled our pails with caramel cake and dulce de leche buttercream. To complete the scene, chocolate shovels, shells, and starfish float along the shore.

This design is one of the more time-consuming in the book. To save time, limit the palette: instead of mixing all of the colors, just choose two or three.

WHAT YOU WILL NEED:

Cake
four 4-inch round Caramel Cakes to make three beach pails (page 79)

Icing
Kaye's Buttercream (page 32) or House Buttercream (page 31), Dulce de Leche (page 101)

Decoration
¼ cup dark wafer chocolate and 3 cups white wafer chocolate to make 3 chocolate shovels, 3 handles, 3 starfish, 3 clam shells, 3 sand dollars, 3 mussels, and 3 oyster shells; 1 cup ground nuts, ground butter cookies, cake crumbs, or graham cracker crumbs for sand; ¼ cup clear edible gel for water.

Colors
red and teal liquid gel colors, and yellow, orange, blue, purple, and pink candy colors

Tips
#89 triple-line tip, #81 mum tip (as small as #79 can be substituted)

Miscellaneous
four 4-inch round cake pans; three 4-inch thin cardboard rounds, or three thick grease-proof paper rounds; one 3⅛-round cardboard or thick paper template; pastry bag; coupler; pastry cones; shell, shovel, and handle templates (page 170); 1 half-sheet pan, parchment paper or cellophane, turntable, four 8-inch (or larger) bases

1. Bake the cakes and let cool. Prepare the Dulce de Leche and the buttercream. Set aside ¼ cup uncolored buttercream. Prepare the colored and flavored buttercream: 1 cup red, about 2½ cups of Dulce de Leche Buttercream (page 33).

2. Trim the domes off of each cake and set aside in an airtight container. Cut each cake into three layers. Stack 4 layers per cake onto three 4-inch cardboard rounds. Fill the cakes with the Dulce de Leche Buttercream as directed in Filling a Cake (page 23). Chill for at least 30 minutes to overnight.

3. Melt the dark wafer and white wafer chocolates separately. Set aside ½ cup white. Using the Color Mixing Chart on pages 44—45, tint the remaining white chocolate: about ½ cup royal blue, 2 tablespoons pale orange, 2 tablespoons coral, 2 tablespoons yellow, 1 tablespoon light brown, 1 tablespoon violet. Using the templates provided, make 3 of each: shovels, handles, starfish, sand dollars, oyster shells, mussels, and clam shells as illustrated in The Chocolate Method (pages 40—43). Set aside to harden.

4. Remove the cakes from the refrigerator. Place the 3⅛-inch round template in the center of the cake. Using the top template and the bottom cardboard round as a guide, with a serrated knife, carve the cake at an angle around the entire circumference of the cake until you have an upside-down pail shape. Make sure the cakes are level, because what is now the top will become the bottom. Crumb-coat the cakes with Dulce de Leche Buttercream as directed (page 24). Chill for at least 30 minutes.

5. Ice the beach pails with red buttercream as directed in Smooth Icing on a Cake (page 27). The tops should have only a scraping of buttercream.

6. Place the remaining red buttercream in a pastry bag with a coupler, and with a #89 tip pipe a strip of lines around the center of each pail.

7. To invert your cakes, hold one cake at a time on its round in your hand and carefully place a covered cardboard round or base onto the top of the cake. Steady the base with one hand and the cake with the other hand and invert. The beach pail should now be right side up. Repeat with the remaining cakes.

8. Remove the cardboard rounds from the top of each cake. Place a dollop of Dulce Buttercream on top of each cake and place the reserved domes on top. Spread more Dulce Buttercream over the top of each cake, then sprinkle with your "sand" material.

9. Change the tip of the red pastry bag to #81 and, with the concave side of the tip overlapping the top edge of the cake, pipe the top rim of the beach pail.

10. Carefully drape the handle over the pail, resting it over the rim and on the side.

11. Mix 1 drop of teal liquid-gel color with the clear piping gel. Spread onto one half of the base. If desired, spread Dulce Buttercream over the other half of the base and sprinkle with nuts and/or crumbs.

12. Place the shells and the shovel around the base of the pail.

13. For fullest flavor, serve the cakes at room temperature.

f l o w e r   p o w e r *

Flowers are just one way to make a rather whimsical treat like the cupcake into a pretty and elegant dessert. I've made the tops of these cupcakes look like roses, chrysanthemums, sunflowers, hydrangeas, peonies, poppies, and Gerbera daisies. Many of the petals are variegated to give them a natural appearance. This is achieved by spreading a thin strip of either a lighter or darker shade of buttercream up one side of a pastry bag, then filling the rest of the bag with the main color. Use the Color Mixing Chart on pages 44–45 to help you mix the colors you want.

By tiering the cupcakes, either on stacked cake pedestals or in a pastry tree (a wire structure used for displaying pastries or cupcakes, available at some baking supply stores and Wilton), you can further enhance the feeling of elegance—perfect for that special day, since more than ever brides and grooms are opting for cupcakes instead of the traditional tiered cake.

For best results, make certain your buttercream has a medium consistency so the petals will hold their shape. Piped flowers, as in nature, are unique and irregular. Don't be intimidated by the piping process; just let the petals flow from the pastry bag. Take a step back from your creation and I am sure you will see how all of the petals fuse into a beautiful flower.

WHAT YOU WILL NEED:

Cake
12 Lemon Coconut Cupcakes (page 136)

Icing
Kaye's Buttercream (page 32) or House Buttercream (page 31). You will need between 2¾ and 5 cups of buttercream depending on the flowers you are making.

Decoration
½ to 1 cup dark wafer chocolate (only needed for some types of flowers)

Colors
See individual flower directions for colors (below).

Tips
Tips are noted in individual flower directions (below).

Miscellaneous
one 12-mold muffin pan, pastry bag, coupler, pastry cones, turntable

1. Bake the cupcakes and let them cool completely. Freeze for 1 hour to overnight.

2. Prepare the icing. Tint the icing according to the individual flower recipe.

3. Follow the directions below for piping out flowers.

4. For fullest flavor, serve the cakes at room temperature.

rose

(SEE VARIATIONS BELOW)

To cover 12 cupcakes you will need 4½ cups buttercream: 1½ cups white and 3 cups pale pink.

Colors: Red or neon pink liquid gel colors

Tip: #104 petal tip (you can substitute #103)

1. Place a coupler into a pastry bag. Using a small metal spatula, spread a strip of white buttercream up one side of the bag's interior. Fill the rest of the bag with pale pink. Try to line up the narrow end of the petal tip with the white strip.

2. Place the cupcake on the center of a turntable.

3. For the first row of petals, spin the turntable clockwise. With the narrow end of the tip running along the outer edge of the cupcake, pipe 6 long petals around the circumference of the cupcake. Allow the tip to stay flush with the cupcake, most likely angled downward with the slope of the dome.

4. Continue spinning the turntable clockwise and pipe a second row of 6 to 8 petals inside the first. The wide end of the tip should touch the previous row of petals. Flare the end of the tip upward from the previous row, approximately 30 degrees.

5. Holding the tip at a 45-degree angle, pipe 6 petals for the third row.

6. For the fourth row of petals, spin the turntable counterclockwise and pipe five almost vertical petals. Pipe 4 to 5 vertical petals for the fifth row. Angle the tip inward approximately 10 degrees and pipe 3 petals for the sixth row.

7. The last row is one petal. To make the petal flare, pull the tip upward slightly, squeezing a little more at the center, and then pull the tip back down toward the starting point and tail off. The petal will resemble a bud.

Variations: To make a ranunculus, pipe an additional 3 rows of petals. Keep the rows and petals tight together.

To make a peony, follow the directions for the rose but apply inconsistent pressure and slightly shake the tip while piping each petal. This will create a ruffled effect.

hydrangea

each petal. To finish each petal, drag the tip toward the center as you release the pressure. The wide end of the tip should remain close to the center. Begin the next petal so that it slightly overlaps the first. Repeat for each blossom.

4. Place the yellow buttercream into a pastry cone and cut a small hole in its tip. Pipe a yellow dot in the center of each blossom.

To cover 12 cupcakes you will need approximately 4 cups buttercream: ½ cup white, 3¼ cups periwinkle, and 2 tablespoons yellow.

Colors: Blue, violet, and yellow liquid gel colors

Tip: # 102 petal tip (you can substitute # 103)

1. Place a coupler into a pastry bag. Using a small metal spatula, spread a strip of white buttercream up one side of the bag's interior. Fill the rest of the bag with periwinkle. Try to line up the narrow end of the petal tip with the white strip.

2. Place the cupcake on the center of a turntable.

3. Most blossoms have 5 evenly spaced petals of equal size, but the hydrangea has 4 petals. Pipe small four-petal blossoms as follows, covering the entire cupcake. Choose a center point for the flower. Place the wide end of the tip at the center point. Place the narrow end of the tip at a 30-degree angle to the cake surface. Pivoting the tip around the center point, pipe the first petal by increasing pressure as you move the tip around. The curvature of the petal occurs not from moving the tip up and back toward the center point, but from increasing the pressure toward the middle of

gerbera daisy

To cover 12 cupcakes you will need 3¼ cups buttercream: 2¼ cups hot pink and ¾ cup bright purple, 2 tablespoons orange, 2 tablespoons yellow.

Colors: Neon pink, violet, yellow, and orange liquid gel colors

Chocolate: ¾ cup dark wafer chocolate

Tip: #104 petal tip (you can substitute #103)

1. Place a coupler into a pastry bag. Using a small metal spatula, spread a strip of bright purple buttercream up one side of the bag's interior. Fill the rest of the bag with hot pink. Try to line up the narrow end of the petal tip with the bright purple strip.

2. Place the cupcake on the center of a turntable.

3. Hold the bag perpendicular to the cupcake. Starting at the outer edge of the cupcake, and the outer edge of each petal, squeeze and move the tip inward. Release the pressure as you move in toward the center point.

4. Fill the cupcake with more petals in the same way, fanning out in a circle from the center point. Overlap the first row of petals with smaller petals to disguise the cupcake's surface.

5. Melt the dark wafer chocolate and pour it into a pastry cone. Cut a medium hole in its tip and fill in the center of the flower.

6. Place the yellow and orange buttercreams into pastry cones. Cut small holes in the tips and pipe yellow and orange dots within the chocolate center.

poppy

1. Place the red buttercream into a pastry bag with a coupler and a petal tip.

2. Place the cupcake on the center of a turntable.

3. Spin the turntable while piping each row of petals. With the narrow end of the tip running along the outer edge of the cupcake, pipe 5 petals around the circumference of the cupcake. Allow the tip to stay flush with the cupcake, most likely angled downward with the slope of the dome. Apply inconsistent pressure and slightly shake the tip while piping each petal. This will create a ruffled effect.

4. Continue spinning the turntable and pipe a second row of 8 petals. The wide end of the tip should touch the previous row of petals. Flare the end of the tip upward from the previous row, approximately 30 degrees. Continue to apply inconsistent pressure and shake the tip.

5. With the tip at a 45-degree angle, pipe 6 petals for the last row.

6. Remove the petal tip and pipe a large red dot in the center of the flower to equalize the height of the cupcake with the petals.

7. Melt the dark wafer chocolate and pour it into a pastry cone. Cut a medium hole in its tip and fill in the center of the flower.

8. Place the yellow buttercream into a pastry cone. Cut a small hole in the tip and pipe yellow dots within the chocolate center.

To cover 12 cupcakes you will need 3⅛ cups buttercream: 3 cups red and ⅛ cup yellow.

Colors: Red and yellow liquid gel colors

Chocolate: ¾ cup dark wafer chocolate

Tip: #104 petal tip (you can substitute #103)

sunflower

To cover 12 cupcakes you will need 2 ¼ cups buttercream: 1½ cups yellow and ¾ cup orange.

Colors: Yellow and orange liquid gel colors

Chocolate: 1½ cups dark wafer chocolate

Tip: #352 leaf tip (you can substitute #67)

1. Place a coupler in a pastry bag. Using a small metal spatula, spread a strip of orange buttercream up one side of the bag's interior. Fill the rest of the bag with yellow.

2. Fill a pastry cone with some of the variegated buttercream from the pastry bag. Set aside.

3. Place the cupcake on the center of a turntable.

4. For the first petal row start ¾ inch from the edge of the cupcake, hold the pastry bag at a 30-degree angle and squeeze, then release the pressure as you move away from the center.

5. Overlap this row of petals with another row, between the petals of the first row. Hold the bag at a 45-degree angle.

6. Melt the dark wafer chocolate and pour it into a pastry cone. Cut a medium hole in its tip and fill in the center of the flower.

7. Cut a small hole in the tip of the pastry cone containing the variegated buttercream and pipe small seeds within the chocolate center.

dahlia

To cover 12 cupcakes you will need 3 cups buttercream: 2 ¼ cups bright purple and ¾ cup pale violet.

Colors: Neon pink and violet liquid gel colors

Tip: #79 tip (you can substitute #80 or #81)

1. Place a coupler in a pastry bag. Using a small metal spatula, spread a strip of bright purple buttercream up one side of the bag's interior. Fill the rest of the bag with violet.

2. Place the cupcake on the center of a turntable.

3. Holding the convex end of the pastry tip down, pipe a row of petals around the outer edge. Start each petal ½ inch from the edge and pull away from the center. For this first row allow the tip to stay flush with the cupcake, angled downward with the slope of the dome. Each petal should be ½ to ¾ inch long.

4. Pipe another row inside the first, overlapping the petals of the first row about halfway. Increase the angle of the petals by approximately 15 to 20 degrees per row. Finish by filling in the center with petals. The petals in the center will be almost vertical.

lemon coconut cupcakes*

Since coconut is wonderful whether it is paired with chocolate, custard, lemon, or lime, we made a light and tangy variation of our Chocolate Coconut Cupcakes that is perfect for a spring celebration or a June wedding. An old-fashioned Kids' Buttercream is all you need to top them off, or make blooming flowers with piped buttercream (see page 131).

Grease the top of a 12-mold muffin pan and line it with paper liners. Preheat the oven to 350°F. Have all ingredients at room temperature.

In the bowl of an electric mixer, beat at high speed until light and fluffy:

- 6 ounces (1½ sticks) unsalted butter
- 1 cup sugar

Add one at a time and beat on medium speed until well creamed:

- 3 large eggs

Add and mix to combine:

- 2 tablespoons lemon zest
- 1½ teaspoons pure vanilla extract

On a piece of wax paper, sift together:

- 1½ cups all-purpose flour
- ¼ teaspoon baking soda
- ¼ teaspoon salt

At low speed, add the dry ingredients to the butter mixture alternately with:

- ¼ cup buttermilk

Add and mix until combined:

- ¼ cup fresh lemon juice

Fold in:

- 1 cup toasted sweetened coconut

Scoop the batter into the prepared molds, filling each to the top of the paper liner. Bake for 20 to 25 minutes, or until a cake tester inserted into the center of a cupcake comes out clean. The tops should spring back when lightly touched. Cool on a wire rack for 5 to 10 minutes before removing the cupcakes from their pan.

a r o s e   i s   a   r o s e . . .*

. . . . Unless it is a cake. Yet again I was inspired by a pan I found in a Williams-Sonoma *store. I wanted to make something unique and was quite excited by my prospects. Unfortunately, my first plan failed. I had wanted to cover the roses with tinted White Chocolate Glaze, but the glaze settled into the crevices between the petals, leaving me with a lovely red blob. Because our Almond Cake is so moist, I decided to leave the rose cakes unglazed, but I did tint the batter pink. I then arranged the baked cakes in a bouquet and made chocolate leaves and stems to tie them all together. Instead of serving the cakes in a bouquet, a simpler alternative is to plate each rose individually with two chocolate leaves.*

. . . .

WHAT YOU WILL NEED:

. . . .

Cake
12 mini rose Almond Cakes to make 1 bouquet (opposite)

Icing
½ recipe Chocolate Glaze (optional, page 34), ¼ cup buttercream (optional; storebought or House [page 31], Kaye's [page 32], or Kids' [page 33])

Decoration
1 cup white wafer chocolate to make leaves and stems, buttercream bow (optional)

Colors
green candy color, pink liquid gel color (optional)

Tip
#104 petal tip (you can substitute #103)

Miscellaneous
one mini rose pan, pastry cones, leaf templates (page 173), 1 half-sheet pan, parchment paper or cellophane, 14-inch or larger base

HOW TO

1. Bake the cakes and let them cool completely.

2. Melt the white wafer chocolate. Using the Color Mixing Chart (pages 44–45), tint the white chocolate: approximately ¼ cup light green and ¼ cup dark green. In a small glass or plastic bowl, set aside approximately 1 tablespoon of the dark green chocolate. Using the templates provided, make 12 small and 12 large leaves. Set aside to harden.

3. Arrange the roses in a cluster of 4 rows offset from the center of the base: 2 roses on top, followed by rows of 3, 4, and 3 below it (refer to the photograph).

4. Remelt the reserved dark green chocolate and pour it into a pastry cone. Cut a small hole at the tip and pipe stems from the bottom of the cluster to the edge of the base.

5. Nestle the leaves into and around the bouquet and stems.

6. Optional: Tint the buttercream pink and place it into a pastry bag with a coupler and a #104 petal tip. First pipe a ribbon around the stems, then pipe a bow: Hold the bag at a 45-degree angle to the surface. With the wide end of the tip pointed down, squeeze, moving the tip up and around to the right, ending at the starting point. Then, starting at the same point, squeeze, moving the tip up and around to the left, again ending at the starting point. At the starting point, squeeze two ribbons down to finish off the bow.

7. For fullest flavor, serve the cakes at room temperature.

almond cakes*

A customer from North Carolina sent us this recipe and requested we make it for her when she was in town. Reminiscent of marzipan, this moist cake was so delicious we're sharing it with you. At the Bakehouse we also bake the Almond Cake in a sheet pan and make it into petits fours.

Grease well and flour one 12-mold mini rose pan. Preheat the oven to 350°F. Have all ingredients at room temperature.

In the bowl of an electric mixer, beat at medium speed until crumbly:
- ¾ cup sugar
- 8 ounces almond paste

Add and mix until light and fluffy:
- 4 ounces (1 stick) unsalted butter

Add one at a time and beat on medium speed until well creamed:
- 3 large eggs

Add and mix to combine:
- 1½ teaspoons rum
- ½ teaspoon almond extract
- 5 drops pink food coloring, or tint to your liking (optional)

Mix together and add to the butter mixture at low speed just until combined:
- ¼ cup all-purpose flour
- ⅓ teaspoon baking powder
- ¼ teaspoon salt

Do not over-mix.

Scoop the batter into the prepared molds, filling each mold three-quarters full. Bake for 20 to 25 minutes, or until golden. The tops should spring back when lightly pressed. Immediately remove the cakes from their pan by placing a parchment-lined sheet pan on top of the baked cakes and inverting. Carefully remove.

basket cupcakes**

Our carrot cupcakes are transformed into a woven basket, complete with
an edible chocolate handle and a spattering of spring blossoms. Fill this treat with piped eggs or
jelly beans and you have yourself an Easter basket. We also like to make these dainty baskets for
baby showers because they are so cute, just like the little bundle of joy that is on the way.

WHAT YOU WILL NEED:

Cake
18 Carrot Cupcakes (page 143)

Icing
1½ recipes Kaye's Buttercream (page 32),
12 ounces semisweet chocolate to make
chocolate buttercream

Decoration
2 cups white wafer chocolate and ⅛ cup dark
wafer chocolate to make 20 handles

Colors
Violet, green, and yellow liquid gel colors and
orange candy color (optional)

Tips
#6, 7, or 8 round tip; #101, 102, or 103 petal tip;
263 small leaf tip

Miscellaneous
three 6-mold muffin pans, pastry bag, coupler,
pastry cones, handle template (page 170), 1 half-
sheet pan, parchment paper or cellophane,
turntable

1. Bake the cupcakes and let them cool completely. Freeze for 1 hour to overnight.

2. Prepare the buttercream.

3. Prepare the colored and flavored buttercream: approximately 4 cups chocolate buttercream, 1½ generous cups of violet, ½ generous cup of green, and 2 tablespoons yellow.

4. Melt the dark wafer and white wafer chocolates together. Add 4 drops of orange candy color to enhance the color. Using the template provided, make eighteen handles, as illustrated in The Chocolate Method (pages 40–43). Set aside to harden.

5. When the chocolate has set, using the same chocolate bag, over-pipe a scalloped edge or rickrack (zigzag) pattern to simulate the braiding of a real basket handle. Set aside to harden. When set, gently flip the handle and pipe the same pattern on the opposite side.

6. Ice the cupcakes with a smooth finish as directed on page 26. The icing on the outer edge of the cupcake should rise at least ½ inch from the paper's edge.

7. Place the chocolate buttercream into a pastry bag with a coupler, and with a round tip pipe a 2 x 2-inch basket weave (see below) around the edge of each cupcake. Placing the cupcake on a turntable will make this easier. Don't go below the paper line.

8. Mark where the handle will go by gently pressing it into the buttercream. If the cupcake is still frozen, use a knife or other small, sharp object to puncture the cupcake in these two spots. This will make it easier to push the handle into the cake later.

9. Place the violet buttercream into a pastry bag with a coupler, and with a petal tip pipe a blossom (see Hydrangea, page 133) in the center of the cupcake. Then pipe approximately 6 more blossoms around it, avoiding the holes made for the handle.

10. Place the yellow buttercream into a pastry cone and cut a small hole in the tip. Pipe yellow dots in the center of each flower.

11. Place the green buttercream into a pastry bag with a coupler, and with a leaf tip pipe leaves sporadically among the blossoms.

12. Stick the chocolate handle into the holes, pressing it halfway into the cupcake.

13. For fullest flavor, serve the cakes at room temperature.

BASKET WEAVE

Holding the bag perpendicular to the cake surface, pipe a vertical line where you want to begin the basket weave. Holding the bag at a 45-degree angle to the cake, pipe equidistant horizontal lines, separated by the width of the tip, overlapping the vertical line by ⅓ inch on each side. Approximately ⅛ inch to the right of the first vertical line, and slightly overlapping the horizontal lines, pipe another vertical line. Pipe another set of horizontal lines, starting in the empty spaces formed between the first set of horizontal lines, overlapping the second vertical line by ½ inch. Continue this pattern.

carrot cupcakes*

YIELD: 18 CUPCAKES

Back in 1988, when my mom opened her first bakery, the Runcible Spoon in Nyack, New York, she offered ten different muffins. This recipe is one of the originals: yet another muffin that is transformed into a delicious cupcake. Bake them for breakfast, ice them with Kids' Buttercream, or make them into adorable little baskets (see page 141).

Grease the tops of three 6-mold muffin pans and line them with paper liners. Preheat the oven to 350°F. Have all ingredients at room temperature.

In a large bowl, mix well:
- 2 cups sugar
- 1¼ cups vegetable oil
- 4 large eggs

On a piece of wax paper, sift together:
- 2½ cups all-purpose flour
- 1 teaspoon baking powder
- 1½ teaspoons baking soda
- 1 teaspoon salt
- 1 tablespoon ground cinnamon
- 1 tablespoon ground ginger

Add the dry ingredients to the wet ingredients and mix to combine.

Add just to combine:
- 1 cup chopped walnuts
- ¾ cup raisins
- 3 cups grated carrots (about 1 pound of carrots)

Scoop the batter into the prepared molds, filling each to the top of the paper liner. Bake for 20 to 25 minutes, or until a cake tester inserted into the center of a cake comes out clean. Cool on a wire rack for 5 to 10 minutes before removing the cupcakes from their pans.

gâteau chapeau***

Before I ever made my first edible hat, I had a name for it: Gâteau Chapeau. Mother's Day was the first holiday to showcase a 3-D bonnet. Since then we have added baseball caps for Father's Day, and witch hats for Halloween. In addition to these Bakehouse favorites, I added a fedora with a feather tucked in its band, perfect for a cool cat.

Cake: To make 4 hats, bake 2 scant 6-inch rounds and 4 mini cones of Pecan Cake (page 149)

Icing: $1/2$ recipe Whipped Chocolate Ganache (page 105), Chocolate Glaze (page 34), $1/4$ recipe Kids' Buttercream for ribbon (optional; page 33)

Decoration: $1/2$ cup white wafer chocolate to make 4 witch buckles, Chocolate Plastic for ribbons (optional; page 109)

Tip: #45 flat tip (you can substitute a #104 petal tip)

Colors: violet liquid gel color and orange and yellow candy colors

Miscellaneous: two 6-inch round pans and one 4-mold mini cone pan, pastry bag, coupler, pastry cones, buckle template (page 170), 1 half-sheet pan, parchment paper or cellophane, turntable, wire rack for glazing, four 6-inch cardboard rounds, four 8-inch (or larger) bases

HOW TO

1. Bake the cakes and let them cool completely. If opting for Chocolate Plastic ribbons, prepare the Chocolate Plastic. If opting for a buttercream ribbon, prepare the Kids' Buttercream. Prepare the Whipped Chocolate Ganache and Chocolate Glaze.

2. To set up the cakes: Cut the 6-inch round cakes horizontally into 2 equal layers. Cut the bottom dome off of the cones. Place each 6-inch layer onto a 6-inch cardboard or thick grease-proof paper round.

3. Crumb-coat the 6-inch rounds with a thin layer of Whipped Chocolate Ganache. Place the remaining ganache into a pastry bag with a coupler and pipe a large point on the top of the cone. With a piece of cellophane, smooth out the ganache where it meets the cake to make a flush connection. Freeze for 1 hour.

4. Melt the white wafer chocolate. Using the Color Mixing Chart on pages 44—45, tint the white chocolate: approximately 1 tablespoon yellow and 1 tablespoon orange. Using the template provided, make 4 buckles as illustrated in The Chocolate Method (pages 40—43). Set aside to harden.

5. Glaze the tops and bottoms of the cakes with Chocolate Glaze as directed in Chocolate Glaze on Cake, pages 29—30. If possible, invert and submerge the tip of each hat into the glaze before glazing as usual. This will ensure that the tip gets covered.

6. Place the bottom of the hat on its base. With the help of a metal spatula, carefully place the cone in the center of the base.

7. Buttercream Ribbon (see Note): Prepare $1/4$ cup violet buttercream. Place the violet buttercream into a pastry bag with a coupler, and with a #45 flat tip pipe a flat ribbon border (see page 163) around the base of the cone. Chocolate Plastic Ribbon: Tint half of the plastic violet. Dust a clean, flat surface with cornstarch. With a rolling pin, roll out the plastic to $1/8$ inch thick. Cut it

into four ¾ x 10-inch strips. Place one end of the strip down on the cake starting at the base of the hat, carefully draping around until it meets itself. Using scissors, cut off any extra plastic.

8 Place the buckle on the ribbon. Pipe 3 chocolate dots (buckle holes) to the right of the buckle.

9 For fullest flavor, serve the cakes at room temperature.

NOTE:
If you are only making witch hats and you don't have buttercream on hand, you can buy a package of vanilla icing at the store and tint it violet.

straw hats

WHAT YOU WILL NEED:

Cake: To make 6 hats, bake 3 scant 6-inch rounds and 6 mini bowls of Pecan Cake (page 149)

Icing: Kaye's Buttercream (page 32)

Tips: #6 or 7 round tip, #103 or 104 petal tip

Colors: yellow, brown, pink, and green liquid gel colors

Miscellaneous: three 6-inch round pans, one 6-mold mini bowl pan, pastry bag, coupler, pastry cones, turntable, six 8-inch (or larger) bases

HOW TO

1 Bake the cakes and let them cool completely. Prepare the buttercream.

2 Cut the 6-inch round cakes horizontally into 2 equal layers. Cut the bottom dome off of the bowls. Place each 6-inch round cake, crumb side down, onto a 6-inch cardboard or thick grease-proof paper round, adhering it with a dollop of buttercream. Place a bowl in the center of each 6-inch round cake, again adhering with a dollop of buttercream. Adhere the cardboard round supporting the cakes to their bases.

3 Set aside ¼ cup uncolored buttercream. Prepare the colored buttercream: approximately 6 cups straw-yellow, ¼ cup pink, 2 tablespoons green, 1 tablespoon yellow.

4 Place the straw-yellow buttercream into a pastry bag with a coupler, and with a #6 round tip pipe a basket-weave pattern. Start with the brim of the hat: pipe the vertical lines so that they are closer together near the top edge and wider apart at the base, like the sun's rays. In a similar manner pipe basket weave on the hat's bowl-top. All of the vertical lines should meet at the apex of the hat. The horizontal lines will be shorter and thinner the closer they approach the top of the dome.

5 Place the pink buttercream into a pastry bag with a #103 petal tip. Pipe a flat ribbon border around the bowl base. Pipe a bow in the front by holding the bag at a 45-degree angle to the cake surface. With the wide end of the tip pointed down, squeeze, moving the tip up and around to the right, end-

ing at the starting point. Then, starting at the same point, squeeze, moving the tip up and around to the left again, ending at the starting point. At the starting point squeeze two ribbons down to finish off the bow.

6. Place the pink, green, and yellow buttercream into separate pastry cones. Cut small holes in the tips of the each. Pipe out green stems and leaves onto the hat. Pipe white daisies on the tops of the stems (see photograph). Pipe yellow dots in the center of each flower. See the photograph for reference.

7. For fullest flavor, serve the cakes at room temperature.

fedoras

WHAT YOU WILL NEED:

Cake: To make 4 hats, bake 2 scant 6-inch rounds and 4 jumbo cupcakes of Pecan Cake (page 149)

Icing: Kaye's Buttercream (page 32); 12 ounces semisweet chocolate to make Chocolate Buttercream (page 33)

Decoration: ¼ cup dark wafer chocolate for accents, Chocolate Plastic (page 109) for ribbon (optional)

Tip: #45 flat tip (you can substitute a #104 petal tip)

Colors: red, yellow, and brown liquid gel colors

Miscellaneous: two 6-inch round pans, one 6-mold jumbo muffin pan, pastry bag, coupler, pastry cones, turntable, four 6-inch cardboard rounds, four 8-inch (or larger) bases

HOW TO

1. Bake the cakes and let them cool completely. Prepare the icing.

2. Prepare the flavored and tinted buttercream: 4 cups Chocolate Buttercream and (optional) ¼ cup dark chocolate buttercream (darken the chocolate by adding red, yellow, and brown liquid gel), 1 tablespoon yellow, 1 tablespoon white, 1 tablespoon red.

3. Cut the 6-inch round cakes horizontally into 2 equal layers. Cut the dome off of the cupcakes. Place each 6-inch round cake, crumb side down, onto a 6-inch cardboard or thick grease-proof paper round, adhering it with a dollop of buttercream. Cut a triangular section out of the top of each large muffin and discard or enjoy as a snack. Crumb-coat the cakes with some of the Chocolate Buttercream as directed on page 24.

4. Ice the cakes with a smooth finish (see page 28).

5. Place an iced 6-inch cake onto its base. Place a cupcake in the center of the 6-inch round.

6. To make a buttercream ribbon, place the dark brown buttercream into a pastry bag with a coupler, and with a #45 flat tip pipe a ribbon border around the base of the muffin. If you like, pipe vertical chocolate stripes on it to simulate grosgrain ribbon.

To make a ribbon of chocolate plastic, tint half of the plastic dark brown. Dust a clean, flat surface with cornstarch. With a rolling pin, roll out the plastic to ⅛ inch thick. Cut it into four ¾ x 10-inch strips. Score it with a knife's edge or fork edge repeatedly into the plastic to give the grosgrain effect. Place one end of the strip down on the cake starting at the base of the hat, carefully draping around until it meets itself. Using scissors, cut off any extra plastic.

7 Melt the dark wafer chocolate and pour it into a pastry cone. Place the red, white, and yellow buttercreams into separate pastry cones. Cut a small hole in the tip of each.

8 Pipe a feather coming out of the hat's ribbon using the chocolate and colored buttercream. Pipe one long white line. From this line pipe parallel lines at a 30-degree angle in red, yellow, chocolate, and white.

9 For fullest flavor, serve the cakes at room temperature.

baseball caps

WHAT YOU WILL NEED:

Cake: To make 12 hats, bake 12 mini bowls of Pecan Cake (page 149)

Icing: Chocolate Glaze (page 34)

Decoration: 3 cups dark wafer chocolate to make 12 baseball cap brims, and ¼ cup white wafer chocolate for stitching

Miscellaneous: two 6-mold mini bowl pans, pastry cones, brim templates (page 170), 1 half-sheet pan, parchment paper or cellophane, twelve 6-inch (or larger) bases

HOW TO

1 Bake the cakes and let them cool completely. Cut the bottom dome off of the bowls, and freeze the cakes for at least 30 minutes. Prepare the Chocolate Glaze.

2 Melt the dark wafer and white wafer chocolates separately. Using the templates provided, make 12 brims as illustrated in The Chocolate Method (pages 40—43). Set aside to harden.

3 Glaze the tops of the cakes as directed in Chocolate Glaze on a Cake (page 29).

4 Invert the brim onto its base, adhering with a dot of glaze. With the help of a metal spatula, place the cap so that it overlaps the brim approximately ¼ inch.

5 Pipe stitching on the brim and hat with white chocolate.

6 For fullest flavor, serve the cakes at room temperature.

p e c a n   c a k e s *

YIELD:
WITCH HATS: 4 witch hats
STRAW HATS: 6 straw hats
FEDORAS: 4 fedoras
BASEBALL CAPS: 12 caps

One of my favorite cakes at the Bakehouse is our hazelnut cake. We fine-tuned our recipe to achieve a lighter consistency and substituted my mom's favorite nut, the pecan. The result is a fragrant and delicious cake. If you don't want to fuss with decorating, for delicious redundancy simply buy a pint of butter pecan ice cream and serve the cupcakes à la mode.

For witch hats, grease two 6-inch round pans and one 4-mold mini cone pan.

For straw hats, grease three 6-inch round pans and one 6-mold mini bowl pan.

For fedoras, grease two 6-inch round pans and 4 molds of a 6-mold jumbo muffin pan.

For baseball hats, grease two 6-mold mini bowl pans.

Preheat the oven to 350°F. Have all ingredients at room temperature.

In the bowl of an electric mixer, beat at high speed until light and fluffy:
- 4 ounces (1 stick) unsalted butter
- 1½ cups brown sugar, packed

Add at medium speed and beat until well creamed:
- 2 large eggs
- 1 teaspoon pure vanilla extract

On a piece of wax paper, sift together:
- 2 cups cake flour
- ½ teaspoon salt
- ½ teaspoon baking powder
- 1 teaspoon baking soda

At low speed, add the dry ingredients to the butter mixture alternately with:
- 1 cup buttermilk

Beat the batter at medium-low speed until it is smooth, then stir in by hand:
- 1 cup finely chopped toasted pecans (see Note)

Pour the batter into the prepared pans.

Fill the mini bowl, mini cone, or jumbo muffin pans three-quarters full. Fill each 6-inch round with 1 cup of batter. Bake the bowl cakes for 12 to 18 minutes, or until a cake tester inserted into the center of a cake comes out clean. Bake the cone, jumbo muffin, and 6-inch round cakes for 20 to 25 minutes, or until a cake tester inserted into the center of a cake comes out clean. Cool on a wire rack for 15 to 20 minutes before turning the cakes out of the pans.

NOTE:
To toast pecans, place the nuts on an ungreased sheet pan. Bake at 350°F for 12 to 15 minutes, or until fragrant. Let cool.

During my first couple of years as a cake decorator I would create a limited-edition three-dimensional cake every week. In the fall I made these apple bushels and our customers loved them. We still make them every apple-picking season. The faux wood slats are created with variegated buttercream, and sweet buttercream apples overflow from the bushel.

. . . . .

WHAT YOU WILL NEED:

. . . . .

Cake
16 jumbo Apple Cupcakes (see page 152)

Icing
3 recipes of Kaye's Buttercream (page 32); Dulce de Leche (page 101)

Decoration
1 cup dark wafer chocolate

Colors
red, brown, green, and yellow (optional) liquid gel colors

Tips
#45 flat tip (you can substitute a #104 petal tip), and a #45 leaf tip

Miscellaneous
3 jumbo muffin pans, pastry bag, coupler, pastry cones, turntable, sixteen 6-inch (or larger) bases

1. Bake the cupcakes and let them cool completely. Do not trim the domes off. Chill for 1 hour to overnight.

2. Prepare the buttercream. Set aside ¾ cup uncolored buttercream. Prepare the flavored and tinted buttercream: approximately 4 cups dulce de leche buttercream (3½ cups buttercream with ¾ cup plus 2 tablespoons dulce de leche), ½ cup dark brown, 4 cups red, and 1 cup green buttercream.

3. Place a dot of dulce de leche buttercream on the underside of each cake and place the cake in the center of its base.

4. With a metal spatula, spread a small strip of dark brown buttercream up one side of the interior of a pastry bag with a coupler. Spread a white strip up the opposite side. Fill the rest of the bag with dulce de leche buttercream. Place the cupcake and its base on a turntable, and with a # 45 flat tip pipe slats up the side of the cake. Keep the tip flush to the cake surface. Start piping each slat at the bottom of the cake and pipe to the top using a consistent pressure. Overlap each slat slightly so no cake will show through. Continue piping until you've covered the entire side of the cake with vertical slats. With a metal spatula, scrape off any excess buttercream that may have come over the top edge.

5. With the remaining variegated dulce de leche buttercream, pipe a rim around the outside top edge and around the center of each bushel.

6. With a spatula, spread a small strip of dark brown buttercream up one side of the interior of a pastry bag. Spread a white stripe up the opposite side. Fill the rest of the bag with red. Pipe one quarter-size apple "hemisphere" in the center of each bushel. Pipe an additional 6 apples around the center one.

7. Place the green buttercream into a pastry bag with a coupler, and with a leaf tip pipe leaves randomly around the top of the bushel.

8. Melt the dark wafer chocolate and pour it into a pastry cone. Cut a small hole in the pastry cone and pipe small nails randomly around the wood slats and pipe stems on the apples. Fill in the spaces between the apples with chocolate to give the effect of shadow.

9. For fullest flavor, serve the cakes at room temperature.

apple cupcakes*

YIELD: **16** JUMBO CUPCAKES

The first incarnation of my mom's Apple Cake was really a cake, but nowadays you will most often find this treat disguising itself on the shelves of the Bakehouse as our apple muffin. If you are not up for the task of decorating a bunch of apple bushels, just whip up a batch of apple muffins instead. You can even slice them in half and serve with fresh Cinnamon Chocolate Whipped Cream (page 113).

Grease 16 molds of three 6-mold jumbo muffin pans. Preheat the oven to 350°F. Have all ingredients at room temperature.

In the bowl of an electric mixer, beat at high speed until light and fluffy:

- 1 cup vegetable oil
- 1 cup granulated sugar
- ¼ cup brown sugar, packed

Add and beat on medium speed until well creamed:

- 2 large eggs
- ½ teaspoon pure vanilla extract

On a piece of wax paper, sift together:

- 2 cups all-purpose flour
- 1½ teaspoons baking soda
- 1½ teaspoons ground cinnamon
- ½ teaspoon ground nutmeg
- ¼ teaspoon ground cloves
- 1 teaspoon salt

Mix the dry ingredients into the sugar and egg mixture at low speed just until combined.

Mix in:

- 2 cups Granny Smith apples, peeled, cored, and grated (from about 1½ apples)
- ½ to ¾ cup chopped toasted walnuts (see Note)

Pour the batter into the prepared molds, filling each mold three-quarters full. Bake for 25 to 30 minutes, or until a cake tester inserted into the center of a cupcake comes out clean. Cool on a wire rack for 15 to 20 minutes before turning the cakes out of the pans.

NOTE:

To toast walnuts, place the nuts on an ungreased sheet pan. Bake at 350°F for 12 to 15 minutes, or until fragrant. Let cool.

flower pots***

I've always wanted to make miniature flower pots. At the Bakehouse we make large (6-inch round by 8-inch tall) flower-pot cakes filled with African violets every Mother's Day. And for St. Patty's Day we fill the pot with golden wild roses (Flower-Pot-of-Gold). After a little brainstorming I decided I would try making the terra-cotta pots out of chocolate instead of cake and tinted buttercream. Three-ounce plastic cups became my mold. A delicious confection of Whipped Chocolate Ganache, cookie crumbs, and a Chocolate Butter Mini-Cupcake simulate the rich soil the buttercream violets sprout from.

WHAT YOU WILL NEED:

Cake
½ recipe of Chocolate Butter Cake (page 155) to make 50 cupcakes

Icing
House Buttercream (page 31) or Kaye's Buttercream (page 32)

Filling
Whipped Chocolate Ganache (page 105)

Decoration
2 ¼ cups dark wafer chocolate and 8 cups white wafer chocolate to make 50 chocolate shovels and flower pots; approximately ½ cup chocolate cookie crumbs (optional)

Colors
purple, green, and yellow liquid gel colors and orange candy color

Tips
#101 petal tip, #263 leaf tip

Miscellaneous
three mini muffin pans, pastry bag, coupler, pastry cones, shovel template (page 173), 1 half-sheet pan, parchment paper or cellophane, fifty 3-ounce plastic drinking cups, fifty 4-inch (or larger) bases

1. Prepare the chocolate ganache. Bake the cakes and let them cool completely. Freeze for 1 hour to overnight.

2. Prepare the buttercream.

3. Melt the dark wafer and white wafer chocolates separately. Mix 3⅛ cups white chocolate with a generous ¼ cup dark chocolate. Add orange candy color drop by drop until you have a terra-cotta color. Using the Color Mixing Chart on pages 44–45, tint the remaining white chocolate gray. Using the template provided, make 50 shovels as illustrated in The Chocolate Method (pages 40–43). Set aside to harden.

4. Cut fifty 3-ounce plastic cups down one side to the base. Tape the slit closed. Pour approximately 2 tablespoons of "terra cotta" into each cup. With a small metal spatula, spread the chocolate so that it covers the entire interior surface of the cup as evenly as possible. Invert the cup onto a wire rack over parchment paper. Let the chocolate drip and set for 3 to 5 minutes. Turn the cups right side up and with a small knife scrape any extra chocolate off the top edge. Place the cups in the freezer for 3 to 5 minutes or just until hard.

5. Remove the cups from the freezer. Remove the tape from the side of the cup. Carefully pull the cup away from the chocolate and remove the pots. Set aside.

6. Whip the chocolate ganache. Remove the cupcakes from the freezer.

7. Place the whipped ganache into a pastry bag with a coupler. Pipe a dollop of ganache in the bottom of each terra-cotta cup. If desired, sprinkle some chocolate cookie crumbs on top (approximately ½ teaspoon per pot) and then pipe more ganache until it reaches two thirds of the way to the top edge. Place one cupcake on the top. The bottom of the cupcake should touch the ganache, and the top of it should slightly rise above the terra-cotta cup.

8. Prepare the colored buttercream: approximately 2 cups violet, 1¼ cups green, and 3 tablespoons yellow buttercream.

9. Place the violet buttercream into a pastry bag with a coupler, and with the #101 tip pipe 1 violet in the center and 5 to 6 violets around the center one. To pipe violets refer to the directions for piping hydrangea on page 133 with one difference: instead of 4 petals, the violet has 5 petals.

10. Place the green buttercream into a pastry bag with a coupler, and with the #263 tip pipe leaves in the empty spaces between the flowers.

11. Place the yellow buttercream into a pastry cone and cut a small hole in the tip. Pipe two yellow dots in the center of each flower.

12. Plate the pots with the shovel at their side. If you are traveling, adhere the pots to a cardboard base with a large dot of melted chocolate; hold in place until set. For an added effect, scoop some chocolate ganache onto the shovel and dip it in chocolate cookie crumbs, and/or spread some chocolate ganache on the base and encrust with cookie crumbs.

13. For fullest flavor, serve the cakes at room temperature.

chocolate butter cake or mini cupcakes*

YIELD: TWO 3-TIERED (2-INCH, 3-INCH, AND 4-INCH) CAKES OR 100 MINI CUPCAKES

This has to be our best cake. We've been baking this amazing recipe for more than twenty years. Take care not to discard the dome of the cake; devour it without shame! It's the moistest and most delicious part.

This recipe does not bake well in standard cupcake molds unless the molds are nonstick Teflon, because even when greased, the tops of the cupcake tend to stick to the top of the pan. However, we had no problems with the mini cupcake pans or other pans if greased and floured.

For tiered cakes, grease and flour two 2-inch, two 3-inch, and two 4-inch round cake pans.

For Flower Pots, cut this recipe in half and grease and flour two 24-mold mini muffin pans plus 2 more molds. Preheat the oven to 350°F. Have all ingredients at room temperature.

In a small bowl, combine:
- ½ cup hot coffee
- ½ cup cocoa powder

Whisk until there are no lumps.

Add and whisk until smooth:
- ½ cup cold water

On a piece of wax paper, sift together:
- 1½ cups cake flour
- 1 teaspoon baking soda
- ¼ teaspoon baking powder
- ¼ teaspoon salt

In the bowl of an electric mixer, beat at high speed until light and fluffy:
- 4 ounces (1 stick) unsalted butter
- 1¼ cups sugar

On medium speed, add slowly and cream well:
- 2 large eggs
- ¾ teaspoon pure vanilla extract

Add the flour mixture to the egg mixture alternately with the cocoa, mixing until smooth.

Scoop the batter into the molds: The 2-inch round uses a scant ¼ cup of batter, the 3-inch round uses a generous ½ cup of batter, and the 4-inch round uses 1 cup of batter. Each mini muffin mold will hold 1 tablespoon of batter. Bake the 4-inch for 20 to 25 minutes, the 3-inch for 20 to 22 minutes, the 2-inch for 15 to 18 minutes, and the mini cupcakes for 12 to 14 minutes. Cool on a wire rack for 15 minutes before turning them out of their pans.

3-d christmas trees **

Every Christmas we make a limited edition of these cakes, but about 6 inches taller. Strung with lights and decorated with festive ornaments and wrapped presents, they will add to the merry atmosphere when placed on your holiday table. Or, instead of a gingerbread house or fruit cake, make these trees as gifts to share with your friends and family.

WHAT YOU WILL NEED:

Cake
6 gingerbread mini cone cakes (see page 158)

Icing
1½ recipes Kaye's Buttercream (page 32)

Filling
Eggnog Cream (page 159; optional)

Decoration
½ cup dark wafer chocolate and 3 cups white wafer chocolate to make doves, stars, bears, rocking horses, candy canes, bulbs, and presents, and ¼ cup edible gel for a garland

Colors
green, blue, and yellow liquid gel colors; and red, yellow, blue, purple, and pink candy colors

Tip
#133 multi-opening tip (you can substitute a #233 tip)

Miscellaneous
two 4-mold mini cone pans, pastry bag, coupler, pastry cones, decoration templates (page 169), 1 half-sheet pan, parchment paper or cellophane, turntable, six 6-inch (or larger) bases

1 Bake the cakes and let them cool completely. Prepare the buttercream.

2 If desired, prepare the filling. To fill the cake, cut each cone in half horizontally and with a small paring knife cut out a 2-inch-long by ¾-inch-deep cone from the bottom of the cake and a 1-inch-long by ¾-inch-deep cone from the top. Fill the holes with a generous amount of eggnog cream and replace the top on the cone. Gently push down on the cake allowing some of the cream to seep out, adhering the two sides. Scrape off any cream that may have come through the seam. Chill for 30 minutes.

3 Melt the dark wafer and white wafer chocolates separately. Set aside 2 tablespoons white chocolate. Using the Color Mixing Chart on pages 44—45, tint the remaining white chocolate: approximately 2 tablespoons each of dark blue, light blue, pink, orange, yellow, red, light green, green, violet, light brown, dark brown. Using the templates provided, make approximately 30 each of the bulbs, stars, bears, rocking horses, and candy canes. Also make 6 of each present and 6 larger stars to top the trees, as illustrated in The Chocolate Method (pages 40—43). Set aside to harden.

4 Prepare the tinted buttercream: approximately ¼ cup yellow and 5¾ cups green. In addition mix 2 drops of yellow liquid-gel color with ¼ cup of clear piping gel.

5 Adhere the cake to its base with a dollop of green buttercream. Place the cake and base on a turntable.

6 Place the green buttercream into a pastry bag with a coupler. Pipe a large point (much like a Hershey's kiss) on top of the cone. Place a #133 tip on the pastry bag and pipe out pine needles as follows: Place the tip ¼ inch from the base, squeeze, and pull downward at a 45-degree angle. Release the pressure when the pine needles are about ½ inch long. Go around the entire base in this manner. Start the next row directly above the last row; the bottom of the tip touches the top edge of the first row. Continue piping overlapping rows. As you get closer to the top, the angle of the tip will change from 45 degrees downward to level to 45 degrees upward. The last row is just one stroke straight up.

7 Place the yellow buttercream and yellow gel into separate pastry cones and cut a small hole into the tip of each. To create a garland, pipe a continuous line of small yellow dots spiraling up and around the cake, then back down again, crisscrossing itself. Pipe swags of gel around the tree.

8 Place the ornaments randomly around the cake and a star on top. Place the presents at the base of the cake.

9 For fullest flavor, serve the cakes at room temperature.

gingerbread cakes*

YIELD: 6 CONES

Gingerbread isn't just a cookie, it also manifests itself as a delicious cake; in fact, this was one of our home testers' favorite recipes. You can bake it in a loaf pan, slice, and serve with Eggnog Cream or go for broke and make a spectacular Christmas tree as on page 156.

Grease 6 molds of two 4-mold mini cone pans. Preheat the oven to 350°F. Have all ingredients at room temperature.

In the bowl of an electric mixer, beat at high speed until light and fluffy:
- 4 ounces (1 stick) unsalted butter
- ¾ cup sugar
- ½ cup molasses

Add at medium speed and beat until well creamed:
- 1 large egg

On a piece of wax paper, sift together:
- 2 cups all-purpose flour
- 1 teaspoon baking soda
- 2 teaspoons ground ginger
- ½ teaspoon ground nutmeg
- 1 teaspoon ground cinnamon
- ¼ teaspoon ground cloves
- ½ teaspoon salt

At low speed, add the dry ingredients to the butter mixture alternately with:
- 1 cup milk

Fold in:
- ¼ cup minced crystallized ginger

Divide the batter evenly among the 6 cones. Bake for 18 to 22 minutes or until a cake tester inserted into the center of a cake comes out clean. Cool the cakes on a wire rack for 5 minutes before turning them out of their pans.

eggnog cream *

This classic yuletide flavor when paired with whipped cream is a perfect accompaniment to our Gingerbread Cake, but it is also great spooned into your evening coffee.

For best results, we recommend preparing the cream right before serving or assembling your cakes. Any leftovers can be stored in an airtight container in the refrigerator for up to 3 days. The cream will break down as it sits in the refrigerator, so rewhip in the bowl of an electric mixer for 1 minute or until medium to stiff peaks form.

In the bowl of an electric mixer fitted with a whisk attachment, whip until stiff:
- 1¼ cups heavy cream
- ¼ cup confectioners' sugar
- 1 teaspoon pure vanilla extract
- Dash of nutmeg (or to taste)

Instead of making a grandiose statement by having a large tiered cake at their wedding receptions, some brides and grooms are opting for a collection of tiered miniature cakes to present to each table or each guest. These little versions of the classic can be just as traditional in their appearance as their larger cousins, or they can take a turn for the whimsical with bright fun palettes and carefree designs.

Of course a tiered cake isn't just for weddings anymore. We make just as many for birthdays. Make an individual tiered cake for that special someone, and let the rest of the party guests eat a regular cake.

Here are three takes on the tiered mini cake: Mariana's Paisley (inspired by a former colleague's cake doodles), Lovely Lilacs, and Dragon Cake.

Cake: Two 3-tiered Chocolate Butter Cakes (each of which has a 2-inch, 3-inch, and 4-inch round layer) (page 155)

Filling: Apricot Mousse (page 167)

Icing: Kaye's Buttercream (page 32)

Colors: yellow, green, orange, neon pink, and violet liquid gel colors

Miscellaneous: Two 2-inch, 3-inch, and 4-inch round pans; two each 2-inch, 3-inch, and 4-inch cardboard rounds; pastry bag; coupler; pastry cones; turntable; drinking straws; two sturdy serving plates or bases at least 3 inches larger than the bottom tier

HOW TO

1. Bake the cakes and let them cool completely. Prepare the icing and filling. Place the cakes on cardboard rounds of the same diameter. Fill and crumb-coat each individual cake as illustrated in Filling (page 23) and Crumbing (page 24). You will need approximately 1½ cups of filling and 1½ cups of buttercream for crumbing all of the round tiers. Chill the filled cakes for an hour.

2. Set aside ¼ cup uncolored buttercream. Prepare the colored buttercream: approximately 2 cups yellow, 2 tablespoons pale orange, 2 tablespoons coral, 2 tablespoons dark coral, 2 tablespoons pale neon green.

3. Ice the cakes with a flat finish (page 26) of yellow buttercream.

4. Place a dot of glue on the center of each base and adhere the two bottom (4-inch) tiers to them.

5. In the center of each bottom tier, press a straw all the way into the center of the cake. (Ideally the cake is level and all points are the same height.) Mark the straw at the buttercream line with a pen or hold it with your finger. You'll use this to create straws that will support the cake. Remove the straw and cut it ⅟₁₆ inch shorter than that line, using scissors. Using this straw as a guide, cut 2 to 4 more straws to the same length. Insert the straws into the cakes, evenly spaced within the area over which the next tier will be placed. Pipe a small dot of buttercream on top of each straw.

6. Center the second (3-inch) tiers on top of the bottom tiers. Cut 1 straw support for each cake (see step 5) and insert them into the center of each cake. Pipe a small dot of buttercream on top of the straws.

7. Center the third (2-inch) tiers on top of the second tiers.

8. Place the remaining colored buttercream into separate pastry cones. Cut small to medium holes in the tip of each. Pipe a dot border on the bottom of each tier (see below for piping dots). Pipe colorful paisley and/or filigree patterns all over the tiers (see below for piping filigree). Use the photograph as a guide, or make up your own pattern.

9. For fullest flavor, serve the cakes at room temperature.

DOTS

Tips: #2 to #12 round tip or pastry cone

Hold the bag perpendicular to the cake surface. Keeping the tip stationary, apply consistent pressure until the dot is the desired size. Release the pressure and tail off gently to the side or in a spiral to give a rounded finish.

LINES AND FILIGREE

Tips: #2 to #7 round tip or a pastry cone

Hold the bag at a 45-degree angle to the cake surface. Touch the tip to the surface where you want to begin piping, then lift the tip up as you begin to apply pressure and move the pastry bag in the desired direction. To end the line, touch the tip to the surface of the cake again and discontinue the pressure.

lovely lilacs

WHAT YOU WILL NEED:

Cake: Two 3-tiered Chocolate Butter Cakes (each of which has a 2-inch, 3-inch, and 4-inch round layer) (page 155)

Filling: Apricot Mousse (page 167)

Icing: Kaye's Buttercream (page 32)

Tips: #2 or 3 round tip, #263 leaf tip, #44 or 45 flat tip

Colors: green, brown, and violet liquid gel colors

Miscellaneous: Two 2-inch, 3-inch, and 4-inch round pans; two each 2-inch, 3-inch, and 4-inch cardboard rounds; pastry bag; coupler; pastry cones; turntable; drinking straws; two sturdy serving plates or bases at least 3 inches larger than the bottom tier

HOW TO

1 Bake the cakes and let them cool completely. Prepare the icing and filling. Place the cakes on cardboard rounds of the same diameter. Fill and crumb-coat each individual cake as illustrated in Filling (page 23) and Crumbing (page 24). You will need approximately 1½ cups of filling and 1½ cups of buttercream for crumbing all of the round tiers. Chill the filled cakes for an hour.

2 Ice the cakes with a flat finish (page 26) of plain white buttercream. Adhere the cardboard rounds supporting the bottom (4-inch) tiers to their bases.

3 To assemble the tiers, follow steps 5, 6, and 7 of Mariana's Paisley (page 161).

4 Place the buttercream into a pastry bag with a coupler, and with the #45 tip pipe a flat ribbon border (see below) around the base of each tier.

5 Prepare the colored buttercream: approximately ¼ cup pale violet, scant ¼ cup violet, 2 tablespoons dark brown, ¼ cup green.

6 Place the brown buttercream into a pastry cone and cut a small hole in the tip. Pipe a branch running up the side of the tiers. The branch should have smaller stems that shoot off it. These stems should have an overall conical form, since on a real tree the stems get fewer and narrower as they grow.

7 With a metal spatula, spread a stripe of light violet up one side of a pastry bag with a coupler. Fill the rest of the bag with violet. With a #2 or 3 round tip pipe small teardrops starting at the outer edges of the branches and pulling in toward the center stem. The petals should be fuller the closer you get to the center stem. Fill in the center of the lilac with dots and add a few 4-petal teardrop blossoms to complete the flower.

8 Place the green buttercream into a pastry bag with a coupler and with a #263 leaf tip pipe leaves sporadically around the lilacs.

9 For fullest flavor, serve the cakes at room temperature.

FLAT RIBBON BORDER

Tips: #44 or 45 flat tip

Hold the bag at a 45-degree angle to the cake surface. With the wide end of the tip down, apply consistent pressure while piping a ribbon flush to the cake surface. Keep the narrow end lightly brushing the surface of the cake to ensure that it adheres.

dragon cake

WHAT YOU WILL NEED:

Cake: Celebration Cake (page 166)

Filling and Icing: Kaye's Buttercream (page 32), Praline Powder (page 167), and 1½ ounces chopped semisweet chocolate to make flavored buttercream

Decoration: ¼ cup dark wafer chocolate and 2½ cups white chocolate to make the dragon's face, scales, legs, and polka dots

Colors: pink and green liquid gel colors and red, orange, yellow, green, blue, violet, and neon pink candy colors

Miscellaneous: Two half-sheet pans; pastry cones; 5-inch and 3-inch square cardboards; dragon templates (page 168); parchment paper or cellophane; turntable; drinking straws; sturdy serving plate or base at least 3 inches larger than the bottom tier

1. Prepare the Praline Powder. Bake the cakes and let them cool completely. Prepare the buttercream. Prepare the flavored buttercream for the filling. To make the praline buttercream, combine 1 cup buttercream and ⅓ cup praline powder. To make the chocolate buttercream, combine 1½ ounces chocolate, melted and allowed to cool to body temperature, and ½ cup buttercream.

2. Cut the cakes as directed in the recipe. Stack the 5-inch cake layers on the 5-inch cardboard square and the 3-inch cake layers on the 3-inch cardboard square. Fill and crumb-coat each individual cake as illustrated in Filling (page 23) and Crumbing (page 24) using praline buttercream between the bottom 2 layers, chocolate buttercream on top of the second layer, and another layer of praline buttercream between the top layers. Each tier will have 4 layers of cake, 2 layers of praline buttercream, and 1 layer of chocolate buttercream. Chill the filled cakes for 1 hour.

3. Melt the dark wafer and white wafer chocolates separately. Reserve 1 tablespoon white chocolate. Tint the remaining white chocolate: approximately ¼ cup neon green, 2 tablespoons teal, 2 tablespoons violet, 2 tablespoons orange, 2 tablespoons yellow, 2 tablespoons red, 2 tablespoons green, 2 tablespoons neon pink. Using the templates provided, trace two dragon heads onto parchment paper. Turn one upside down and one right side up. Place another piece of parchment over them. Make the two dragon heads, plus 4 feet,

multicolored teardrop-shaped scales, spikes, and pink and green polka dots as illustrated in The Chocolate Method (pages 40–43). Set aside to harden.

4 Prepare the colored buttercream: approximately 1½ cups light green and ½ cup pale pink. Reserve approximately 1 tablespoon of each color and tint it one shade darker. Place the darker colors into separate pastry bags.

5 Ice the cakes with a flat finish (page 27), the bottom tier in green and the top tier in pink. Pipe pinpoint dots on the tiers in the same hue as the icing. Adhere the cardboard squares supporting the bottom (5-inch) tier to its base.

6 In the center of the bottom tier, press a straw all the way into the center of the cake. (Ideally the cake is level and all points are the same height.) Mark the straw at the buttercream line with a pen or hold it with your finger. You'll use this to create straws that will support the cake. Remove the straw and cut it 1/16 inch shorter than that line, using scissors. Using this straw as a guide, cut 4 more straws to the same length. Insert the straws into the cake, evenly spaced within the area over which the next tier will be placed. Pipe a small dot of buttercream on top of each straw.

7 Stack the top tier so that it is kitty-corner to the bottom tier.

8 Stick the pink chocolate polka dots to the bottom border of the pink cake and the green chocolate polka dots to the bottom border of the green cake.

9 Mark where the dragon head will be on the side of the top tier. It should come up over the top edge approximately 2 inches. Line up the other head so that it will be directly behind the first head, ½ to ¾ inch away, with the back or underside facing the front. With a sharp knife, score the top of the cake where it will be inserted. Slowly and carefully press the dragon head into the cake, until it lines up directly behind the other. Place any leftover green buttercream in a pastry bag with a coupler. Pipe buttercream on the back side of the dragon, then stick the forward-facing dragon head into the buttercream directly in front of the inserted head.

10 Pipe an undulating line from the dragon's neck down to the bottom tier, tailing off before you reach the base.

11 Place the spikes into the buttercream between the heads.

12 Starting at the bottom, stick the scales onto the buttercream (the points face upward). Overlap the rows, and offset them, so the points are disguised (refer to the photograph). Continue until you reach the dragon's neck and have covered all of the buttercream.

13 Stick the legs into the side of the dragon (refer to the photograph).

14 For fullest flavor, serve the cakes at room temperature.

celebration cake**

My mom has been making this cake since I was a child and I always loved to eat the scraps she trimmed off. I was so enamored of this unique cake that, for my fifth-grade French class, I entered it in a language fair baking contest at a local college. Suffice it to say, it won!

Grease and flour a half-sheet pan. Preheat the oven to 350°F. Have all ingredients at room temperature.

In a food processor, combine and finely chop:

- 6 ounces (1½ cups) toasted hazelnuts (see Note)
- 5 ounces (1 cup) toasted whole almonds (see Note)
- ¼ cup all-purpose flour

Transfer to a bowl and add:

- ¾ cup sugar

In the bowl of an electric mixer at medium speed, use a whip attachment to beat until frothy:

- 1¼ cups egg whites (from 10 to 12 eggs)
- ½ teaspoon cream of tartar
- ¼ teaspoon salt

Continue beating at high speed while gradually adding:

- ¼ cup sugar

Beat until very stiff.

Fold in the nut mixture.

Pour the batter into the prepared pan. Using an offset spatula, spread the batter evenly onto the sheet pan. Bake for 17 to 22 minutes, or until golden brown. Cool the cake in its pan on a wire rack. Using an offset spatula, loosen the edges and bottom of the cake from the pan. To make the tiered Dragon Cake on page 164 cut the cooled cake as follows: Measuring the horizontal (or 16-inch) side of the cake with a ruler, lightly score the cake into two 5-inch strips and two 3-inch strips. From these strips cut out four 5-inch squares and four 3-inch squares (you will have extra 3-inch squares and 2 x 5-inch strips). To fill and assemble the cakes follow the Dragon Cake directions.

To assemble and ice a plain Celebration Cake cut the cake into four 6 x 8-inch pieces. Stack the layers on a 6 x 8-inch piece of cardboard. Prepare 2 cups of praline buttercream and 2 cups of chocolate buttercream. Fill the cake with 2 layers of praline buttercream and 1 layer of chocolate buttercream as described in Filling a Cake (page 23). Spread a thin layer of chocolate buttercream onto the sides of the cake and press on chopped nuts into the buttercream (approximately 1 cup). Dust the top with powdered sugar.

NOTE:
To toast the hazelnuts and almonds, place the nuts on an ungreased sheet pan. Bake at 350°F for 12 to 15 minutes or until fragrant. Let cool.

praline powder*

We use this recipe to flavor our praline buttercream, but we recommend topping your ice cream with this delicious concoction, too. Feel free to add your favorite nut in place of almonds.

In a small saucepan, bring to a boil:
- ½ cup sugar
- 2 tablespoons water

Dip a clean pastry brush in cold water and wash down the sugar crystals that form on the sides of the pot. Continue boiling on high heat until caramelized or the mixture has become a nut-brown color, about 7 minutes. Do not stir. If the sugar mixture colors unevenly, shake the pan. Take care, as this sugar mixture gets very hot.

Remove from the heat and stir in:
- ½ cup sliced almonds

Immediately pour onto a sheet pan lined with parchment paper or a silicone mat and let cool completely.

Break the praline into pieces and place into a food processor. Process until fine.

apricot mousse*

YIELD: 1½ CUPS

A little tang and a lot of yumminess. For best results, we recommend preparing the Apricot Mousse right before serving or assembling your cakes.

In the bowl of an electric mixer fitted with a whisk attachment, whip until stiff:
- ¾ cup heavy cream
- 3 tablespoons confectioners' sugar
- ½ teaspoon pure vanilla extract

In a small bowl, stir until smooth:
- Scant ¼ cup apricot jam

Gently fold the jam into the whipped cream.

To achieve the correct size for your little cakes, each
of the templates should be increased to four times
their size, or by 400 percent on your photocopier.

DRAGON CAKE (PAGES 164—165)

3-D CHRISTMAS TREES (PAGES 156—157)

SPIDERS (PAGES 122—123)

LADYBUGS (PAGES 122—123)

BE MINE CAKES (PAGES 110—111)

BASKET CUPCAKES
(PAGES 141—142)

SHARK CAKES (PAGES 125—126)

ACORN CUPCAKES
(PAGE 99)

WITCH HAT (PAGE 145)

A DAY AT THE BEACH (PAGES 128—129)

BASEBALL CAP (PAGE 148)

A ROSE IS A ROSE . . . (PAGES 137—138)

YUMMY YUMMY
BUMBLEBEE CUPCAKES
(PAGES 119—120)

FLOWER POTS (PAGES 153—154)

CONSTRUCTED CUPCAKES
(PAGES 116—117)

list of suppliers

The suppliers listed below stock baking and decorating tools and ingredients that are not readily available in supermarkets.

WILLIAMS-SONOMA
Retail locations throughout the United States
877-812-6235
www.williams-sonoma.com

In addition to carrying a wide range of bakeware (including many of the pans used in this book) and many specialty baking ingredients, this national chain also carries great decorating starter kits.

WILTON INDUSTRIES, INC.
2240 West 75th St.
Woodridge, IL 60517
800-794-5866
www.wilton.com

Decorating tools, bakeware, display equipment, wafer chocolate, and food coloring.

NEW YORK CAKE AND BAKING DISTRIBUTORS, INC.
56 West 22nd St.
New York, NY 10010
Phone: 800-942-2539 or 212-675-7955

Decorating supplies including food coloring, pastry bags, and tips.

KING ARTHUR FLOUR BAKER'S CATALOGUE
58 Billings Farm Road
White River Junction, VT 05001
800-827-6836

Flagship Store:
135 Route 5 South
Norwich, VT 05055-0876
802-649-3361
www.kingarthurflour.com

Everything from cake pans to electric mixers, specialty ingredients to chocolate, decorating tools, and display equipment.

NORDIC WARE
www.nordicware.com

This is the source for a wide range of bakeware, including Bundt pans, unique mini shaped pans, muffin tins, and much more. Check it out.

THE FOODCRAFTER'S SUPPLY CATALOG
P.O. Box 442-OKD
Waukon, IA 52172-0442
800-776-0575
www.kitchenkrafts.com

A wide range of baking and decorating tools from candy-making equipment to bakeware and display.

PFEIL AND HOLING
58-15 Northern Blvd.
Woodside, NY 11377
Phone: 800-247-7955
www.cakedeco.com

This is where the Bakehouse purchases the majority of our decorating tools and colors.

index

Note: Page numbers in *italics* refer to illustrations

KIDS' CAKES
from the
WHIMSICAL BAKEHOUSE

And Other Treats for
Colorful Celebrations

Liv Hansen & *Kaye Hansen*

PHOTOGRAPHS BY
Ben Fink

Clarkson Potter/Publishers
New York

For the kid in all of us . . .

Thank you to everyone who has ever baked one of our cakes or tried his or her hand at decorating with chocolate. You made three a charm and our fourth effort even more special. For the Riviera Bakehouse staff, who home-tested our recipes and sampled treat after treat (Kim Winder, Sung Yung Cho, Jaime Raucci, Sara Romeo, Becca DeAngelis, Nicole Vellucci, Gina DiBattista, Mike DeVito, and Halle and Andrea Lerner), thank you for your encouragement and hard work. And none of this would be possible without the support of Carla Glasser (our agent), the brilliance of Ben Fink (our photographer), and the guidance of Aliza Fogelson (our editor). Thank you, thank you, and thank you!

CONTENTS

INTRODUCTION

KAYE This book is for the kids and for the kid in us all. I know I am still a kid at heart and I think that deserves a party.

LIV Great idea! It's time to celebrate the wonder and imagination of childhood, where pixie dust is sugarcoated and pirate's booty is made of gilded chocolate. Whether you are hosting a themed celebration, like our Best Sleepover Ever (page 53); having some friends over for a playdate any day; or spending precious time with your child in the kitchen, the recipes and decorations in this book are kid friendly and fun.

KAYE The year is full of opportunities and excuses to bake and decorate—and you're right, it's not just for birthdays. Maybe you want cake or cookies or pie, but you aren't throwing a party. The recipes on these pages are perfect for festivities great and small. Why not celebrate Friday (and use up those overripe bananas) with Banana Chocolate–Chocolate Chip Cake (page 57)! Make Funnel Cakes (page 117) and invite the kids over for an end-of-the-school-year get-together. Let the aroma of Pumpkin Spice Cake (page 140) fill the air on Thanksgiving Day, and roll out play dough (see page 40) with your grandchildren while the turkey roasts.

LIV In addition to a great collection of fifteen cake recipes, we've added cupcakes, cookies, pies, and even breakfast treats—the perfect sweet ending to a sleepover party. The flavors we offer up are kid approved, like chocolate fudge, cinnamon swirl, root beer float, and apple pie. If you are throwing an enchanted tea party, not only can you transform our Citrus Sponge Roll (page 41) into a Woodland Fairies Cake (page 42) but you can also send guests home with sugar cookie Magic Wands (page 50). We've even included a section called What, No Cake? for those of you who wish for something unexpected on your birthday.

KAYE If you decide to have a party, to really set the mood, choose a theme. We've organized the book into thematic chapters like Pretty in Pink: Indulgent Sensations for Your Little Divas and Step Right Up: A One-Ring Circus Filled with Yummy Attractions to offer plenty of inspiration.

LIV I've been decorating cakes professionally for the past fifteen years, so even before I had a child myself, I knew what party themes were most popular with kids. I have made countless chocolate animals, fire trucks, and treasure chests. This book is a collection of some of the most requested themes at the bakery, from dinosaurs to makeup. Even the youngest of children will give you a clue as to what they are interested in, and by age five they will outright tell you what they want. For my son's second birthday I made him cupcakes with silly Richard Scarry vehicles on top since his favorite book was *Cars and Trucks and Things That Go*. At four, without any parental involvement, he was already planning his fifth birthday: *Star Wars*.

KAYE This is not to say that the little ones should make all the decisions. Instead, just encourage them to share their ideas and vision. As children get older they can play a more integral part in planning the festivities. When I was growing up I got to watch my mother bake birthday cakes ten times a year (one for me and each of my siblings). We usually chose her pinwheel cake, but if it was our special day, we wouldn't have to fight our sisters or brothers for the chance to lick the spatula. When I was old enough I was given my own responsibilities. The first time I made whipped cream I added 2 tablespoons of salt instead of sugar. My siblings were furious. Liv, you and I spent time together in the kitchen, too. As a young girl you were always there to observe or help out, from grinding wheat to make flour for our bread to cracking eggs or just licking icing off of the beaters. As you got older you became my assistant, carving watermelons for fruit-salad bowls, piping my buttercream roses; and by age thirteen you were helping me decorate my first wedding cakes.

LIV I say get your kids involved as soon as you can—the younger the better. My son, who has been mixing batter since he could stand on a chair and reach the kitchen counter, loves to grease the pans, sift the flour, and add the ingredients. Even little tasks can boost their ego, give them confidence in the kitchen, and encourage a lifelong love of baking and cooking. For my son's fourth birthday I cheated a little and made two cakes— a tyrannosaurus for him to decorate and a stegosaurus for me to decorate. He helped me fill them, and then I iced them. But he decorated the T-rex by himself, squeezing on googly eyes and inserting sharp chocolate teeth and scales along the back. It took some self-control, on my part, to not tell him how or what to do, but in the end, I must admit that his tyrannosaurus, served next to my stegosaurus, had more life, verve, and expression. Although it was not classic perfection, it was a different kind of perfection, which I treasure.

Sometimes it's all about just letting the mess happen. It's not permanent, and you can even make cleanup part of the fun with bubbles and spray bottles filled with water. Keeping with the spirit of inclusiveness, we've sprinkled "Kids can" sidebars throughout the book. Here we show you great ways to get your children involved with baking and decorating, from cutting out balloon cookies to piping out chocolate wheels.

KAYE I think we can learn a thing or two from children. They are so uninhibited. Adults tend to get hung up on details and imperfections, but if you just let the baking and decorating process unfold as it may, you will probably be happier with the results: less pressure and more pleasure.

LIV My decorating style lends itself well to kids' cakes. It is all about fun and fantasy—but not the visual flawlessness that can be found in fondant cakes. And kids' cakes, I feel, allow me to loosen the confines of what a decorated cake should be. Children delight in cakes that resemble something, and partygoers will fight for the decorations whether they are polka dots or miniature fairies encrusted on the side. So, channel the kid inside and have fun with your creation. Feel free to personalize and tweak any of my designs. See them as a springboard; or, even better, draw your own templates for chocolate designs to match your party's theme.

KAYE The introductions to each themed chapter suggest ideas for your party, including fun ways to decorate your table and activities. The recipes and designs range from simple to advanced, but by working step-by-step, even a novice can create an elaborately decorated cake or tackle a multistep recipe. Whenever possible we offer "plain and simple" variations, which are noted throughout the book.

LIV Before moving on to the themed chapters, take time to read The 1, 2, 3s: Getting Started. This section gives invaluable information about our favorite recipes for icings and fillings, introduces you to basic decorating techniques such as icing and piping, and explains the Chocolate Method, which is used throughout the book.

KAYE When we started writing books, it made sense for Liv to write about the decorating techniques and for me to write the recipes. We've continued that tradition in this book, but this time around Liv created some of the recipes, too; those are designated by her signature.

LIV And, if you haven't noticed yet, my son . . .

KAYE and my grandson . . .

LIV was a big inspiration in writing this book; he is mentioned often. Enjoy!

THE 1, 2, 3s: GETTING STARTED

 Let's think of this chapter as elementary school. It's a great place to start your baking and decorating adventures. If you are confident in your basic sweet skills, then feel free to skip a grade. If not, walk before you run; baby steps are welcome. Our 1, 2, 3s section starts with a core selection of fillings and icings. These recipes are indispensable to us at the bakery, and you will find them equally so. Each recipe is suited for different applications, and some are so easy you're sure to get an A+.

 To find detailed directions and helpful hints on how to make a level cake, a stable cake, and a smooth icing, check out our section on assembling, filling, and icing a cake like a pro.

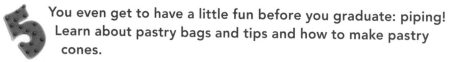 If you don't know already, chocolate is a basic Whimsical Bakehouse decorating medium. Learn about confectioners' chocolate, how best to store and melt chocolate, and all about our Chocolate Method.

If you need a splash of color in your life, head over to our Color Mixing Chart (page 37) to see how the rainbow of food coloring gives life to plain old buttercream and chocolate.

You even get to have a little fun before you graduate: piping! Learn about pastry bags and tips and how to make pastry cones.

Refer to these pages whenever needed.

Icing Recipes

Are you someone who snitches icing right out of the bowl? Come on, admit it. I think I don't crave icing anymore because I've worked with it for so long, but I know some folks who want it piled high on their cupcake—enough to satisfy a few people. Whip up a batch of one of these versatile icings for your next cake.

A bakehouse secret: We mix equal parts House Buttercream (page 13) and Kaye's Buttercream (below) when making roses and other flowers. The pure butter content in Kaye's Buttercream, when chilled, holds its shape wonderfully and lends stability. The House Buttercream allows you to make a richer and more varied color palette. For best results, mix the colorant into the House Buttercream and then add the Kaye's.

Don't worry, though—for those of you who don't have the time or space to make both, you'll find that each kind works fine on its own.

To use chilled buttercream icing, bring it to room temperature and beat at medium speed in the bowl of an electric mixer until smooth and creamy. To speed up this process you can lightly reheat the buttercream in a double boiler before beating.

Kaye's Buttercream

In the battle of buttercream this Italian meringue reigns supreme. The satiny texture is a delight to work with. It holds up in all kinds of weather and is trusted for assembling and frosting all of our wedding cakes. The flavor melts on your tongue, leaving a wonderful sweetness and, thanks to the pure butter content, no greasy after-coating in the mouth. It is light and delicate yet rich and voluptuous.

Kaye's Buttercream is great for tinting with pastel colors, but when you want to create a vibrant or rich palette we recommend using House Buttercream (page 13) or Kids' Buttercream (page 14).

CONTINUES

Here are some tips for adjusting the consistency of Kaye's Buttercream in the summer or in the heat:

⁕ After adding the sugar syrup to the egg whites, let the bowl cool to room temperature (you can touch the side of the bowl to be sure) before adding the butter, even if it means whipping for 30 minutes or more.

⁕ Add cold butter instead of room-temperature butter.

⁕ Whip the buttercream longer, after all of the ingredients are added, to incorporate completely and "thicken" slightly.

Kaye's Buttercream can be stored in an airtight container at room temperature for up to 3 days and in the refrigerator for up to 3 weeks. —Liv

Yield: approximately 8 cups

Have all ingredients at room temperature.

In a small saucepan, bring to a boil:
   ½ cup water
   2¼ cups sugar

Use a clean pastry brush and cold water to wash down any sugar crystals that form on the sides of the pan as the water heats. When the sugar begins to bubble, set a timer for 7 minutes and let it boil.

After 5 minutes, in the bowl of an electric mixer, begin to whip at high speed:
   1 cup egg whites (about 12 large egg whites)

Whip until stiff. They should be done when the timer for the sugar goes off.

With the mixer on high speed, slowly beat the sugar syrup into the egg whites, pouring the syrup to the side of the bowl to avoid getting any sugar on the whip.

Continue to beat until the bowl is cool to the touch, about 10 minutes. Slowly add:
   1½ pounds (6 sticks) unsalted butter, cut into 1-inch pieces

When the buttercream begins to splash out of the bowl, reduce the speed to low.

Mix in at low speed:
   1 teaspoon pure vanilla extract

Beat until light and fluffy. At some points the mixture might look curdled. Just keep beating; it will become smooth again.

♥ Chocolate Buttercream

In a bowl, combine 2 to 3 ounces melted, body-temperature (100°F) semisweet, white, or milk chocolate per 1 cup Kaye's Buttercream or House Buttercream. Mix until smooth and completely blended, scraping down the sides of the bowl to prevent the chocolate from hardening and causing unmelted flecks in the buttercream.

♥ Raspberry Buttercream

Stir in ¼ cup (or to taste and color) raspberry puree per 2 cups Kaye's Buttercream or House Buttercream. Mix until smooth and completely blended. Seedless raspberry jam can be substituted for the puree, but the flavor is not as strong. To intensify the flavor, use a couple of drops or up to ¼ teaspoon raspberry extract.

House Buttercream

Due to its bright white color, our House Buttercream is our icing of choice whenever we need to mix vibrant or rich colors. Unlike Kaye's Buttercream, this icing contains high-ratio shortening, which enables it to hold more air when beaten, creating a fluffier texture. In the past we recommended substituting regular vegetable shortening for high-ratio shortening, if you couldn't find it; but due to reformulation of many shortening brands to reduce trans fats, for best results try to find the high-ratio. Some common brand names are Quick Blend and Sweetex. You can purchase the shortening at any good cake decorating supply store, or online at Web sites such as countrykitchensa.com or cookscakeandcandy.com.

If you don't have high-ratio shortening, you can still use vegetable shortening, but the buttercream may not accept color as readily and the consistency may be softer. To firm up the buttercream, you can add butter 1 tablespoon at a time until the icing is a spreadable consistency.

House Buttercream can be stored in an airtight container at room temperature for up to 3 days and in the refrigerator for up to 3 weeks. —Liv

Yield: approximately 9½ cups

In the bowl of an electric mixer at low speed, stir together:
> 6 cups confectioners' sugar
> ½ teaspoon salt
> 1 teaspoon pure vanilla extract

With a whisk attachment, add and whip at low speed:
> 1 cup boiling water (¾ cup on hot days—otherwise the buttercream will be too liquid/soft)

Whip until smooth and cool.

Add and whip until smooth:
> 2¾ cups high-ratio shortening
> 6 ounces (1½ sticks) slightly chilled unsalted butter, cut into 1-inch pieces, plus extra to add as needed for consistency

Increase the mixer speed to medium-high. Whip until light, fluffy, and doubled in volume (10 to 20 minutes). If the buttercream still appears too soft, add butter 1 tablespoon at a time until it is a spreadable consistency.

- -

Salt brings out or intensifies the flavors in food. At the Bakehouse, we use kosher salt for all of our baked goods. If you substitute table salt, which has a finer grain than kosher salt, reduce the amount of salt by half.

Kids' Buttercream

This classic, no-fuss buttercream is a sweet sensation with children, and I have to admit, it is the one frosting I will lick off my fingers. Kids' Buttercream is surprisingly versatile: It makes a yummy filling or icing, tints beautifully, and is perfect for piping borders or simple shapes. However, we don't use this icing for delicate piping applications because it has a dense and slightly gritty texture that tends to break (instead, try Kaye's Buttercream, page 11, or House Buttercream, page 13). —Liv

Meringue powder can be found at baking supply stores and in some supermarkets.

Kid's Buttercream can be stored in the refrigerator in an airtight container for 1 week.

Yield: approximately 3 cups

In the bowl of an electric mixer at medium-high speed, beat until creamy:
> 8 ounces (2 sticks) unsalted butter at room temperature

Add all at once and beat at low speed until smooth:
> 4 cups (1-pound box) sifted confectioners' sugar
> 1 tablespoon meringue powder
> 1 teaspoon pure vanilla extract
> ¼ teaspoon salt

Add and beat until light and creamy:
> 2 tablespoons milk

♥ Kids' Chocolate Buttercream

In a bowl, combine 2 to 3 ounces melted, body-temperature (100°F) semisweet chocolate per 1 cup Kids' Buttercream. Mix until smooth and completely blended, scraping down the sides of the bowl to prevent the chocolate from hardening and causing unmelted flecks in the buttercream.

• •

Matt's Fudge Icing

My uncle Matt's delectable fudge icing had to be included, once again, in our recipe collection—it's that good! We love it on our Sour Cream Chocolate Cake (page 89) or atop any of our cupcakes. When I use this at home, my son will eat just the fudge and leave the cake.

Matt's Fudge Icing can be stored in the refrigerator in an airtight container for 2 weeks. To use the chilled icing, bring it to room temperature and beat at medium speed in the bowl of an electric mixer until smooth and creamy. To speed up this process you can lightly reheat it in a double boiler before beating. —Liv

Yield: approximately 2¼ cups

In a small saucepan over low heat, mix together:
- ¼ cup sugar
- 2 large egg yolks
- ¾ cup heavy cream
- 1 teaspoon pure vanilla extract
- A pinch of salt

Whisk until the mixture is slightly thickened and coats the back of a wooden spoon (175 to 180°F on a candy thermometer).

Remove from the heat and whisk in until melted:
- 8 ounces finely chopped semisweet chocolate
- 3 ounces (¾ stick) unsalted butter, cut into 1-inch pieces

Whisk in
- ¼ cup light corn syrup
- 2 tablespoons sour cream

Transfer to a bowl, cover with plastic wrap, and chill for 1 hour to overnight.

· ·

Royal Icing

This amazing icing is the "glue" that holds gingerbread houses together and is the colorful frosting that you find on decorated cookies. You can tint it, pipe with it, spread it with a spatula, adhere candies or sanding sugar to it, or thin it with water to create smooth flooded designs (see pages 144–45).

Yield: approximately 4 cups

In a large bowl of an electric mixer fitted with a whip attachment, whip to stiff peaks:
- ¼ cup meringue powder
- ½ cup cold water

Add and mix at low speed with a paddle attachment, until combined:
- 4 cups (1-pound box) confectioners' sugar

Continue mixing at high speed for 5 to 8 minutes, or until the icing is stiff.

Add and mix on low speed until combined:
- ½ teaspoon strained fresh lemon juice

Cover the bowl with a damp cloth while you are working with or coloring batches of icing, or immediately place it in an airtight container or a pastry cone; otherwise, a hard crust will quickly form as it dries.

Note: If you are making a gingerbread house or other assembled three-dimensional cookies, I recommend adding an extra tablespoon of meringue powder and an additional cup of confectioners' sugar. This will firm up the frosting, making your structure even more stable. —Liv

Marshmallow Fondant

I can't believe I am actually including a fondant recipe in my book. I normally don't work with it because I prefer buttercream's flavor, but so many people I know recommended trying marshmallow fondant not only because it is easy to make, but also because it tastes better than traditional fondant.

   Marshmallow Fondant can be stored in the refrigerator for up to 3 weeks. To use the chilled fondant, bring it to room temperature. To speed up this process, warm the fondant in the microwave for a few seconds. —Liv

In a large microwave-safe bowl, place:
   16 ounces mini marshmallows
   2 tablespoons water

Microwave for 30-second intervals, stirring in between, until melted. It will take 2 to 3 minutes to melt, but times will vary based on the power of your microwave. Stirring the marshmallows vigorously will often melt any remaining small pieces.

Stir in
   Approximately 5 drops food coloring (or color and amount of your choice; see Note)

Over the top of the melted marshmallows, sift:
   3 cups confectioners' sugar

Stir the mixture to combine.

Have on hand:
   ½ cup confectioners' sugar
   ½ cup vegetable shortening, at room temperature

Dust a work surface with the confectioners' sugar. Generously grease your hands with shortening. Knead the fondant mixture.

Continue kneading, and gradually add, until it is a smooth and malleable consistency:
   Up to 1 cup confectioner's sugar

Regrease your hands and dust the work surface as needed.

If the mixture is dry and tears easily, add:
   Water, tablespoon by tablespoon, up to an additional 3 tablespoons

Knead until the fondant is no longer sticky, is firm yet elastic, and does not rip. You can test this by rolling out a small piece ¼ inch thick and placing it over a measuring cup. If it tears, add more water and continue to knead, 8 to 10 minutes in total.

Check to make sure there are no small clumps of sugar. If there are, knead and add more water. Wrap the fondant in plastic wrap, and then seal it in a zip-top bag, pressing out as much air as possible. Let it set overnight at room temperature.

To cover a cake, on a work surface dusted with confectioners' sugar, roll out the fondant approximately ¼ inch thick.

Note: The color will lighten slightly when the sugar is added, so add a drop or two more than you think you will need.

Filling Recipes

To keep it simple, you can use the icing as your filling: Chocolate cake filled and iced with Matt's Fudge Icing (page 14) is always a hit. But why not add different flavor components—mix it up a little by whipping up a filling that complements your cake and icing? The easiest option is whipped cream, which goes with just about any cake (or pie); but there are plenty of other choices, such as Cookies and Cream, Whipped Chocolate Ganache, or Caramel Pudding, to name a few.

Whipped Cream

The light, fluffy texture of whipped cream is the perfect counterpoint to our rich cakes, and if you don't plan on making a complex design, it is a delicious and simple topping, frosting, or filling. To make it sweeter, add an additional 2 tablespoons of sugar. We even like it without sugar—a nice contrast to the sweetness of our fresh fruit pie.

Keep in mind that, unlike buttercream, whipped cream breaks down if kept out, especially in the heat. For best results we recommend preparing the whipped cream right before serving or assembling your cakes. Chocolate appliqué designs do not adhere well to the sides of a cake decorated with whipped cream, so keep the design contained on the top of the cake.

Any leftovers can be stored in an airtight container in the refrigerator for up to 3 days. The whipped cream will break down as it sits in the refrigerator, so rewhip it in the bowl of an electric mixer for 1 minute or until it forms soft to medium peaks (for icing) or stiff peaks (for fillings).

Yield: approximately 3 cups

In the bowl of an electric mixer at high speed, whip until stiff:

> **2 cups heavy cream**
> **4 tablespoons confectioners' sugar, sifted**
> **½ teaspoon pure vanilla extract**

♥ Raspberry Mousse

Gently fold ¼ cup raspberry puree into 1 recipe Whipped Cream (above). To use fresh raspberries, puree 1 quart berries with 1 tablespoon confectioners' sugar. Strain and use as above. A fine seedless raspberry jam can be substituted.

CONTINUES

Most of the fillings we use at the bakery are whipped-cream based—simple and delicious. The whipped cream we use for our "mousse" filling is whipped to *very* stiff peaks. We don't let the cream turn into butter, but we whip it until it is no longer smooth, has an air-bubbly consistency, and sticks to an inverted spoon or the whip without oozing. To maintain the stiff peaks, gently fold in the added flavor (raspberry puree, Oreos, caramel, etc.); do not overmix as this may deflate the mousse. Fill the cake right away; do not let the mousse sit for long or it may collapse or further aerate, reverting to a near liquid state when you spread it with a spatula.

If you "ring" the cake with buttercream, even if the mousse is slightly soft (but not at all runny) the buttercream will hold the mousse in place. Just handle the cake with care and do not jostle it unnecessarily.

Any cake sealed with buttercream and filled with one of our mousses or custards will last for at least 1 week in the refrigerator. Cakes filled with fresh fruit will stay fresh for 1 or 2 days. However, my mom, Kaye, will eat a cake (filled with mousse) that is 2 weeks old and claim it is still good—even delicious. —Liv

♥ Cookies and Cream Mousse

Gently fold 20 Oreos (or cookies of your choice), crushed into medium pieces, into 1 recipe Whipped Cream (page 17). Do not overcrush Oreos. If the crumbs are too fine, the whipped cream may look gray, rather than white with chocolate chunks.

♥ Creamsicle Mousse

Gently fold ¼ cup frozen orange juice concentrate into 1 recipe Whipped Cream (page 17).

Fresh Fruit Filling

Fresh fruit is best paired with whipped cream (or try whipped chocolate ganache for a richer alternative). The cream binds the fruit to the cake, making the layers more stable, and it adds that irresistible creaminess. The most requested fruit at the bakery is strawberries, but other fruits work well too. Try whole raspberries, whole blackberries, ripe sliced mangos, ripe sliced peaches, chopped pine-apple, or sliced bananas (do not toss with sugar). You can also substitute canned fruits like peaches or pineapple, but drain off the juices and do not add any additional sugar. To fill a cake, layer the fruit on the cake, then spread whipped cream (or ganache) on top. Alternatively, to prevent the fruit from moving, you can pipe on the cream filling.

In a bowl, combine:
    2 pints (2 to 3 cups) sliced strawberries
        (or substitute other fruits)
    1½ tablespoons sugar

Let sit at room temperature for 30 minutes to let the juices form.

Whipped Milk or White Chocolate Ganache

This recipe proves that a filling can be simultaneously rich and light.

Yield: approximately 6 cups

In a double boiler or in a medium metal bowl placed over a pot of barely simmering water, melt:

> **8 ounces chopped milk chocolate or white chocolate**

In a small saucepan, heat over medium-high heat:

> **4 cups (1 quart) heavy cream**

Whisk one-third of the cream into the chocolate until smooth. Slowly whisk in the remaining cream. Refrigerate overnight or freeze for a couple of hours to set.

Whip the chilled ganache until stiff.

Chocolate Pudding

Our Chocolate Pudding makes a great dessert, whether it is simply scooped into a bowl, made into a chocolate cream pie (use our pie crust as the shell, see page 157, and top with Whipped Cream, see page 17), or the filling of our Cauldron Bubble (page 141). However, it isn't the most stable cake filling. Folding 3 cups of whipped cream into 2½ cups of chocolate pudding lightens the pudding's consistency so that it can be used as a filling.

Our Chocolate Pudding can be stored in the refrigerator in an airtight container for 3 or 4 days.

Yield: approximately 5 cups

In a medium bowl, whisk until smooth:

> **2 extra-large eggs**
> **2 extra-large egg yolks**

Sift together and whisk into the eggs:

> **2 tablespoons cocoa powder**
> **2 tablespoons cornstarch**
> **2 tablespoons sugar**

In a medium saucepan, bring to a boil:

> **2 cups milk**
> **½ cup heavy cream**
> **⅓ cup sugar**
> **A pinch of salt**

Slowly whisk the hot milk mixture into the egg mixture. Return the mixture to the saucepan and cook over medium-low heat, whisking constantly, until it boils. Continue whisking and boil for 1 minute. Remove from the heat and pour into a heat-proof bowl containing:

> **4 tablespoons (½ stick) unsalted butter, cut into pieces**
> **8 ounces semisweet or bittersweet chocolate, coarsely chopped**
> **1 teaspoon pure vanilla extract**

CONTINUES

Whisk the mixture until smooth and then, using a sieve, strain the pudding into a clean bowl. Cover the top of the pudding with plastic wrap to prevent a skin from forming on the surface.

Let the pudding sit until it reaches room temperature and then refrigerate until completely cooled, a few hours or overnight.

. . . .

Caramel Pudding

Fill a pie shell with our Caramel Pudding and sliced bananas for a delicious twist on banana cream pie or scoop into glass bowls and serve plain and simple.

Like our Chocolate Pudding, our Caramel Pudding is not a stable cake filling, but fold in some whipped cream (½ recipe Whipped Cream, page 17, with 1 recipe Caramel Pudding), and voilà!

Our Caramel Pudding can be stored in the refrigerator in an airtight container for 3 or 4 days.

Yield: approximately 3½ cups

In a medium saucepan over medium heat, bring to a boil:
> ½ cup granulated sugar
> ¼ cup water

Continue cooking at medium-high heat, swirling occasionally, until the mixture is a dark amber color, about 15 minutes.

In a second medium saucepan over medium heat, whisk together until well blended:
> 2½ cups milk
> ½ cup packed light brown sugar
> ¼ cup cornstarch

Remove from the heat and whisk in:
> 3 egg yolks
> ½ teaspoon kosher salt

Carefully (the mixture will bubble up) pour the milk mixture into the caramelized sugar, whisking constantly. Continue whisking until the mixture thickens, about 5 minutes. Boil for an additional minute.

Remove from the heat and stir in:
> 2 tablespoons unsalted butter
> 1 teaspoon pure vanilla extract

Transfer the pudding to a bowl. Cover the top of the pudding with plastic wrap to prevent a skin from forming on the surface. Let the pudding sit until it reaches room temperature and then refrigerate until completely cooled, a few hours or overnight.

The Basics of Cake Assembly

In most cases, assembling a cake is a four-part process: cutting or carving, filling, crumbing, and icing. Of course, you could skip all of these steps and just eat your cake plain—maybe with a scoop of ice cream or a dollop of whipped cream—but in this book all of our decorated cakes follow these four steps. If you are familiar with our first book, *The Whimsical Bakehouse: Fun-to-Make Cakes that Taste as Good as They Look,* then this will be old hat (although I have added some new helpful tips); but for our newbies, I recommend you read through this section. To start, some helpful hints and some useful tools for working with any cake.

* Never work with or ice a warm cake, because they crumble easily and melt the icing.

* Chilling the cake in the refrigerator for a few hours or overnight firms up the cake (which decreases the number of crumbs), making it much easier to work with. You can also wrap the cooled cake tightly in plastic wrap and freeze it for up to two weeks, letting it thaw when ready to use. We do not find that this changes the texture or taste of the cake—just as long as you bring the cake to room temperature before serving.

* For the fullest flavor, we recommend serving all of our cakes at room temperature.

Helpful Tools for Icing a Cake

Turntable: This is a valuable tool in the decorator's arsenal. With it you can cut, fill, and ice a cake more efficiently—and it helps you to get a beautifully smooth icing. If you decorate often, rather than purchasing a cheaper plastic turntable, I highly recommend Ateco's heavy-duty metal one.

Cardboard: All of the cakes we make are assembled on cardboard bases. This may be a round of the same size as the cake or it might be a sheet of cardboard cut into a shape, such as a fire truck. Whatever the size or shape, this support is crucial to creating a stable cake. The cardboard also makes it easier to handle the cake and gives a clean edge for icing. You can purchase precut rounds in a variety of sizes, or if you can't get your hands on the size you need, trace your cake pan (or cake) onto a sheet of corrugated cardboard and cut out the shape with scissors or a matte knife.

Metal Spatula: Metal spatulas come in a variety of sizes. When filling and icing my cakes, I prefer to work with offset spatulas as opposed to flat spatulas. The angled blade helps your hand avoid contact with the cake, and it makes for easier access to tight spaces. I use two sizes; I could not decorate without a 4½-inch, which I lovingly refer to as my "baby-bent." It is great for frosting cupcakes and shaped cakes, and for spreading filling. The other is a 10-inch, a standard for filling and icing cakes.

Bench Scraper: To get the icing super smooth, in addition to my metal spatulas, I use a metal bench or dough scraper. Just make sure the scraper's handle is flush with the metal sides, as one with a rolled metal handle will be. The reason it works so well: One side of the metal scraper rests flat on the turntable, while the perpendicular edge runs flush with the cake, making for a steadier hand and a smooth finish.

Trimming, Cutting, and Carving a Cake

The first step to assembling your cake, after it has cooled, is to trim, cut, and/or shape it.

Trimming: Most cakes form a rounded dome when they are baked. Some designs use the dome as part of the final shape, so consult the individual directions before trimming; but in many cases, you'll want a flat cake and will need to level it off. For best results, use a serrated bread knife; I like to work with a 12-inch blade. If you baked your cake in multiple pans, trim the dome off of each cake. If the bottom of the cake has baked dark, trim a thin layer off of there, too. Once the dome is trimmed, center the cake on its cardboard base. If any part of the cake protrudes over the cardboard edge, trim it, ideally creating a ⅛-inch (no more than a ¼-inch) distance between the cake's side and the cardboard edge.

Cutting: To make an even and level cut, rotate the cake, either on a turntable or with your hand. Keeping the knife horizontal and your arm locked, lightly score the cake where you plan to cut. Then with one hand lightly resting on the cake to hold it steady, rotate the turntable (or your hand) as you use a sawing action to cut the cake along the guideline. Again, remember to lock your arm; this keeps the knife at the same height throughout. Do not be tempted to cut straight across the cake in one swipe or to force the knife's blade. You may get lucky, but in most cases the cut will be uneven. Instead, be patient and, using a gentle sawing action, cut in the round, working your way to the center from all sides. Safety tip: To avoid cutting yourself, make sure your hand is on the top of the cake at all times and no part of your hand rests on the side of the cake. All of the round cakes in this book are cut into three layers. If you baked your cake in one pan, after trimming the dome, you will have to cut it into three equal layers. If you baked your cake in two pans, then cut the higher of the two cakes in half, leaving the lower one as is.

All of the shaped cakes in this book are filled. Depending on the specific design, they are made up of between one and three layers of cake. Before you cut the layers, start by cutting the shape.

Some of the cakes, such as the Abracadabra! (page 122) and the Treasure Chest (page 84), are shaped but don't involve intricate carving. Instead, they are beveled slightly with a serrated knife. Others, such as the Sand Castle (page 92) and the Fire Truck (page 100), use a cardboard template. The cardboard will act as a guideline for cutting out the shape and as the base for assembling the cake. To cut long, straight lines, use a serrated bread knife. To cut out small areas or details, it is best to use a small serrated paring knife (or if you don't have one, a steak knife will work just as well).

Filling

Because we use a wide variety of fillings, which range in density, we start each cake by piping a buttercream reservoir, which we flood with filling to ensure that the layers remain level and in place. I refer to the process of creating a reservoir as "ringing." Ring the cake with the same icing you plan on using in the crumb coat (see page 25).

There are exceptions to our filling technique: If you are filling and icing a cake with the same thing, such as buttercream inside and out, then you do not need to ring the cake. Also, if you plan on cutting many very thin layers of cake (¼ inch high), then just spread thin layers of filling without ringing—otherwise the cake will be too high and there will be too much buttercream.

1 Adhere the bottom layer of cake to the cardboard with a drop of buttercream. Carefully set aside the top one or two layers.

2 Fill a pastry bag, with a coupler inside, with buttercream. Pipe a ring of buttercream around the edge of the bottom layer, keeping the ring as close to the edge of the cake as possible (this will get you maximum filling and minimum buttercream in every bite). The ring of buttercream should be as tall as the coupler is wide; if the ring is too short, pipe another ring on top of the first to create a sufficiently high border.

3 Fill the reservoir you've created with filling and spread the filling so it is level with the buttercream ring. For maximum stability, don't allow the filling to extend above the border.

4 Place the second layer of cake on top of the first, making sure it is centered and level. If your cake has three layers, ring and fill the second layer as above. Center the third layer on top of the first two. Press gently with your hand to level the cake.

At the Bakehouse, when making a layer cake, we often bake the cakes in two pans as opposed to one. This prevents the batter from sinking or collapsing in the middle, especially for cakes 12 inches and larger. It also reduces the baking time, which in larger cakes can prevent overbrowning on the bottom, top, and sides. Most of the cakes in this book are small enough that it is not an absolute necessity (as in our 8-inch, 6-inch, and 4-inch tiered Circus Cake), but whenever possible it yields more consistent results. For the most part, the baking times in the recipes are calibrated for two pans. Feel free to make adjustments to the baking times when using just one pan.

Helpful Hints for Working with an Offset Spatula

* The goal is to create even pressure across the entire length of the spatula's blade. If you are pressing harder at one end, you will leave tracks in the icing and there may be holes where there is no icing.

* Grip the top of the handle between the thumb and fingers, extend the pointer finger, and press it into the angled metal portion of the blade.

* Practice pressing the spatula on a flat surface. See how angling your hand changes the portion of the blade that touches the surface.

* Touch the entire blade to the surface. Now play with the amount of pressure you apply with your pointer finger. As you apply more pressure, the back end of the blade may lift off the surface. You want to have equal pressure on both ends of the blade—a balance between the angle of the hand and the pressure of your finger.

* Now another important element is added: the lateral angle of the blade. You don't want to ice a cake with the entire blade flush on the icing. This will sometimes cut into the icing and even the cake, reexposing the crumbs. Instead, angle the spatula (between 15 and 45 degrees) so that you spread the icing with one edge of the blade.

* As you run your blade to the right across the icing surface, press the left edge of the spatula down and reverse for the other direction.

* Scraping off your spatula after each pass will prevent you from redepositing icing on the cake. Always have a pot or bowl of very hot water on hand. After every pass of the spatula or scraper, dip it in the hot water, and then dry it off. The heat will melt and smooth the surface. This will also eliminate small air bubbles.

Crumbing

A crumb coat is a thin layer of icing applied over the entire cake that seals in any stray or excess crumbs. Once chilled, this layer will prevent crumbs from appearing in your final coat of icing. The smoother your crumb coat, the smoother your final coat of icing will be.

CRUMBING A STANDARD ROUND CAKE:

1 Place the filled cake in the center of the turntable or work surface.

2 Place a small amount of icing on top of the cake (about ½ cup for a 9-inch round). With a metal spatula, spread the icing evenly over the entire top of the cake so that it extends about ½ inch over the edge all around. Use the excess icing that comes over the edge to help cover the sides. Load your spatula with icing, invert it, and run the entire edge of the spatula along the side of the cake, from top to bottom. Reload the spatula as needed until the sides are covered.

3 To create a thin, smooth coat, rest the bottom of the spatula on the bottom edge of the cake and the middle/top of the blade on the top edge of the cake. Without lifting the edge of the spatula, spin the turntable and remove the excess buttercream. A lip of excess buttercream should form around the top edge of the cake. Use your spatula to gently sweep the excess buttercream toward the center around the entire circumference of the cake. No icing should extend over

the cardboard base. Note: If you do not have a turntable, instead of turning the cake, move the spatula evenly around the side of the cake, if possible in one fluid motion.

4 Chill the cake. Cakes crumbed in buttercream should be refrigerated for at least 30 minutes, or until the cake has set and the buttercream has hardened. Cakes crumbed with whipped cream or mousse should be placed in the freezer until set.

CRUMBING A SQUARE OR ANGULAR CAKE:

For icing detailed and small angled portions of a shaped cake, use a small offset spatula.

1 When crumbing a cake with angular sides, cover the entire surface of the cake with icing as you would with a round cake (step 2). Just make sure all of the corners have enough icing on them so that they stay level and don't droop.

2 Smooth out one side. Run the bottom edge of the spatula along the side of the cake. Make sure that some icing goes over the corner. Use this lip of icing to start smoothing the next side. Working in one direction, go around in this fashion until all of the sides are smooth. The first edge may now have another lip; just scrape this excess icing off.

3 A lip of excess buttercream should form around the top edge of the cake. Use your spatula to gently sweep the excess buttercream toward the center around the entire circumference of the cake until the top is

smooth and level. No icing should extend over the cardboard base.

4   Chill the cake. Cakes crumbed in buttercream should be refrigerated for at least 30 minutes, or until the cake has set and the buttercream has hardened. Cakes crumbed with whipped cream or mousse should be placed in the freezer until set.

Usually I recommend smoothing the sides first and creating a lip on the top of the cake, but for some tight angles you can reverse this. Ice the top, then slice off the excess icing with a downward stroke of your spatula.

CRUMBING AND ICING A CURVED CAKE:

1   When crumbing and icing (done as separate steps) a cake with curves, first cover the entire surface of the cake with icing.

2   To remove the excess icing and create a smooth finish, hold a 2 x 10-inch strip of cellophane or acetate at both ends and drag the long edge of it over the cake, starting at the bottom.

3   Continue around the circumference of the cake until it is smooth. Unlike a metal spatula, the cellophane will curve to the shape of the cake. If you do not have cellophane or acetate, a strip of standard white paper will suffice.

4   To ice a roll, hold a 2 x 10-inch strip of cellophane or acetate at both ends and wrap it around one end of the roll. Press your thumbs into the strip at the points where the cake meets the work surface. This will make the strip taut around the circumference of the roll. Keeping the strip taut, drag it across the length of the cake.

Icing a Cake

Creating a flat finish of icing takes practice, but with the correct tools and a few helpful hints, the process is much easier. Unless you can hold a cake on your fingertips and rotate your wrist, a turntable will help you immensely in getting a smooth finish. Remember, whether you are using a spatula or a scraper, you must apply even pressure over the entire surface of the tool. And don't forget the hot water.

For best results the icing should be a smooth spreadable consistency; do not use cold icing as this will create a lumpy or rough texture. Also, if the icing has been sitting for some time, make sure to restir it to remove any air bubbles that may have formed. Your final coat of buttercream should be thin—just thick enough to cover the crumb coat.

ICING A STANDARD ROUND CAKE:

The majority of the icing finishes in this book are smooth. With a little practice and patience, you, too, can master this look.

1   Prepare the icing for the final coat, coloring your buttercream as desired. Place the cake in the center of the turntable.

2   Place a small amount of icing on top of the cake (approximately ¾ cup for a 9-inch round cake). With a metal spatula, spread the icing evenly over the entire top of the cake so that

it extends about ½ inch over the edge all around. Use the excess icing that comes over the edge to help cover the sides. Load your spatula with icing, invert it, and run the bottom edge of the spatula along the contour of the cardboard, being careful to keep the spatula upright. Hold the spatula perpendicular to and flush against the cardboard to ensure even distribution of the icing. Reload the spatula as needed until the sides are covered (using about 2 cups of buttercream in total for a 9-inch cake).

3 Smooth the sides by holding the spatula upright against the side of the cake (the bottom of the blade should run along the cardboard edge). Slowly spin the turntable without lifting the spatula from the cake's surface. Try to spin the turntable at an even rate; choppy movements will create linear imprints in the icing. Remove any excess buttercream with the spatula. The icing can go out to but not over the cardboard round.

4 A lip of excess buttercream should form around the top edge of the cake. Often I notice a slight buckling of the buttercream beneath the lip; this buckle gives me a clue as to where the buttercream meets the cake top, so you have a better idea of where to position your spatula. Line up your offset spatula with the lip buckle, but a few inches away from it. Do not start each pass with your spatula resting on the lip; this may cause the lip of frosting to mush down, thus messing up the sides of the cake. Move the spatula (angle the blade about 15 to 30 degrees—

the wide angle facing the lip) in toward the cake edge, slicing off some frosting (if the spatula is lined up well you will slice off excess frosting without hitting the cake underneath) and spreading it toward the center of the cake. If you continue passing your spatula all the way across the cake top, you would redeposit frosting on the opposite edge, so after scraping and spreading I recommend slowly lifting your spatula up at an angle again near the center of the cake. I describe the motion of the spatula as an airplane coming in for a landing and then taking off again near the center of the cake. Clean off the spatula after each pass.

5 Adhere the cake's cardboard base to a cake plate or other base. If the base is disposable or you are going to be traveling with the cake, use glue; otherwise, place the cake on the base you will be serving from.

6 Chill the cake until one to six hours before serving, depending on the temperature. For fullest flavor, we recommend serving our cakes at room temperature.

ICING A SQUARE OR ANGULAR CAKE:

Icing an angular cake is much like crumbing it, but this time around you want the finish smooth and just thick enough that you don't see any of the cake.

1 Prepare the icing for the final coat, coloring your buttercream as desired.

2 Follow the directions for crumbing an angular cake, with one main exception. In step 2, instead of running your spatula along the side of the cake, run the bottom edge of the spatula along the contour of the cardboard, being careful to hold the spatula perpendicular to and flush against the cardboard to ensure even distribution of the icing. The icing should not extend over the cardboard base.

3 Adhere the cake's cardboard base to a cake plate or other base. If the base is disposable or you are going to be traveling with the cake, use glue; otherwise, place the cake on the base you will be serving from.

4 Chill the cake until one to six hours before serving, depending on the temperature. For fullest flavor, we recommend serving our cakes at room temperature.

OLD-FASHIONED ICING ON A CAKE OR CUPCAKE

Easy as pie . . . or a piece of cake . . . You get the idea.

To ice, simply place a nice-size dollop of frosting on top of your cake or cupcake; for a standard cupcake we recommend 2 tablespoons of icing.

With a small metal spatula, spread the icing so it covers all of the exposed cake. Create a textured pattern on the cake by applying light pressure while moving the spatula randomly about the surface of the icing, then glide the spatula off at a 45-degree angle to end the pattern.

Piping

Piping is an underlying element in all of my cake decorating, whether I am ringing a cake, making a simple shell border, or creating a beautiful blooming blossom. The following section discusses the fundamentals of piping with buttercream (for chocolate see page 31).

THE 1-2-3s OF PIPING

Icing Consistency: Piping applications are affected by the consistency of your icing: hard or soft, cold or warm, smooth or lumpy. Soft buttercream flows easily, making it ideal for line work. Most other piping applications need icing of a medium consistency that is fluid yet holds its form. Flowers need a medium to firm icing to hold the petal's shape, but keep in mind that if the icing is too stiff it will break or crack while being piped. You can often firm up or soften buttercream by chilling it in the refrigerator for a few minutes or by lightly melting it over a double boiler. To remove any lumps, whisk or stir the buttercream. If icing has sat for a while in a pastry bag or bowl, restir it before piping with it; otherwise you are more likely to get air bubbles, which can cause small explosive spatters.

Pressure: Pastry bag pressure is influenced by two factors: the twisting and squeezing. Guide the bag with your nondominant hand or pointer finger, while squeezing at the top of the bag with your dominant hand. Twist the top of the bag occasionally to maintain pressure. Beware: If you squeeze in the middle of the bag, the icing will most likely leak out of the top of the bag, creating a (yummy) mess!

By altering the amount of pressure with which you squeeze, you can control the flow of the buttercream. Although some piping applications call for irregular bag pressure and irregular rhythm, your goal, in most cases, is to apply consistent pressure while moving the tip or bag at a steady pace or rhythm. Whenever I teach, I tell my students to do warm-up exercises. Using a small round tip (#4, 5, or 6), pipe lines back and forth across a piece of parchment paper. If the line breaks it probably means that you are moving the bag too quickly and not applying enough pressure. If your line squiggles or forms loops it probably means you are applying too much pressure and not moving the bag quickly enough. Keep practicing until your line is even and without breaks or loops. To end a buttercream line or embellishment, abruptly stop applying pressure

to the bag and quickly spiral the tip, pull the tip downward, or pull the tip to the side. To create a point at the end of a petal or on top of a dot, gradually release the pressure as you continue to move the bag.

Now, keep in mind that gradual is a relative term, because in actuality, all of these movements are in the milliseconds. If you move too slowly you will get long, exaggerated, and often misshapen forms. Just as with the lines, find a balance between pressure and speed. These actions are referred to as tailing off, and they end piping applications with a clean stroke. Note: Do not overfill your pastry bag. Not only is it more likely that buttercream will ooze out the top and make a mess, but you also have less control of the bag. To start, I recommend filling the pastry bag half full.

Tip and Bag Placement: Tip placement, unless otherwise noted, is usually at a 45-degree angle to the cake. Two common exceptions are dots and rosettes, for which the tip is perpendicular to the cake surface. To begin, touch the pastry tip to the surface of the cake where you want to start piping, allowing the icing to adhere to the surface. Lift up the tip slightly as you begin to apply pressure. Do not drag the tip along the surface of the cake, as this will indent the surface; instead, lightly touch the surface of the cake or hover just above it as you pipe. For some more advanced piping applications, you may have the bag at one angle and the tip at another. For instance, when piping a blossom, the bag is held at a 45-degree angle and, while the wide end of the petal tip rests on the cake surface, the narrow end of the tip is angled up at a 45-degree angle.

TOOLS

Pastry Cones: These wee cones are indispensable. I use them for detailed piping applications, for writing on cakes, and for chocolate work. I make mine out of cellophane, but you can also use parchment paper. The only downside to parchment is that the point sometimes decays or frays with use, whereas the cellophane maintains its shape. Cut rolls of parchment paper or cellophane into 10- or 12-inch squares, and then cut these squares in half diagonally. With the hypotenuse, or longest side, of the triangle facing up, hold each of the two acute-angled points separately between your thumb and fingers. First curl the top right point downward, wrapping under itself until it lines up with the left side of the right angle. Hold this in place while you wrap the top left point down and around the back of the pastry cone until it lines up with the right side of the right angle. Adjust the cellophane with your thumbs inside and your pointer fingers outside until a sharp point forms. Tape close to the base to maintain the cone shape. Note: You can purchase precut squares online; see page 171.

Pastry Bags: These cone-shaped bags make piping decorations a breeze. We recommend 12-inch polyester bags, which can be washed and reused. Disposable plastic ones are also available. If you do not have a pastry bag handy, you can always make a parchment or cellophane pastry cone or, in a pinch, you can use a sturdy zip-top bag (cut a hole in one of the bottom corners).

Coupler and Ring: The coupler, a plastic insert, allows you to change tips with ease. The ring screws onto the outside of the bag and coupler to secure the tip in place. As an alternative, you can place a tip directly inside a bag without a coupler. Just make sure the hole is not too big, or the tip will slip right out.

Tips: There is a special tip for almost every piping application. For a good selection of tips, I recommend buying a starter set. Tips can also be purchased individually. Before starting any design, make sure you have the appropriate tips. When applicable, in the recipes I noted alternative tips that can be used to achieve similar piping results. Check the suppliers listed on page 171 to order individual tips or sets. If you buy tips individually, I recommend getting a #104 petal tip, a #20 star tip, a #8 round tip, and a #352 leaf tip; with these four tips you can do almost anything in this book.

♥ *Kids can* ♥

Consider learning the 1-2-3s of piping with your kids. If they are very young they will love the tactile aspects: squeezing the bag, attaching tips to a coupler, and of course getting buttercream on their fingers. Just beware; speaking from experience, kids tend to eat their "mistakes." If your children are a little older, have them experiment with different tips and see what fun designs they can come up with.

Confectioners' Chocolate and the Chocolate Method

At the Bakehouse we use a wide variety of chocolates: unsweetened chocolate, semisweet chocolate, milk chocolate, white chocolate, baker's chocolate, cocoa powder, and chocolate chips. But this section is dedicated to confectioners' chocolate, which is also called wafer chocolate, compound chocolate, candy melts, or chocolate coating. Technically, confectioners' chocolate is not chocolate because it does not contain chocolate liquor, and the cocoa butter is partially or completely replaced with vegetable fats. This product does not need to be tempered, so it stays shiny after resolidifying, is easy to handle, and sets up quickly, making it ideal for the at-home decorator. It comes in dark chocolate, white chocolate, and a limited range of colors. If you are looking for the true taste of chocolate, you will have to temper your own semisweet, milk, or white chocolate.

Confectioners' chocolate is the product I use to make all of my "Chocolate Method" appliqués. I developed the Chocolate Method as a way to increase efficiency at the bakery. It ended up being a very versatile and fun decorating technique. The process is similar to painting on glass because everything is done in reverse; details like highlights and shadows are applied first, followed by the background. Using a template as a guide, melted chocolate is piped or painted onto parchment paper or cellophane. When the design is complete it is set aside to harden, and then it's carefully flipped to reveal the image. I will illustrate how to use chocolate in a variety of ways to achieve different effects, from making basic silhouettes with overpiping, like the bed frame on page 56, to multicolor designs that are outlined with either chocolate or color, as in our Miss Pink wig on page 70. Chocolate appliqué decorations, although flat, do not have to lack dimension. A sense of depth can be created by shading as seen in a chocolate portrait (page 76), or by constructing a chocolate design in segments and assembling and layering the pieces after they have hardened, as in our chimp cupcake on pages 130–32.

Each of the above-mentioned techniques (silhouette with overpiping, multi-color appliqués, shading and portraiture, and assembled pieces) has brief written directions with the corresponding recipes. For detailed directions, including setup and thorough descriptions, and step-by-step photos, refer to the shading and portraiture chocolate method on page 76. These directions, with slight alterations, can be used as a guide for all of the Chocolate Method decorations in this book as well as ones you make on your own. You may have to change the palette, remove or add details, or adjust the amount of melted chocolate, but in essence it is the same process. For best results when working with the Chocolate Method, read through the following common questions and helpful hints.

Common Questions and Helpful Hints

WHAT TOOLS DO I NEED TO WORK WITH THE CHOCOLATE METHOD?

* **Pastry Cones:** At the Bakehouse we like to make our small pastry cones out of cellophane instead of parchment paper because they maintain a clean, sharp point as you work (see page 30 for directions on how to make a cone).

* **Cellophane:** At the Bakehouse we often use cellophane instead of parchment paper to create our designs. Not only is it easier to see the template through the clear surface, but it leaves the chocolate nice and glossy. Parchment paper can be substituted, and it is recommended when you are making a design that will get a brushing of luster dust.

* **Parchment Paper:** This versatile paper is not only good for lining baking pans, but it is also a great surface for piping chocolate designs. If you plan on dusting your chocolate with luster dust, then parchment is a must since it leaves the chocolate with a matte finish that easily accepts the metallic coating.

* **Paintbrush:** Soft sable or acrylic brushes are used to paint with melted chocolate. For detailed shading I recommend using a #0, 1, or 2 brush.

* **Heating Pad:** To keep chocolates warm in the pastry cones, we use standard heating pads found at pharmacies. The temperature is hot, but it doesn't scald the chocolate as a double boiler or portable stove might do if the temperature isn't perfectly regulated.

WHAT DO YOU USE TO TINT CHOCOLATE?

Since adding small amounts of water to chocolate will cause it to seize (when chocolate resolidifies and becomes lumpy), you cannot use water-based food coloring like liquid, liquid gel, or paste. Instead, use oil-based candy colors. I recommend Chefmaster and Wilton brand candy colors.

WHAT TEMPERATURE SHOULD THE WAFER CHOCOLATE BE?

Most important, store chocolate in a cool, dry place—not in the refrigerator. If your chocolate is exposed to prolonged humidity it may be lumpy when melted. It is best to work with chocolate at room temperature (68 to 70°F).

The melting point of confectioners' chocolate is approximately 115°F. When it is melted it should be in a fluid state. Confectioners' chocolate can easily be melted in a double boiler or in a microwave, but you should never melt chocolate directly over a heat source.

To melt chocolate in the microwave: Place the chocolate wafers in a heat-proof glass or other microwave-safe bowl. For 1 to 2 cups of chocolate, microwave in 30-second intervals, stirring in between to ensure that the chocolate does not burn. It will take approximately 1½ minutes to melt, but times will vary based on the room temperature, the amount of chocolate you are melting, and the power of your microwave. Stirring chocolate vigorously will often melt any remaining small pieces.

To melt chocolate in a double boiler: Find a metal bowl that fits snuggly into a medium-size pot, or use a double boiler. Fill the pot one-third full with water and, over low heat, bring to a light simmer (hot but not boiling). Place the wafers in the bowl. Place the bowl on the pot. Do not let the bottom of the bowl touch the water. Heat the chocolate, stirring often, until all of the chocolate has melted (approximately 15 minutes). Remove from the heat.

To keep chocolates warm in the pastry cones, we use standard heating pads (set to high) found at pharmacies. However, placing your chocolate bags on a sheet pan placed over a pot of barely simmering water will do. I have found that the dark chocolate requires slightly more heat to stay workable. If you fold the heating pad in half, covering the chocolates, the temperature will get hotter; check the chocolates, however, to make sure they do not overheat.

If chocolate gets too hot it can start to bake and get hard and unworkable. Also, if you pipe with very hot chocolate it may remelt other piped chocolate elements as it is piped next to or on top of them. This can cause the other chocolate details to blur or melt into each other.

If painting with chocolate, use a sheet pan over a pan filled with barely simmering water as a palette to remelt any chocolate on the paintbrush. You have to work quickly, since the chocolate on the brush will dry quickly.

A chocolate design can take anywhere from 5 minutes to 1 hour to set completely, depending on the room temperature and the size of the design. In general, the designs in this book will take between 5 minutes and 15 minutes to set.

If you are in a rush and you need your design to set quickly, you can flashfreeze the chocolate. Place the design (on its pan) in the freezer for approximately 1 minute, or just until set. Do not keep it in the freezer any longer, because when removed, the design will sweat and leave water marks.

HOW DO YOU MEASURE THE CHOCOLATE?

All the measurements listed in "What you will need" are calibrated in unmelted cups, but you can measure the wafer chocolate by the ounce or by the cup in the melted state. Approximately 6 ounces of unmelted wafer chocolate is equivalent to approximately 1 cup unmelted wafer chocolate or ½ cup melted wafer chocolate. When making designs it is always a good idea to melt extra chocolate, and make extra designs, just in case a design breaks or you make a mistake and need more.

HOW DO I PREVENT MY CHOCOLATE DECORATIONS FROM BREAKING?

The final design should be anywhere from ⅛ to ¼ inch thick. The larger the design, the thicker it should be to ensure stability and ease of handling. If the design is too thin, it will be too fragile to flip.

To prevent the decoration from breaking along the seams, it is important that the colors overlap. Also, don't worry if you go outside the lines a little; not only will the initial outline maintain the definition of the design, but overlapping the outline will add stability. Worst-case scenario, you can carefully carve off the excess chocolate with a sharp paring knife, or score along a straight line and crack the excess off along the score.

Before flipping a design, make sure it is completely set. If any part is still slightly soft, it will stick to the parchment or cellophane and not peel up.

While making your designs, be careful not to shift the parchment paper or cellophane, since this may cause the chocolates (if still in the liquid state) to ooze, blur, or change shape. If you are making more than one of a design and you only have one copy of a template, do not move the template until the chocolate of the first design has set. You can also trace one template and attach a long parchment tab, or handle, to it so that you can more easily move the template under the parchment paper to pipe out multiples without disrupting those you have already made. Yet another option is to trace or make as many photocopies of the template as you need. This may become problematic, however, when you need forty of one design. Whichever way you choose, begin by placing the template onto a sheet pan or a flat surface. Cover the template with parchment paper or cellophane, and lightly secure with one or two pieces of tape.

HOW DO I CONTROL THE LINE QUALITY?

Although piping with chocolate and piping with buttercream share some basic rules (such as holding the bag with one hand and guiding with the other) they also have many differences. Most notably, chocolate has to be in the liquid state to pipe. This may take some getting used to. You do not need to apply as much pressure to the pastry cone; the chocolate will often flow on its own.

I always recommend practicing on a piece of parchment paper before attempting any designs. Start with a very small hole (an almost imperceptible 1/32 inch). When cutting the hole at the tip of the pastry cone, make sure the cut is straight across; if it is at an angle, the chocolate may come out loopy or the angled point may touch the surface and cause a split line as you pipe. When the hole is this small, you may have to squeeze a bit harder than with a larger hole. If the chocolate does not flow easily, make sure the chocolate at the tip has not cooled. If it has, with your finger, massage the tip against the double boiler, being careful not to burn your finger. Pipe back and forth on the parchment paper, noticing the change in the thickness of the line as you squeeze harder or lighter.

Cut a larger hole at the tip of the pastry cone and notice how the chocolate flows more easily, but also how you have slightly less control. The larger the hole, the faster you will need to move the pastry cone across the surface. Find a tip size that you are comfortable working with. Most designs can be done with different line weights. A heavier line may give the design a more playful quality, and a thin line may lend itself more to realistic subjects. See each set of chocolate method directions for more information on lines, and see Shading and Portraiture (page 76) for more information on fine line work.

If you are a novice, you may notice that the beginning of each line has a dot. With practice, the size of this dot will diminish or disappear altogether. To help reduce the dot size, clean the tip on a blank piece of parchment paper before starting the line. Also, choose to start each line where the dot will be least visible, such as at a corner where other lines intersect.

To end a chocolate line, stop applying pressure and tilt the entire bag upward to change the direction of flow and create an abrupt end. Or, to create a point, drag the tip on the surface of the cellophane or parchment as you release pressure.

WHY DO MY CHOCOLATE DECORATIONS, WHEN FLIPPED, HAVE AIR POCKETS OR THE TEXTURE OF THE PIPED LINES?

A Chocolate Method decoration is supposed to be smooth and flat on the flipped and decorated side. If you see the texture of the piped chocolate or excessive air bubbles, it may be because the chocolate was not in the desired liquid state while you were making the decoration.

If the chocolate is too cool as you pipe, it acts more like icing, keeping a linear shape. It does not flood into the area being filled or piped like a liquid would. I recommend having two pastry bags of each color of chocolate. While you are working with one bag, have the other bag warming on a heating pad or on a sheet pan placed over a pot of barely simmering water. Switch bags often to ensure that you are always working with warm chocolate.

Chocolate is temperamental. It has to be kept slightly warmer than body temperature or it begins to set. I have found that white chocolate is the perfect working temperature if it rests on a heating pad at high heat and dark chocolate prefers a slightly hotter surface, such as a portable stovetop or a double boiler.

Humidity also affects the way chocolate melts. If your chocolate was exposed to excessive or prolonged humid conditions, you may have difficulty melting it; instead of melting, it will seize. If the seizing is not severe, you can counteract it by whisking a few drops of vegetable oil into the melted chocolate.

Another reason textural lines or air bubbles may appear in your chocolate designs is the size of the hole in the pastry cone. The larger the area you are trying to fill in, the larger the hole in your pastry bag should be. Keep in mind that you don't want the hole to be so big that you are unable to control the flow of chocolate. If you try to fill in a larger area using a very small hole, the first rows or lines of chocolate you piped may start to set before the other layers are in place. This creates a lacy effect with many holes. Try to work as quickly and efficiently as you can without sacrificing quality. To increase efficiency, have all of the chocolate and colored chocolates you will need to complete a design melted, poured into pastry cones, and ready to go. If you have to stop mid-design to melt chocolate this could affect the quality of your final design.

A Splash of Color

With children in mind, the colors in this book are vivid, energetic, playful, and rarely muted: happy yellows, joyful oranges, calming blues, fiery reds, and pretty pinks.

The buttercream colors opposite are mixed from a palette of red, neon pink, sunset orange, lemon yellow, neon green, leaf green, teal, royal blue, sky blue, violet, black, and buckeye brown liquid gel colors. The chocolate colors are mixed from a palette of red, pink, orange, yellow, green, royal blue, sky blue, violet, and black candy colors. Candy color is not available in brown; for those formulas, use melted dark wafer chocolate in place of brown coloring. You may not be able to mix a true sky blue or teal depending on the range of colors available in the brand you buy; if these colors are important for your designs, I recommend buying a bag of pretinted wafer chocolate or a jar of paste color for buttercream. When mixing colors, whatever colorant you are using, always err on the side of too little color as opposed to too much. Add color drop by drop. If a color is too dark, and you want to make it lighter, adding white buttercream or white chocolate doesn't always solve the problem. More often than not you end up adding cups of buttercream before reaching the desired color. Instead, start over and use the food coloring cautiously.

If you don't need a wide range of colors, you can just use blue, yellow, and red food coloring. These primary colors, in varying amounts and when mixed together in different proportions, can give you pinks, greens, oranges, purples,

Kids can

Kids love mixing colors. There is something magical about watching white buttercream, with the addition of just a drop or two of food coloring, transform into pink or blue or yellow as you stir.

and more. Liquid gel, paste, and candy colors can be purchased online, at baking supply stores, and at some craft stores (see the list of suppliers on page 171). If you can't find liquid-gel colors, paste colors work just as well. The liquid colors found in grocery stores, such as McCormick's brand, can also be used, but the palette is limited and they are less concentrated.

Use this chart as an approximate guide for mixing colors. Your results may vary depending on the brand and type of coloring you use. These formulas are based on drops of Chefmaster liquid gel colors per ¼ cup of House Buttercream and drops of Chefmaster (except for Wilton's "sky" blue) candy colors per ¼ cup of melted white wafer chocolate.

COLOR	BUTTERCREAM	WAFER CHOCOLATE
red	5 red	10 red
light pink	scant drop neon pink or 1 red	scant drop pink or 1 red
pink	2 neon pink	1 pink
dark pink	3 neon pink + 1 red	2 pink + 1 red
neon pink	5 neon pink	3 pink
raspberry	2 red + 3 neon pink	5 red + 3 pink
burgundy	4 burgundy + 1 neon pink	1 pink + 1 red + 1 purple
orange	3 orange	4 orange
light orange/peach	scant drop orange	1 orange
yellow-orange	2 yellow + 1 orange	5 yellow + 2 orange
dark orange	3 orange + 3 red	4 orange + 5 red
coral	1 orange + 2 neon pink	2 orange + 1 pink
yellow	2 yellow	4 yellow
sandy yellow	2 yellow + scant drop orange + scant drop brown	5 yellow + 1 orange + 1 drop dark chocolate
green	3 green + 1 brown	4 green + 12 drops dark chocolate
light green	scant drop green + scant drop brown (optional)	1 green + 2 drops dark chocolate
lime green	2 green + 4 yellow or 3 neon brite green	3 green + 5 yellow
dark green	4 green + 1 brown + 1 blue	4 green + 10 dark chocolate + 1 blue + 1 yellow
teal	4 teal or 1 green + 2 sky blue	2 sky blue + 1 green
light blue	1 royal or sky blue	1 royal or sky blue
sky blue	3 sky blue	2 sky blue
blue	5 royal blue	6 royal blue
purple	3 violet	3 violet
lavender	1 violet	scant drop violet or 1 pink + 4 drops dark chocolate
tan	scant drop brown + scant drop yellow	scant drop yellow + 2 drops dark chocolate
light brown	1 brown	15 drops dark chocolate + 1 orange (optional)
dark brown	5 brown	45 drops dark chocolate + 2 orange (optional)
gray	1 black	1 black

CONGRATULATIONS! YOU'VE GRADUATED FROM CAKE AND BAKE 101; NOW HAVE FUN!

The Enchanted TEA PARTY

Magical Delicacies for Your Fairy Princess

Nestled in a blooming garden, a table is set with tiny teacups and itty-bitty scones, all atop a delicate tulle tablecloth. Pitchers of pink lemonade await the dancing fairies, and edible magic wands are wrapped in silk ribbons for guests to take home. Laughter and the patter of little footsteps are heard, as fairies run by with their wings flapping behind them.

This is an Enchanted Tea Party—perfect for your little fairy princess. If the weather is warm, host this fanciful gathering outdoors, where the children can run free. Prepare sweet treats for the sweet girls. The teacups? Some are real, for sipping

lemonade, and some are "fairy cakes"—little cupcakes decorated to look like teacups. In the center of it all is a Woodland Fairies cake, replete with chocolate fairies flitting about a fallen log.

If your fairy princess is still just a wee thing, why not make some pixie play dough (see recipe on page 40) for her and her friends to roll, cut, and mold? What makes this play dough so magical? The calming peppermint scent, the pretty pink color, and the spattering of glitter.

And to top it all off, have a box filled with shimmering fairy wings and skirts for dressing up.

PIXIE PLAY DOUGH

Playing with this dough is like aromatherapy for the young. As the children mold and cut, the aroma of peppermint infuses the air and scents their hands. This dough is not edible, but if your little ones are tempted to taste it, no fear: There are no harmful ingredients. It's just salty. To make plain play dough, omit the peppermint extract and glitter.

In a medium pot, mix together:

2 cups all-purpose flour
1 cup salt
2 cups water with 2 drops pink food coloring
2 teaspoons cream of tartar
2 tablespoons vegetable oil
1 teaspoon peppermint extract

Place the pot over low heat and stir until the play dough pulls away from the sides of the pot. Set aside. When cool to the touch add:

1 tablespoon edible glitter (or to your liking)

Knead until smooth.

CITRUS SPONGE ROLL

Our Citrus Sponge Roll is a favorite at Passover, and when flavored with orange instead of lemon and rolled with chocolate mousse, it transforms into a delicious Christmas Yule Log.

Yield: 1 sponge roll

PLAIN+SIMPLE Lightly frost the filled roll with whipped cream, and then roll in sliced almonds or flaked coconut. Alternatively, fill with raspberry jam.

Grease the bottom of a half-sheet (12 x 16-inch rimmed) pan and line it with parchment paper. Grease the parchment paper and the sides of the sheet pan with *melted butter*. Preheat the oven to 400°F. Have all ingredients at room temperature.

In the bowl of an electric mixer, using a whip attachment, beat until frothy:

- 6 extra-large egg yolks
- 2 extra-large egg whites

Slowly whisk in:

- 1 cup sugar
- 1 tablespoon plus 1 teaspoon fresh lemon juice
- 2 teaspoons grated lemon zest

Continue beating until the egg mixture has tripled in volume and ribbons form when the whip attachment is lifted.

Transfer the batter into a large bowl.

Sift over the bowl and gently fold in:

- ½ cup plus 2 tablespoons potato starch

In the bowl of an electric mixer, using a whip attachment, beat until stiff peaks form:

- 6 extra-large egg whites
- ⅓ cup plus 1 tablespoon sugar
- Pinch of salt

Gently fold the egg white mixture into the egg and potato starch batter.

Pour the batter into the prepared pan and spread evenly with a spatula. Bake for 7 to 9 minutes, or until the cake begins to pull away from the sides of the pan. The top should spring back when lightly touched. Cool in the pan on a wire rack.

When the cake has cooled to room temperature, run the blade of a metal spatula around the edge of the pan to loosen it. Invert the cake onto a piece of clean parchment paper or a slightly damp kitchen towel. Carefully peel away the parchment paper the cake was baked on. Invert the cake again. Using a rubber or metal spatula, spread the filling of your choice evenly over the entire surface of the cake. Beginning at one long edge, roll the cake over the filling, keeping the spiral as tight as possible. Wrap in plastic wrap and freeze for 1 hour.

WOODLAND FAIRIES CAKE

If you have any little pixies living in your house, this edible woodland scene will delight them. Our Citrus Sponge Roll is decorated to look like a log and is home to enchanted chocolate fairies and blooming flowers.

To simplify this cake, use fewer colors and make fewer and/or simpler fairies.

Serves approximately 16 people

· WHAT YOU WILL NEED ·

Cake: **Citrus Sponge Roll (page 41)**

Icing: **½ recipe Kaye's Buttercream (page 11)** and approximately **8 ounces semisweet chocolate** to make chocolate buttercream

Filling: **3 to 4 cups Whipped Cream (page 17), Whipped Milk Chocolate Ganache (page 19), or Creamsicle Mousse (page 18)**

Decoration: **⅛ cup dark wafer chocolate** and **1½ cups white wafer chocolate** to make 5 fairies, **pearl luster dust and/or edible glitter**

Colors: **pink, purple, yellow, green, and sky blue candy colors** and **purple, yellow, teal, and green liquid gel colors**

Tips: **#8, 9, or 10 round tip, #352, 65, 66, or 67 leaf tip, #103 or 104 petal tip**

Miscellaneous: **2 half-sheet pans, pastry bag, coupler, pastry cones, fairy templates (page 160), parchment paper or cellophane, 8 x 16-inch (or larger) base**

1 Bake the sponge roll and let it cool completely. Prepare the buttercream.

2 Prepare the filling of your choice and fill the sponge roll as directed in the recipe on page 41. Wrap in plastic wrap or roll in parchment paper and freeze for at least 1 hour.

3 Melt the dark wafer and white wafer chocolates separately. Set aside ¼ cup white chocolate. Using the Color Mixing Chart on page 37, tint the remaining white chocolate: approximately

2 tablespoons each of pink, lavender, light sky blue, yellow, green, and the skin tone of your choice (such as light peach, light brown, or medium brown). Pour the chocolates into separate pastry cones. Using the templates provided, make 5 fairies as illustrated in The Chocolate Method: Shading and Portraiture (page 76). Set aside to harden.

4 Using a serrated knife, cut the ends of the sponge roll at parallel 45-degree angles. Adhere the sponge roll to the base with a dollop of buttercream. Attach one of the beveled pieces, with a dab of buttercream, to the sponge roll, a couple of inches from one end (see photograph).

5 Prepare the tinted buttercream: approximately 2 tablespoons light green for grass and vines, ¼ cup teal green for leaves, and 2 tablespoons yellow and ¼ cup lavender for flowers. Prepare the chocolate buttercream: Melt the semisweet chocolate. Mix ¾ cup of buttercream with a scant tablespoon of melted chocolate to make a light chocolate icing for the ends of the log. Mix 2½ cups buttercream with the remaining chocolate to cover the log.

6 Ice the cake with a textured finish: Cover the entire surface of the sponge roll with chocolate buttercream, and then run the tip of an offset spatula up and down the length of the roll, simulating the texture of bark.

CONTINUES

7 Place the light chocolate buttercream in a pastry bag with a coupler and a #10 round tip. Starting at the outer edge, pipe a spiral on each of the three cut ends. Try to cover all of the cake when piping.

8 Place the green and yellow buttercream into separate pastry cones and cut a small hole in each. Pipe green vines and blades of grass randomly around and on the log. Place the lavender buttercream in a pastry bag with a coupler, and with a #104 tip pipe, blossoms (see below) on the vines. Pipe yellow dots in the center of each blossom. Place the teal buttercream in a pastry bag with a coupler, and with a small leaf tip, pipe leaves (see below) among the blossoms and trailing from the vines.

9 While the buttercream is still soft, arrange the fairies on the log.

10 Sprinkle the top of the cake with edible glitter. Optional: Load a medium paintbrush with luster dust, place the brush approximately 6 inches from the cake, take a deep breath, and exhale with one short burst of air. Repeat in different spots until the cake is shimmering. Be forewarned: Dust gets everywhere, so I recommend doing this outside, if possible.

LEAVES

Tips: any leaf tip (such as #352, 65, 66, or 67)

Hold the bag at a 45-degree angle and lightly touch the tip to the surface of the cake where you want the leaf to be placed. Squeeze and hold the tip in place until the base is the size you want; this can be small or large depending on the amount of pressure you apply. Continue squeezing the bag as you pull it up at a 30- to 45-degree angle; release pressure and continue to pull up at the same angle to form the leaf's point.

BLOSSOMS

Tips: any round tip (such as #4, 8, or 10)

These blossoms have 5 evenly spaced petals of equal size. Choose a center point for the flower. Hold the pastry bag at a 45-degree angle and place the wide end of the tip at the chosen center point on the iced cake. Place the narrow end of the tip at a 30-degree angle to the cake surface. Pivot the tip around the center point. Pipe the first petal. The curvature of the petal forms not from moving the tip up and back toward the center point, but more from increasing the pressure toward the middle of each petal. To finish each petal, drag the tip toward the center as you release the pressure. The wide end of the tip should remain close to the center at all times. Begin the next petal so that it slightly overlaps the first. Repeat for each blossom.

CINNAMON SWIRL CUPCAKES

Cinnamon is my favorite spice, so I am always thinking up ways to incorporate it into new recipes. These scrumptious cupcakes are reminiscent of cinnamon coffee cake—but lighter. While we were testing recipes for this book, this was one of Liv's favorite recipes to sample.

Yield: 24 cupcakes

PLAIN + SIMPLE A dollop of cream cheese frosting or fudge on top transforms these from a snack-time treat to a delicious dessert.

Grease the top of two standard 12-cup muffin pans and line them with paper liners. Preheat the oven to 350°F. Have all ingredients at room temperature.

On a piece of wax paper, sift together:

- 3 cups cake flour
- 1 tablespoon baking powder
- ½ teaspoon kosher salt

In the bowl of an electric mixer, beat at high speed until light and fluffy:

- 6 ounces (1½ sticks) unsalted butter
- 2 cups sugar

Add slowly and beat on medium speed until well creamed:

- 4 extra-large eggs
- 1 teaspoon pure vanilla extract

At low speed, add the dry ingredients to the butter mixture alternately with:

- 1 cup milk

Transfer 2 cups of the batter to a medium bowl and mix in:

- 1½ teaspoons ground cinnamon

Scoop the plain batter into the prepared pans, filling each two-thirds full. Add approximately 1 rounded tablespoon cinnamon batter. Swirl together gently with a small knife or a toothpick. Bake for 20 to 24 minutes, or until golden.

The tops should spring back when lightly pressed. Cool on a wire rack for 5 to 10 minutes before removing the cupcakes from the pans.

TEA PARTY CUPCAKES

For your tea party, delight the children with these edible teapots and cups, alongside a real miniature tea set.

The directions below are based on a tea set that has white as the main color (just like the one I had as a child). For cups and handles to have green or pink bases, adjust the amounts accordingly.

Yield: 24 cupcakes

.... WHAT YOU WILL NEED ....

Cake: 24 Cinnamon Swirl Cupcakes (page 45)

Icing: 1 recipe Kids' Buttercream (page 14)

Decoration: 2 cups white wafer chocolate to make teacup and pot tops and handles

Colors: green and pink candy colors and neon green and pink liquid gel colors

Miscellaneous: two standard 12-mold muffin pans, half-sheet pan, pastry cones, teacup and -pot templates (page 161), parchment paper or cellophane

1 Bake the cupcakes and let them cool completely. For best results, freeze for at least 1 hour. Prepare the buttercream.

2 Melt the white wafer chocolate. Set aside ½ cup of the melted white chocolate. Using the Color Mixing Chart on page 37, tint the remaining white chocolate: approximately 2 tablespoons light green and 2 tablespoons pink. Using the templates provided, make 4 teapot handles, spouts, bases, and tops and 20 teacup handles and bases as illustrated in the Assembled Chocolate Method (pages 130 and 133, step 3).

3 Set aside 2 cups Kids' Buttercream. Using the Color Mixing Chart on page 37, tint the remaining buttercream: approximately ½ cup pink and ½ cup lime green.

4 Ice 4 of the cupcakes with a white old-fashioned finish (page 28). Ice the remaining cupcakes as follows: spread white buttercream on three-fourths of the cupcake. Spread pink or green on the top quarter of each cupcake. This section will act as negative space.

5 Place the remaining buttercreams in separate pastry cones. Pipe swirling colors (to serve as the steam) in contrasting colors in the negative space and pipe a line in white or color where the two colors meet. This will act as the brim of the cup.

6 Adhere the chocolate pieces to the cupcakes, pressing to set when needed. If the icing has set already, put a dot of icing on the underside of each segment and place it right side up on the cupcake. Place the bases on the bottom of each cupcake; for the teacups this is directly opposite the dark pink strip. The handles, tops, and spouts will overhang the edge slightly.

♥ *Kids can* ♥

The first thing I ever decorated, completely by myself, was a cupcake. I think the small size is unintimidating, especially for kids, so bake a batch of cupcakes, give your children an offset spatula (or even a butter knife) and buttercream, and let them experiment with frosting.

SUGAR COOKIES

This basic sugar cookie dough is strong enough to be cut into any shape, and the cookies are durable enough to stand up to a lot of decorating. Make mask-shaped cookies for your Halloween party, a cookie card for the birthday boy or girl, pirate faces for your little buccaneer, or magic wands for your fairy princess.

Yield: approximately 24 to 30 wands, 12 masks, 20 pirate faces, or 4 cookie cards

Line 2 cookie sheets with parchment paper. Preheat the oven to 350°F. Have all ingredients at room temperature.

In the bowl of an electric mixer at medium speed, cream:

> **4 ounces (1 stick) unsalted butter**
> **⅔ cup sugar**

Add and thoroughly incorporate:

> **1 extra-large egg**
> **½ teaspoon pure vanilla extract**

On a piece of wax paper, sift together:

> **1¾ cups plus 2 tablespoons all-purpose flour**
> **½ teaspoon baking powder**
> **½ teaspoon kosher salt**

Add the dry ingredients to the butter mixture. Mix until the dough comes together.

Wrap in plastic and chill for 30 minutes.

On a lightly floured board, roll the chilled dough out to ¼ inch thick. Slip parchment paper under the rolled dough and transfer it to a half-sheet pan. Chill for 30 minutes. Cut out shapes (see below).

If making magic wands: Cut out stars using a star cookie cutter (2 inches to 3 inches across; larger stars need longer handles). Arrange the stars 1 inch apart along the long sides of the cookie sheets. Carefully insert lollipop sticks into the hollow created between two points of the star about ½ inch deep.

If making a mask: Using the mask image on page 165, cut out a cardboard template. Place the template on the dough. Cut out the mask by running a paring knife around the edge of the template. Carefully slide a metal spatula under the cookie to transfer it to the cookie sheet. Arrange the masks 1 inch apart along the long sides of the cookie sheets. Carefully insert Popsicle sticks into the bottom left side about ½ inch deep.

If making pirate faces: Cut out circles using a 3-inch round cookie cutter. Arrange the circles 1 inch apart on the cookie sheets.

If making cookie cards: Using a paring knife or a pastry wheel, cut out 4 x 6-inch rectangles. Using the small end of a #12 round tip or any round cutter approximately ¼ inch in diameter, cut 2 circles out of the left side of each cookie, 1 inch from the top and 1 inch from the bottom (make sure the holes line up). Using a cookie cutter, cut out a heart, circle, or small shape of your choice from the center of half of the cookies. Carefully slide a metal spatula under the cookie to transfer it to the cookie sheet. Arrange the cards 1 inch apart on the cookie sheets.

Bake for 10 to 15 minutes, or until lightly browned. Let the cookies cool on the pans for 5 minutes, then transfer the cookies to a wire rack to cool completely.

♥ When we mention half-sheet pans, we are referring to 12 x 16-inch baking sheets (aka jelly roll pans) that have a 1-inch rim around all four sides. A pan that is missing a lip on at least one edge is a cookie sheet. When working in the chocolate method or baking cookies, either type of sheet pan will work, but for baking cakes you must use a rimmed pan.

MAGIC WANDS

The Good Witch of the North and the queen fairy agree that these star wands are magically delicious. The pixies at your party will love them, too. Send the sparkly pink wands home as party favors, or let the children decorate their own with royal icing and sanding sugar. They are sure to cast a spell on all who hold them.

.... WHAT YOU WILL NEED ....

Cookie: **Sugar Cookies (page 48)**

Icing: **1 recipe Royal Icing (page 15)**

Decoration: **pink and/or white sanding sugar, 6- or 8-inch lollipop sticks for magic wands, and ribbon for decoration (1 to 2 feet per wand, depending on whether a knot or bow is tied)**

Colors: **pink liquid gel colors**

Miscellaneous: **half-sheet baking pan, pastry cones, star cookie cutter**

1 Bake the cookies and let them cool completely. Prepare the Royal Icing. Keep the icing covered with a damp cloth.

2 Prepare the colored icing: approximately 1 cup light pink, ½ cup medium pink, ½ cup neon pink.

3 To prevent breaking when decorating, hold the cookie, not the lollipop stick. Spread a thin layer of colored icing over the entire cookie. Immediately pour white or pink sanding sugar over the top or dip the cookie into a bowl of sanding sugar, pressing gently to adhere. Shake or dust off any excess sugar.

4 Place 2 tablespoons of each color icing into separate pastry cones. Cut a small hole at the tip of each pastry cone. Pipe dots or lacy borders around the edge of each cookie, write the initials of the birthday fairy, or make a design of your own. Let dry overnight.

5 Tie a bow with long trails around the handle of each wand.

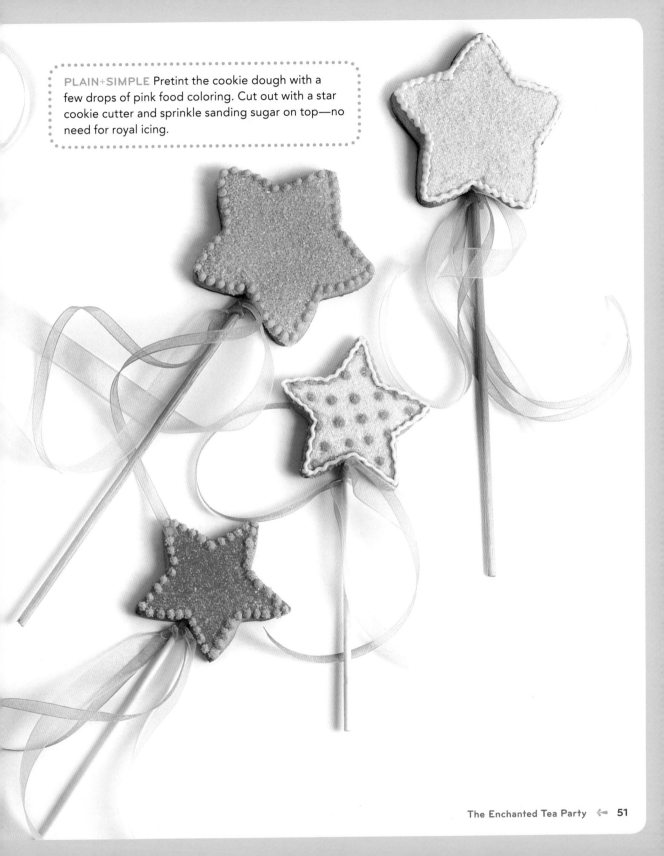

PLAIN+SIMPLE Pretint the cookie dough with a few drops of pink food coloring. Cut out with a star cookie cutter and sprinkle sanding sugar on top—no need for royal icing.

The Best SLEEPOVER EVER

From Nighttime Munchies to a Breakfast Bonanza

The easiest way to host a proper sleepover party is to settle the kids onto the couch or throw pillows, serve "Half-Moon" Black and White Cookies (page 58), and play an age-appropriate movie. If you want to keep it simple, classic salt-and-butter popcorn, one of my favorite snacks, is equally delicious. When the movie is over, there is always charades; or, for older children or teens, set a table with candles, turn out the lights, and play Ouija or foretell the future with tarot cards and palm reading. And the night's grand finale: CAKE! What could be more perfect for a sleepover party than a three-dimensional bed decorated with your child's favorite colors or patterns? Then it's time for bed—HA! Let the giggling begin.

In the morning, wake the kids with the delicious aroma of Banana Bear Pancakes, Oven French Toast, and Cinnamon Bread. These breakfast treats are classic and kid friendly—full of banana, cinnamon, chocolate, and, of course, sugar—and they're so irresistible you'll want to make them every weekend.

Here's an idea you might not have thought of: my friend Jamie toyed with the idea of having a girls' sleepover, but the girls she had in mind were all grown-up moms. Sometimes you just need to get together with your best friends, wear comfy pj's, eat good food (yes, I mean cake), and relax.

BED CAKE

A couple of years ago, my friend Laura asked me to make a cake for her daughter Katie's birthday. She was hosting a faux-sleepover party. Guests came wearing pajamas and toting their pillows. But there was no sleeping, just fun: pillow fights, popcorn, and this 3-D bed cake.

The headboard and footboard for this bed are made of chocolate. The decorating directions with this recipe guide you through the Silhouette and Overpiping Chocolate Method process. Of all the ways of working with chocolate, this is the easiest. Whether you are making a silhouette portrait in profile or just a polka dot, simply piping one color yields great results. If you want to add details and other colors, overpipe with tinted white chocolate, as shown here.

You'll find more detailed information on working with the Chocolate Method on pages 31 to 35 (Confectioners' Chocolate and the Chocolate Method) and page 76 (Shading and Portraiture).

Serves 12 to 15 people

······························· WHAT YOU WILL NEED ·······························

Cake: 9 x 13-inch Banana Chocolate–Chocolate Chip Cake (page 57)

Icing: ½ recipe Kaye's Buttercream (page 11), 8 ounces semisweet chocolate to make chocolate buttercream, and 1 recipe Marshmallow Fondant (page 16)

Filling: 4 bananas and 1 recipe Whipped Cream (page 17)

Decoration: ½ cup dark wafer chocolate and 2½ cups white wafer chocolate to make bed frame

Colors: sky-blue liquid gel color and yellow and blue candy colors

Miscellaneous: 9 x 13-inch baking pan, 6½ x 9-inch cardboard rectangle, pastry bag, coupler, pastry cones, headboard and footboard templates (page 161), half-sheet pan, parchment paper or cellophane, 9 x 12-inch (or larger) base

1 Bake the cake and let it cool completely. For best results, freeze for 1 hour or chill in the refrigerator for a few hours.

2 Prepare the buttercream and sky blue marshmallow fondant (see recipe instructions for tinting).

3 Using a serrated knife, cut the cake in half vertically, so that you have two 9 x 6½-inch pieces.

Cut off the domes and set them aside. Using the same knife, slice one of the layers of cake in half horizontally. Stack the 3 layers of cake on the cardboard rectangle.

4 Prepare the whipped cream and slice the bananas (about ¼ inch thick). Flavor the buttercream with the semisweet chocolate (see page 12). Fill

CONTINUES

PLAIN+SIMPLE Instead of using a rolled marshmallow fondant, make the blanket with buttercream, either iced or piped in a basket weave with a round tip (it will look like a hand-knit blanket).

the cakes with layers of sliced bananas and whipped cream (see page 23). Spread a thin layer of chocolate buttercream on top of the cake and adhere one of the reserved domes. Using a small serrated paring knife, bevel the sides of the cake slightly; eliminating the sharp angles will make it easier to lay the fondant on top. Crumb coat the cake with chocolate buttercream as directed on page 25. Adhere the cardboard rectangle supporting the cake to your base. Chill the filled cake for 30 minutes, or until the buttercream has set.

5 Melt the dark wafer and white wafer chocolates separately. Using the Color Mixing Chart on page 37, tint the white chocolate: approximately 2 tablespoons blue, 2 tablespoons yellow, and 1 cup medium brown. (To make the brown, mix approximately 1 cup white chocolate with 1 tablespoon melted dark chocolate. Add more, teaspoon by teaspoon, to get the desired shade.) Pour the tinted chocolates into separate pastry cones.

6 To make the headboard and footboard using the Silhouette and Overpiping Chocolate Method: Cut a medium hole (1/16 to 1/8 inch in diameter) in the brown pastry cone and a small to medium hole (1/32 to 1/16 inch) in each of the remaining pastry cones. The larger the hole, the more difficult it is to control the flow of the chocolate, but if the hole is too small it will take a long time to fill in the template. Using the templates provided, trace/fill in the bed frame; ideally each line of the bed frame can be done in one stroke. The chocolate should be approximately 1/8 inch thick, but it can be thicker. Set aside to harden. When the chocolate has set, following the photograph for guidance if necessary, pipe blue and yellow decorative details on the bed frame. Set aside to harden. When the chocolate has set, gently flip the design and overpipe additional blue and yellow details. Set aside to harden.

7 Dust a clean, flat surface with confectioners' sugar. With a rolling pin, roll out the fondant into a rectangle 1/4 inch thick and approximately 17 x 20 inches. Gently slide your hands under the fondant, lift, and drape the rectangle evenly over the cake. To facilitate this you can roll the fondant onto a rolling pin and then, starting at one side, unroll the fondant over the cake. Using scissors, trim off any extra fondant, but leave enough so none of the buttercream underneath is visible. Then press the fondant on the short sides flush against the cake. Trim the bottoms, if needed, with a paring knife, so they end at the bottom of the cake. With your hands, mold the long sides so the blanket flares or undulates.

8 To make the pillow, roll out a 3 x 4-inch rectangle of fondant. Place a 1 x 1½-inch chunk of fondant in the center of the rectangle. Fold the short sides around the chunk so they meet in the middle. Invert so the seam is on the bottom. Lightly press your fingers on either short side of the pillow. Place the pillow on one end of the bed. If desired, pipe a colored chocolate border around the edges of the pillow.

9 Pipe a few dots of buttercream or melted chocolate on the backside (below the bed height) of the headboard and footboard. Gently adhere the headboard to the top of the bed where the pillow is, and the footboard to the bottom of the bed.

• •

♥ *Kids can* ♥

My son loves to mash, squash, and puree, and I'm quite sure your kids will love getting the chance to "play" with their food, too. Place the bananas in a bowl. Let your kids mash the bananas, using a fork, a pestle, or even their (clean) hands. —Liv

BANANA CHOCOLATE–CHOCOLATE CHIP CAKE

I buy bananas every week but somehow they are always the last fruit to be eaten, and by the time the weekend rolls around, they are brown and inevitably overripe. Not wanting to waste, I bake banana muffins, banana pancakes, and banana cake. According to my son and husband, chocolate makes everything better, so chocolate chips replace walnuts in our banana muffins, and cocoa powder and chocolate chips make this banana cake over-the-top delicious. —Liv

Yield: one 9 x 13-inch cake

PLAIN+SIMPLE Slice the cake in half and layer it with bananas and whipped cream—no frosting necessary. Dig in!

Grease and flour a 9 x 13-inch pan. Preheat the oven to 350°F. Have all ingredients at room temperature.

In the bowl of an electric mixer, beat at high speed until light and fluffy:
   8 ounces (2 sticks) unsalted butter
   1½ cups firmly packed light brown sugar
   ½ cup granulated sugar

Add and cream:
   3 extra-large eggs

Add:
   2 cups mashed banana (about 3 large bananas)

(Don't worry if the batter looks curdled.)

On a piece of wax paper, sift together:
   2¾ cups cake flour
   ¼ cup cocoa powder
   1½ teaspoons baking powder
   ¾ teaspoon kosher salt

Mix the dry ingredients into the butter and egg mixture at low speed just until combined.

Stir in:
   ½ cup mini chocolate chips

Pour the batter into the prepared pan. Bake for 45 to 50 minutes, or until a cake tester inserted into the center of the cake comes out clean. Cool the cake on a wire rack for 15 to 20 minutes before turning it out of the pan.

"HALF-MOON" BLACK AND WHITE COOKIES

"Cookie" might be a bit of a misnomer, since these classic New York–New England deli treats are more like mini sponge cakes. Half of the "cookie" is covered in a simple vanilla icing and the other half in chocolate. I've taken it a step further here, and, with a slight flourish of a pastry cone, transformed them into the phases of the moon. —Liv

Yield: approximately 12 cookies

Line a half-sheet pan with parchment paper. Preheat the oven to 350°F. Have all ingredients at room temperature.

On a piece of wax paper, sift together:
- 1 cup all-purpose flour
- 1¼ cups cake flour
- ¾ teaspoon baking soda
- ¾ teaspoon kosher salt

In the bowl of an electric mixer, beat at high speed until light and fluffy:
- 4 ounces (1 stick) unsalted butter
- ¾ cup sugar

Add and cream:
- 1 extra-large egg
- 1 extra-large egg yolk
- ¾ teaspoon pure vanilla extract

In a bowl, mix together:
- ¼ cup buttermilk
- ¼ cup milk

Add the dry ingredients and milk alternately to the butter mixture and combine.

Scoop the batter into a pastry bag with a #803 large round tip or a coupler with a #12 tip. Pipe the batter onto the prepared pan in 3-inch circles, starting from the center and spiraling outward. Leave at least a 1-inch space between each circle. Bake for 10 to 12 minutes, or until golden. The tops should spring back when lightly touched. Let the cookies cool in their pans for 5 minutes, then transfer them to a wire rack to cool completely.

Prepare the icing.

White Icing

Sift into a medium bowl:

> 2 cups confectioners' sugar, plus additional as needed

Slowly whisk in:

> 3 tablespoons water, plus additional as needed

Black Icing

Sift into a medium bowl:

> 1¾ cups confectioners' sugar, plus additional as needed
>
> ¼ cup cocoa powder

Slowly whisk in:

> 5 tablespoons water, plus additional as needed

The icings should be thick enough for a small offset spatula to stand up in them (better to be too thick than too thin). If either icing is too thin, add more confectioners' sugar 1 tablespoon at a time; if it becomes too thick, add water 1 teaspoon at a time. Use the glaze immediately or place plastic wrap directly on the surface of the glaze to prevent a crust from forming on the top of the icing. It can be stored in the refrigerator for 1 week.

To ice a traditional black and white cookie, using an offset spatula, spread white icing on half of the cookie and black icing on the other half. To make a crescent moon pattern, pour 2 tablespoons each of white and black icing into 2 separate pastry cones. Pipe a white line around two-thirds of the circumference of an un-iced cookie. Starting at the topmost line, create a point and start piping another line curving downward but inset about ½ inch, flaring out for a nose, coming straight back in, flaring slightly for lips, and ending back at the bottom line with another point. Flood this area with white icing. Fill in the negative space with black icing. Pipe chocolate details, such as eye, brow, nostril, and lips.

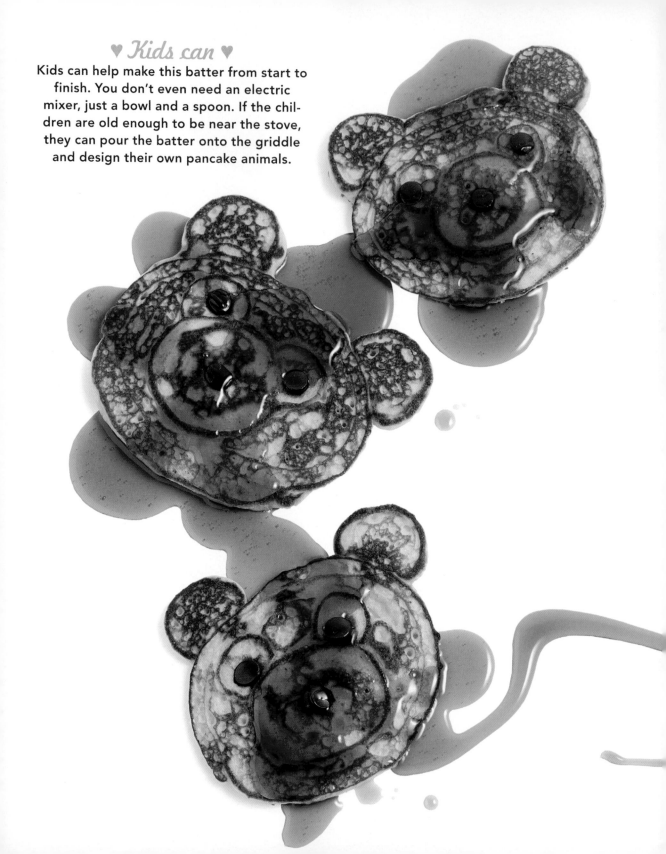

♥ *Kids can* ♥

Kids can help make this batter from start to finish. You don't even need an electric mixer, just a bowl and a spoon. If the children are old enough to be near the stove, they can pour the batter onto the griddle and design their own pancake animals.

BANANA BEAR PANCAKES

When I was a little girl my mom made me teddy bear pancakes, then I made them for myself, and now I make them for my son. My mom, the queen of overripe and spotted bananas, always sliced a few extra to add on top. This time around, they are pureed so they more thoroughly incorporate into the batter, adding a wonderful and aromatic flavor. —Liv

Yield: approximately 12 pancakes

Have on hand a griddle or a frying pan. Have all ingredients at room temperature.

Sift into a bowl:
    2 cups cake flour
    2 teaspoons baking powder
    ½ teaspoon kosher salt
    2 tablespoons sugar

In a separate bowl, mix together:
    3 extra-large egg yolks
    6 tablespoons melted unsalted butter
    1¼ cups milk
    ½ cup mashed bananas (about 1 banana)

Add the egg mixture to the dry ingredients and whisk until just combined. Do not overmix; the batter will be slightly lumpy.

In the bowl of an electric mixer, beat at high speed until soft peaks form:
    3 extra-large egg whites

Gently fold the egg whites into the batter.

To make bear pancakes, pour the batter into a squeeze bottle.

Have on hand:
    ¼ cup vegetable shortening or nonstick spray
    ¼ cup chocolate chips

Heat a griddle or a frying pan over medium heat and grease the pan with shortening or nonstick spray (butter has a tendency to burn).

To create the outline of the eyes and the snout when the pancake is turned over, squeeze out a 2-inch oval of batter onto the hot pan and pipe two dots above the oval, offset from each other. Let cook for approximately 15 seconds. Overpipe a large circle, covering the oval and dots. Pipe 2 "ears" on the top, offset from each other. Flip the pancakes when bubbles form (1 to 2 minutes per side). Press chocolate chips into the center of the eyes and oval (nose). Repeat with the remaining batter. Remove the pancakes and serve immediately.

CINNAMON BREAD

Bread was my first love—baking wise. It is much more forgiving then baking a cake. You can add more or less sweetener, more or less fat, and the end result will still be great. I prefer to knead the dough by hand for the therapeutic value. The whole process can be done without a mixer, but feel free to use one with a dough hook.

I always make two loaves of bread at a time, because one will always disappear before it cools and the other is great for French toast or to slice and save in the freezer for later.

Yield: 2 loaves of bread

In a large bowl, combine:
- **1 cup warm water**
- **1 tablespoon sugar**
- **1 packet active dry yeast**

Let rest for 5 minutes, or until bubbles form.

Add and stir to combine:
- **4 tablespoons melted unsalted butter, cooled to lukewarm**
- **2 teaspoons kosher salt**
- **3 tablespoons sugar**
- **1 cup milk**

Add and stir until a dough forms:
- **4½ cups all-purpose flour**

Turn the dough out onto a floured board. Knead the dough until it is smooth and no longer sticky (approximately 10 minutes), adding as needed:
- **Up to ½ cup all-purpose flour**

Butter a medium bowl. Transfer the dough, upside down, to the bowl. Then turn it right side up to ensure that all of the dough surface is coated with butter. Cover with a damp cloth or plastic wrap. Set the dough in a warm area and let it rest until it is doubled in size (1 to 2 hours depending on the warmth of the area).

Grease two 5 x 9-inch loaf pans with melted butter.

In a small saucepan, melt:
- **2 ounces (½ stick) unsalted butter**

In a small bowl, combine:
- **1 cup sugar**
- **1½ tablespoons ground cinnamon**

Punch down the dough. Divide the dough in half to make 2 loaves. On a lightly floured work surface, spread the dough into a 9 x 12-inch square. Brush with melted butter. Sprinkle 5 tablespoons of the cinnamon sugar over the dough.

Starting at a shorter edge, roll the dough tightly, pressing with the palm of your hand as you go. When the spiral is complete, pinch the seam of the dough to seal it. Place the rolled loaf in the pan. Butter the top and sprinkle with an additional tablespoon of cinnamon sugar. Repeat with the remaining dough. Let rise until doubled in size (approximately 1 hour). Preheat the oven to 350°F.

Bake for 30 to 35 minutes. Test for doneness by taking the bread out of the pan and tapping the bottom with your knuckle. You should hear a hollow sound when it's done.

♥ *Kids can* ♥

I grew up on homemade bread, so I was always there to help my mom with various steps of the bread-making process, from kneading to punching down the dough. But one of my favorite things to do was mix the water, sugar, and yeast and then check for bubbles. I was fascinated by the fact that yeast is alive; it eats sugar and releases carbon dioxide, which creates the telltale bubbles. So, let the kids help out; they may even learn something. —Liv

OVEN FRENCH TOAST

You can prepare this breakfast bread pudding the day before. We make ours with our Cinnamon Bread (page 62) but a good loaf of day-old challah or brioche would be wonderful. Instead of adding chocolate chips, try blueberries, raspberries, raisins, or even chopped nuts for a delicious accent.

Butter a 9 x 13 x 2-inch baking dish. Have all ingredients at room temperature.

Cut into ½-inch-thick slices:
    1 loaf of Cinnamon Bread or bread of your choice

If the bread is fresh, spread the slices on an unlined sheet pan and toast in the oven for 5 minutes at 350°F. Let cool.

In a medium bowl, whisk together:
    6 extra-large eggs
    3 cups milk
    1 teaspoon pure vanilla extract
    ¾ cup packed light brown sugar

Arrange the bread slices in the buttered baking dish, overlapping as needed. Pour the egg mixture over the top.

Sprinkle on top:
    ½ cup chocolate chips

Cover with plastic wrap and chill for 2 hours or overnight.

Preheat the oven to 400°F.

In a small saucepan, melt:
    2 ounces (½ stick) unsalted butter
    ¼ cup real maple syrup

Drizzle the maple butter over the bread mixture. Bake for 20 to 25 minutes, or until puffy, set, and golden brown. If desired, serve with more maple syrup.

Pretty IN PINK

Indulgent Sensations for Your Little Divas

It's time to indulge in all things pink and girly: glitz and tutus, hearts and sweethearts, sparkles and glitter galore.

If your little girl has a little diva inside, why not throw a makeup party? Pamper the guests with facials and makeovers. Keeping to the theme of sweet luxury, give out flavored lip gloss or Lipstick Cookies (page 69) for party favors. Keep everything pink: serve pink lemonade, salmon salad sandwiches (instead of tuna), watermelon, and of course our Miss Pink Cake (page 70). If the girls are young and still enjoy dressing up, gather old high heels, dresses, and scarves, and let them strut their stuff on the catwalk.

If your little one is so cute you want to "bite her cheeks off" (a favorite Hansen-Hudson family saying), then why not make a chocolate portrait of your adorable child, as on our Sweetheart Cheesecake (page 75)? Maybe your child has a crush on a movie star; surprise her with a chocolate portrait of her teen idol.

♥ Kids can: Pink Punch ♥

Maybe you are a mom who doesn't mind a little mess. If so, let your child make his or her own fruit punch. Back in the day, I used to mix up concoctions of all the liquids in my fridge—sometimes gross, sometimes absolutely mouthwatering. My son has followed in my footsteps, making his own personalized punch: grape, cranberry, passion fruit, lemonade, and water (we always dilute our juices). —Liv

♥ Kids can ♥

Let the kids add the food coloring and watch as
plain dough transforms into pretty pink dough.
When it comes time to decorate, the kids can even
help dip the lipsticks into the melted chocolate.

LIPSTICK COOKIES

Kids are sure to run this trompe l'oeil lipstick across their lips before devouring it. Pink-tinted butter cookies are dipped halfway in chocolate and overpiped with some golden lines. Serve alongside your Miss Pink Cake (page 70).

Yield: approximately 2 dozen lipstick cookies

PLAIN+SIMPLE Roll the dough into a large log, roll the log in sanding sugar, chill, slice, and bake.

Line 2 cookie sheets with parchment paper. Preheat the oven to 350°F. Have all ingredients at room temperature.

In the bowl of an electric mixer at medium speed, mix until fully incorporated:
 8 ounces (2 sticks) unsalted butter
 ½ cup sugar

Add and thoroughly incorporate:
 1 extra-large egg
 1 teaspoon pure vanilla extract

Add **pink food coloring** drop by drop until you have the desired color.

On a piece of wax paper, sift:
 3½ cups cake flour

Add the flour to the butter mixture. Mix until the dough comes together. Wrap the dough in plastic and chill for 30 minutes.

On a lightly floured board, roll the dough into 12-inch logs ½ inch in diameter. Chill the logs for 30 minutes to an hour. Cut the logs into 3-inch pieces, cutting one end on a diagonal. Arrange the cookies ½ inch apart on the cookie sheets.

Bake for 10 to 15 minutes, or until lightly colored. Let the cookies cool on the pans for 5 minutes, then transfer the cookies to a wire rack to cool completely.

In separate glass bowls, place in a microwave:
 2 cups dark wafer chocolate
 ½ cup white wafer chocolate

Melt the chocolate at 30-second intervals (approximately 3 passes in the microwave), stirring in between.

To the white chocolate, add and mix to combine:
 4 drops yellow candy color

Pour the yellow chocolate into a pastry cone and cut a small hole at the tip. Keep the chocolates warm on a heating pad or on a sheet pan set over a barely simmering double boiler.

Dip the cookies halfway into the dark chocolate; try to create a straight edge where the cookie and chocolate meet. Place the cookies on a parchment-lined half-sheet pan. Set aside to harden. Overpipe yellow stripes on the chocolate.

MISS PINK CAKE

When I was little I didn't like pink. I even cried when my mom bought me a pink raincoat for my tenth birthday. But I have grown and learned to embrace the color pink in all its facets, from baby pink to screaming neon. I even have a lucky fuchsia shirt. This playful cake pays homage to the Miss Pink in your life, whoever she may be.

Perfect for a makeup party or other girly event, our Raspberry Swirl Cake is decorated with chocolate makeup, a pink wig, and girly accessories.

A Multicolor Chocolate Method appliqué, like the wig on this cake, can utilize many hues or shades of just one. Here I chose to use a combination of light pink, neon pink, raspberry, and burgundy, but you could just as well mix it up with neon green, purple, and orange. Usually when working with the chocolate method, dark chocolate acts as the line that defines a shape. For added effect, I used colors to outline the wig instead. It creates a sense of unexpected whimsy and vibrancy. Just be careful to choose colors that have enough contrast.

The mirror that is also included in the Miss Pink Cake has no outlines at all; the two shades of pink run right up to each other. If you are daring, try to make more complex designs with abutting colors—just remember to overlap all the colors so the decoration doesn't break along the seams.

You'll find more detailed information on working with the Chocolate Method on pages 31 to 35 (Confectioners' Chocolate and the Chocolate Method) and page 76 (Shading and Portraiture).

Serves approximately 12 people

WHAT YOU WILL NEED

Cake: **8-inch round Raspberry Swirl Cake (page 73)**

Icing: **½ recipe Kaye's Buttercream (page 11) or House Buttercream (page 13)**

Filling: **1 recipe Raspberry Mousse (page 17)**

Decoration: **1½ cups white wafer chocolate to make wig, makeup, and other Miss Pink decorations**

Colors: **sky blue, pink, red, and violet candy colors (to simplify, only use pink) and neon pink liquid gel colors**

Tips: **#8, 9, or 10 round tip**

Miscellaneous: **8-inch round baking pan, 8-inch cardboard round, pastry bag, coupler, pastry cones, Miss Pink templates (page 160), half-sheet pan, parchment paper or cellophane, turntable, 10-inch (or larger) base**

PLAIN+SIMPLE Instead of making chocolate appliqué decorations, cover the cake with piped buttercream lips (to go with your lipstick cookies).

1 Bake the cake and let it cool completely. For best results, freeze for 1 hour or chill in the refrigerator for a few hours. Prepare the buttercream.

2 Prepare the Raspberry Mousse and fill and crumb coat the cake as directed on pages 23–25. Chill the filled cake for 30 minutes, or until the buttercream has set.

3 Melt the white wafer chocolate. Using the Color Mixing Chart on page 37, tint the white chocolate: approximately 2 tablespoons light pink, 2 tablespoons neon pink, and 2 tablespoons burgundy. Pour the colored chocolate into separate pastry cones. Keep the chocolates warm on a heating pad or on a sheet pan set over a barely simmering double boiler.

4 Using the templates provided, make one wig, assorted makeup and accessories, hearts, and lips. To make the wig using the Multicolor Chocolate Method Appliqué technique: Cut a small hole (1/32 to 1/16 inch in diameter) in the burgundy pastry cone. Use the burgundy chocolate to trace the outline and interior lines of the wig. Cut a medium hole (1/16 to 1/8 inch in diameter) in the light and neon pink pastry cones. Fill in the wig with the two pinks. Let the chocolate flow up to the outline by itself, pushing it with the tip if need be. Make sure the colors overlap each other; this will prevent the design from breaking along the seams. The chocolate should be approximately 1/8 inch thick, but it can be thicker. Set aside to harden.

5 Prepare the colored buttercream: approximately 1/2 cup neon pink and 2 cups light pink. Ice the cake with a flat finish as directed on pages 26–27. Adhere the cardboard round supporting the cake to your base.

6 Place the neon pink buttercream in a pastry bag with a coupler, and with a #10 round tip, pipe a lip border (see below) around the base of the cake.

7 Pipe a dab of buttercream onto the underside of the wig. Invert it and set it carefully in the middle of the cake. Place the makeup, accessories, hearts, and lips randomly around the top and sides of the cake.

LIPS

Tips: any round tip (such as #4, 8, or 10)

Hold the bag nearly perpendicular to the cake surface and lightly touch the pastry tip to the surface of the cake where you want to start piping. Lift up the tip slightly as you begin to apply light pressure and move the bag to the right at a 45-degree angle. Increase pressure as you move the bag up and down to form the shape of the upper lip, and then release pressure as you move the bag down to the right and tail off. Start the lower lip below the starting point of the upper lip, applying light pressure as you move the tip downward at a 30-degree angle, increasing pressure toward the center of the lip, and then decreasing pressure to tail off at the end point of the upper lip.

RASPBERRY SWIRL CAKE

The tang of raspberry swirled together with the rich buttery goodness of our pound cake makes a dreamy combination. And the pink tint imparted to the batter by the raspberries is perfect for our Miss Pink Cake.

Yield: one 8-inch layer cake

PLAIN+SIMPLE Bake the pound cake in a Bundt pan for 55 to 60 minutes (covering after 45 minutes) or until a cake tester inserted into the center comes out clean. Let the cake cool, slice it, and serve it with fresh raspberries and whipped cream.

Grease and flour two 8-inch round cake pans. Preheat the oven to 350°F. Have all ingredients at room temperature.

In the bowl of an electric mixer, beat at high speed until light and fluffy:
- **10 ounces (2½ sticks) unsalted butter, melted and cooled**
- **3 cups confectioners' sugar**

Add and cream at high speed until light and fluffy:
- **3 extra-large eggs**

On a piece of wax paper, sift together:
- **2¾ cups cake flour**
- **1 teaspoon baking powder**
- **¼ teaspoon kosher salt**

Add the dry ingredients to the butter and egg mixture and mix on low speed until smooth.

Remove half (approximately 2½ cups) of the batter and place it in a medium bowl. Add to the medium bowl and mix to combine:
- **¼ cup milk**
- **½ teaspoon pure vanilla extract**

In a food processor or blender, puree:
- **1 cup raspberries (fresh or frozen)**

Strain the raspberry puree (to remove any seeds) into a small bowl. Stir in:
- **½ teaspoon natural raspberry extract**

Add the raspberry mixture to the batter in the bowl of the electric mixer and mix to combine.

Using a large ice cream scoop or spoon, scoop the two batters alternately into the prepared pans. Fill one pan two-thirds full and the other pan one-third full. Using a cake tester or paring knife, make a circular pattern in the batter. This will create a pinwheel or swirled pattern. Bake the less full pan for 20 to 24 minutes and the fuller pan for 30 to 35 minutes, or until a cake tester inserted into the center of the cake comes out clean.

Cool the cakes on a wire rack for 15 to 20 minutes before turning them out of their pans.

Basic Piped Forms

A great alternative to Chocolate Method decorations are piped designs. Here are some basic forms to practice:

- Lines—The best starting place for a novice decorator is with piping lines. From there, you can pipe words, linear shapes (flowers), lace, and many other details. This one form, when manipulated, will teach you almost all you need to know about piping. By changing the amount of pressure you apply to the pastry bag, even using just one size tip, you can change the line's width—perfect for a "crazy" border or cloud border. Lines can be piped with round tips or even flat, star, or petal tips.

- Dots—This fundamental form is used for polka dots, animal heads, ears, and eyes, rattles, baseballs, and various other structural elements. Hold the bag perpendicular to the cake surface. Keeping the tip stationary, apply consistent pressure until the dot is the desired size. Release the pressure and tail off gently to the side or in a spiral to give a rounded finish.

- Teardrops—This shape is the basis for shell and bead borders, hearts, balloons, ballet slippers, booties, daisy petals, fish, and other tapered forms. Hold the bag at a 45-degree angle to the cake surface. Rest the tip where you are going to begin piping the bead. Without moving the bag, apply heavy, consistent pressure, allowing the tip to rise as the icing builds. Once the bead has formed, decrease the pressure while dragging the tip downward, forming a tail. For large teardrop shapes, such as balloons, booties, and ballet slippers, the angles may differ slightly: Instead, hold the bag at a 75-degree angle. Lift up the coupler (no tip necessary) slightly as you begin to apply heavy pressure and hold in place until a ball forms, release pressure as you drag the tip downward, forming a point at the end. The bag angle may change slightly, nearing perpendicularity, as you near the point. One variation of the teardrop is the point; instead of dragging the tip downward, pull upward. This is great for grass, animal manes, ears, and fins.

For more information on piping, see pages 28–30.

SWEETHEART CHEESECAKE

When I think of birthday cake I don't usually think of cheesecake, but some cheesecake lovers would have nothing else. My cousin Andre is among them, and appropriately, he is the father of Lina, who adorns our Sweetheart Cheesecake.

Nothing wows a crowd like a realistic portrait made in chocolate. For your sweetheart, add hearts, stars, or chocolate balloons. If your little one has dreams of stardom, pipe a stage curtain behind the portrait and emblazon it with stars, or pipe a billboard with your future sensation's name in lights.

Serves approximately 20 people

WHAT YOU WILL NEED

Cake: **10-inch Classic Cheesecake (page 81)**

Decoration: **approximately ½ cup dark wafer chocolate and 3 cups white wafer chocolate to make**

portrait and hearts (optional: ¼ cup frosting to adhere the portrait to the cake)

Colors: **pink candy colors or colors to match your portrait**

Miscellaneous: **10-inch baking pan, half-sheet pan, pastry cones, portrait of your choice, cellophane, sheet of blank white paper, paintbrush, 12-inch (or larger) base**

---

1 Bake the cheesecake and let it cool completely. Place the cake on its base.

2 Melt the dark wafer and white wafer chocolates separately. Using the Color Mixing Chart on page 37, tint the white chocolate: approximately 2 tablespoons light pink and 2 tablespoons medium pink, leaving the remaining chocolate untinted. Place the chocolates in separate pastry cones. Cut a small hole at the tip of each. Make a chocolate portrait as directed on page 72. Pipe out pink hearts. To make a chocolate heart: Lightly squeeze and hold in place until a dot forms, then release pressure as you drag the point at a 45-degree angle down to the right,

forming a teardrop shape. Pipe another equal-size ball to the right of the first and touching the first, and release pressure as you drag the point at a 45-degree angle down to the left, forming a teardrop shape. The two points of the teardrops should fuse, forming the point of the heart.

3 If you have any buttercream on hand, place a dollop on the underside of the portrait. If not, pipe a dot of chocolate onto the underside of the portrait. Invert it and set it carefully in the middle of the cheesecake. Place a dot of chocolate on the back of each heart and adhere them randomly around the top and sides of the cake.

The Chocolate Method
SHADING AND PORTRAITURE

There are a few considerations when choosing a portrait to replicate in chocolate. Black-and-white images are often easier to work from. The photograph should have good contrast and a range of values from white to black. If the image is washed out or blurry it can be more difficult to copy.

If you'd like to add color, I recommend keeping the colors as simple as possible. In addition, mix the colors a shade lighter than they appear in the photograph, skin tones in particular. For light skin I generally use small amounts of orange candy color for tinting. For olive skin I start with the orange base and add small amounts of green, yellow, or chocolate. For brown skin tones, start with the orange base and add dark chocolate, drop by drop. Usually all of the shading, regardless of the skin tone, is done with painted dark chocolate. Highlights can be painted using thin layers of a lighter version of the base skin tone or white. Blush tones can be added to cheeks, but if the color is too bright it can look tacky, or if the brushwork is not smooth the skin can have a ruddy appearance.

Try to paint each shadow in one fluid stroke. There is a fine line between too much shadowing and too little. Too much and the face can look overworked, muddy, or choppy; too little and it lacks definition. I recommend keeping it simple, but this does not mean omitting key shadows. Certain shadows, like the one that often appears below the lower lip, give facial structure. The shadow near the bridge of the nose adds depth to the eye socket, and shadows on the neck help to define the jawline.

When I teach students how to paint chocolate shadows on a portrait, I encourage them to turn the image upside down; this abstracts the face and prevents the painter from overthinking what a face "should" look like. Sometimes there is a line around the eye but often it is not visible in the photograph; instead it may be a spattering of lashes or a deep shadow on top. The biggest challenge—and the biggest help—is to think of what you are painting as a grouping of lights and darks, not as a face.

Photograph of your favorite star, heartthrob, or child

Half-sheet pan

Cellophane

½ cup dark wafer chocolate and approximately 2 cups (more or less depending on your image) white wafer chocolate

Pink candy color (or colors to match your portrait)

1 sheet of blank white paper the approximate size of the photograph you are painting

Soft-bristled paintbrush, preferably acrylic or sable #1 or 2

Pastry cones

Small glass or other microwave-safe bowls

Rubber spatulas

Small saucepan with a cake pan or cookie sheet on top to act as a "double boiler" and palette

Optional: Heating pad to keep the chocolate pastry cones at their ideal temperature

1 Place the photograph on a sheet pan or flat surface. Cover the photograph with cellophane. If necessary, lightly secure the cellophane with one or two pieces of tape.

2 Melt the white and dark wafer chocolates separately (see pages 32–33 for how to melt chocolate). If desired, tint a small amount of the white chocolate for accents (I used 2 tablespoons of pink) or, if making a color portrait, tint the white chocolate accordingly.

3 Pour the dark, white, and tinted chocolates into separate pastry cones. Keep the chocolates warm on a heating pad or on a cake pan or cookie sheet placed on top of a saucepan filled with barely simmering water. The temperature should be adjusted often. If the heat is too high the chocolate will bake and seize; if the heat is too low it will not stay in the necessary liquid state.

4 Cut a very small hole in the dark chocolate pastry cone.

5 With a fine line, trace the outline of the face and hairline. Trace all other visible lines: where black and white areas meet, eyelashes, nostrils, hair, pupils, and the like. Place a sheet of white paper between the photograph and the cellophane. See if you are missing any lines. Remove the white paper. If you were missing any lines, trace them now; if not, it's time to start shading.

CONTINUES

6 Pipe some dark chocolate onto the palette. Dip the paintbrush into the chocolate and move the bristles in a crosshatch pattern across the palette to evenly load the brush with chocolate. The more chocolate you have on your brush, the darker the shadow will be. Try to paint in one fluid stroke because excess brushstrokes or movement can cause a ruddy or dirty complexion. Similarly, do not overlap shadows until the initial shadow layer has set. This means planning where you will start each line of shadow beforehand. Usually you will get only one or two passes of the brush before you have to remelt the chocolate on the palette. Some shadows will be semitransparent. Practice on the side before moving onto the portrait. Once much of the original photograph is obscured, place the white paper between the cellophane and the photograph again. Remove the original photograph.

7 Now start to layer shadows and darken the image as needed by referring to the original photograph. When overlapping a layer of previously painted shadow, do not press too hard with the brush because the warm chocolate may remelt the under layer. By overlapping shadows in this manner you can go from light to dark, creating a mottled effect.

8 For hair, you can cover a large area with chocolate brushstrokes, let set, and then gently carve negative space back into it with the other end of your brush or with a toothpick.

Note: If there are any large areas of solid black in the photograph, fill them in with piped dark chocolate, but save this step for last. As large and thick areas of chocolate set they may warp off the cellophane, and later when you fill in colors next to this area, the colors may bleed under the warped section. Similarly, any large area of any color should be filled after all of the other details are complete.

9 If desired, paint in subtle colored accents.

10 Once you feel the image is complete, it is time to cover it with white chocolate. Cut a medium to large hole in the white chocolate pastry cone. Pipe the chocolate over the entire photograph, being careful not to let the tip scrape against the cellophane as this may smear, blur, or erase the dark chocolate. Instead, hover the pastry tip slightly above the cellophane. Make sure the white chocolate is at least 1/8 inch thick. If it is too thin the piece is more likely to break when handled. Also make sure the white chocolate is about body temperature. If it is too hot it will remelt the dark chocolate, causing blurring or erasure. Set the portrait aside to harden.

11 When the chocolate is hardened, carefully flip the design and gently peel off the cellophane.

Kids can make this easy-as-pie crust for you. Just give them a bowl and a spoon and let the stirring begin. They can even try molding the crust into the bottom of the pan.

CLASSIC CHEESECAKE

When it comes to cheesecake, I like mine New York–style, baked in a graham cracker crust. And it's not just me who loves this classic; whenever I take it to a party, it's the first dessert to go. To make it extra special, don't be afraid to add some crushed Oreos to the batter.

Yield: one 10-inch round cheesecake

Grease a 10 x 3-inch round cake pan and line the bottom with parchment paper. Preheat the oven to 350°F. Have all ingredients at room temperature.

Graham Cracker Crust

In a medium bowl, mix:

- 1½ cups ground graham crackers
- 2 tablespoons sugar

Stir in:

- 4 tablespoons plus 2 teaspoons melted unsalted butter

Pour the graham cracker crust into the prepared pan. Press firmly onto the bottom and one-third of the way up the sides.

Filling

In the bowl of an electric mixer, beat at medium speed until smooth, scraping down the bowl often:

- 2½ pounds cream cheese (five 8-ounce boxes)

Gradually beat in:

- 1¾ cups sugar
- 3 tablespoons all-purpose flour

When the sugar and flour are combined, scrape the bowl again and add at low speed:

- ¼ cup heavy cream
- ½ cup sour cream
- 2 tablespoons fresh lemon juice
- 1 teaspoon pure vanilla extract

Mix well, scraping the bowl down often. When the mixture is combined, add, one at a time:

- 4 extra-large eggs

Pour the filling into the prepared crust.

Place the prepared pan in a larger pan and fill the larger pan halfway with hot water. Bake for 1 hour and 20 minutes, or until lightly golden and set. Remove the cheesecake from its water bath and let it sit at room temperature for 1 to 2 hours before unmolding. To remove the cheesecake from the pan, run a paring knife around the edge of the cake, close to the pan so as not to break the crust. Cover the top of the cheesecake with plastic wrap and place a cake round or flat plate on top. Invert the cake onto the plate. Slowly lift off the cake pan and peel off the parchment paper. Place another cake round or flat plate on top and invert again. Carefully peel the plastic wrap off without pulling off the skin of the cheesecake.

Digging for TREASURE

Adventurous TREATS *for* *Young Explorers*

What is your idea of treasure? Is it a chest filled with jewels, a rare dinosaur fossil, or your child? OK, that was a trick question, but why not indulge your little "treasure's" favorite fantasy for a day? Does she want to be a paleontologist digging for T. rex skeletons? Does he dream of sailing the seven seas in search of gold? Or does she simply want to shovel sand to find a beautiful seashell?

Start by transforming your home. If it's the Caribbean of yesteryear you want to re-create, hoist the Jolly Roger flag and fill the sandbox. Dress the table with netting and booty (fake jewels), or get a large roll of kraft paper and help your child draw a treasure map; this can be your tablecloth. For fun, plan a treasure hunt. Give written clues that guide the kids on a hunt through your yard or house. Each clue leads them to an X with a small offering, maybe pirate patches for all the children, handkerchiefs to wrap around their heads, or golden chocolate coins. The final clue leads them back to the table, where a three-dimensional treasure chest cake and pirate cookies await.

If it's an excavation site you envision, simply hide small toy dinosaurs in the dirt or in a sandbox, and let them dig. The best discovery of the party will surely be the Dinosaur Cake (page 90). You can make it scarier or cartoonier depending on the age of the birthday child.

If it's fun in the sun and sand you are after, host a beach party, even if you're not at the shore. Invite guests to bring towels and wear their bathing suits. Relax poolside or sprinkler-side, toss beach balls and lounge on floats, and dig your toes into the sand (-box). Make a sand castle with cake, buttercream, and graham cracker "sand."

TREASURE CHEST CAKE

Don your eye patch and whip up this treasure of a cake. The faux wood-grain buttercream, gold-studded chocolate "leather" binding, and gilded coins will have your guests thinking they've found a real pirate's booty.

Serves 12 to 15 people

· ·
WHAT YOU WILL NEED
· ·

Cake: **9 x 13-inch Freckled Orange Cake (page 86)**

Icing: **approximately ½ recipe Kaye's Buttercream (page 11), 10 ounces semisweet chocolate to make chocolate buttercream**

Filling: **1 recipe Whipped Cream (page 17) or ½ recipe Whipped Milk Chocolate Ganache (page 19)**

Decoration: **2 cups dark wafer chocolate and ½ cup white wafer chocolate to make trimming and lock, foil-wrapped chocolate coins, or candy necklaces, candy rings, and assorted candies of your choice**

Color: **yellow candy color**

Miscellaneous: **9 x 13-inch baking pan, cardboard cut to 5¼ x 7½ inches, pastry bag, coupler, pastry cones, lock template (page 165), half-sheet pan, parchment paper or cellophane, 10 x 12-inch (or larger) base**

1 Bake the cake and let it cool completely. For best results, freeze for 1 hour or chill in the refrigerator for a few hours.

2 Prepare the buttercream and melt the semisweet chocolate. Prepare the chocolate buttercream, stirring in 8 ounces of melted chocolate. Place ¼ cup of the chocolate buttercream in a small bowl and mix it with the remaining 2 ounces of melted chocolate.

3 Using a serrated knife, cut the cake in half vertically so that you have two 9 x 6½-inch pieces. Cut off the domes and set them aside. Stack the two cakes. Use a serrated knife and, keeping the knife horizontal, cut one layer of the cake in half. Place the uncut layer in the middle of the two cut layers. Place the cardboard rectangle on the top.

Using the cardboard and the bottom of the cake as a guide, trim the cake at an angle (the cake will look flared). Invert so that the cardboard is now underneath the cake.

4 Prepare the Whipped Cream or a filling of your choice. Fill the cake as directed on page 23. When filled, spread ¼ cup of buttercream on top. Place one of the reserved domes on top. Repeat buttercream. Using a serrated knife, trim the domes so that they are higher at the center and flush with the top edge around the sides. Crumb coat the cake as directed on page 25. Chill the filled cake for 30 minutes, or until the buttercream has set.

5 Melt the dark wafer and white wafer chocolates separately. Using the Color Mixing Chart on

page 37, tint the white chocolate yellow. Pour the chocolates into separate pastry cones. Using the template provided, make the lock as described in the Multicolor Chocolate Method Appliqué technique (page 72, step 4). In addition, on the half-sheet pan, pipe four ½ x 10-inch strips of chocolate, four ½ x 8-inch strips of chocolate, and eight ½ x 6-inch strips of chocolate. These strips should be approximately ¼ inch thick. Set aside to harden. When the chocolate has set, pipe yellow dots along the strips. If you notice the chocolate warping off the pan, carefully place a piece of parchment paper and another half-sheet pan on top of the set chocolate. Do not press down as this may crack the chocolate; instead, let the weight of the pan slowly flatten the chocolate.

6 Ice the cake with chocolate buttercream. Adhere the cardboard rectangle supporting the cake to your base.

7 Place the darker chocolate buttercream in a pastry cone and cut a small to medium hole in the tip. Pipe faux wood grain around the sides of the chest: horizontal lines, undulating parallel lines, and some swirled knots.

8 Score, then cut or break the chocolate strips. You should have four 9-inch strips, four 6-inch strips, and eight 4-inch strips, but be sure to double-check the measurements against the sides of your cake before making the final cut. Adhere the chocolate strips to the edges of your cake. Each side of the cake will have four strips: one at the top edge, one at the bottom edge, and one on each side edge. Place the side pieces on first, flush with the base and approximately ½ inch from the top border. Place the top strip so it rests on the top of the two side segments. Place the bottom strip on last. If needed, pipe a line of buttercream on the underside to secure the chocolate in place. Adhere the lock to the front of the cake, centered directly beneath the top strip.

9 Arrange the coins or candies on the top of the cake (using buttercream as glue if necessary). Fill in the spaces between the coins with chocolate to give the effect of shadow.

PLAIN+SIMPLE Bake the batter in cupcake liners, frost, and place a couple of gold coins and a dusting of graham cracker crumbs on top of each cupcake.

FRECKLED ORANGE CAKE

My four-year-old son and I were leaving the bakery when he said he wanted to make an orange cake. I promised him we could make it when we got home. So, true to my word, as soon as we arrived home I took out the butter and eggs from the fridge and he grabbed some oranges from the bowl on our counter. After gathering the remaining ingredients, we mixed and mixed. Even though my son loves the mixing and pouring, he rarely eats his creations—unless they are chocolate. So, I decided at the last minute to add some grated chocolate. I thought it was delicious, and he agreed. —Liv

Yield: one 9 x 13-inch cake

PLAIN+SIMPLE VARIATION Bake in a Bundt pan and drizzle with chocolate.

Grease and flour a 9 x 13-inch pan. Preheat the oven to 350°F. Have all ingredients at room temperature.

In the bowl of an electric mixer, beat at high speed until light and fluffy:
> **8 ounces (2 sticks) unsalted butter**
> **2 cups sugar**

Reduce the speed to medium.

Add one at time, mixing well after each addition:
> **4 large eggs**

Add and mix to combine:
> **1 tablespoon finely grated orange zest**

On a piece of wax paper, sift together:
> **3 cups all-purpose flour**
> **½ teaspoon baking powder**
> **½ teaspoon baking soda**
> **1 teaspoon kosher salt**

In a small bowl, combine:
> **¼ cup fresh orange juice (from approximately 1 orange)**
> **¾ cup milk**

Add the dry ingredients and the juice mixture alternately to the egg and butter mixture.

Add and mix until evenly distributed:
> **1 cup (approximately 3 ounces) grated or finely chopped semisweet chocolate**

Pour the batter into the prepared pan. Bake for 45 minutes to 1 hour, or until a cake tester inserted into the center comes out clean. Cool on a wire rack for 15 minutes before turning out of the pan to cool completely.

PIRATE COOKIES

This rather youthful buccaneer is ready for adventure. The skull and cross-bones emblem on his chocolate sugar cookie hat warns that he is mischievous, but that cherubic face tells you it's all in fun.

To create a swarthy pirate or change the skin color, knead one table-spoon at a time of chocolate sugar cookie dough into the plain sugar cookie dough, until you have the desired tone. For added fun, cut out additional cookie circles, cut the circles in half, and use them to form the pirate's torso. Pipe colored stripes across the shirt with tinted chocolate or royal icing.

Optional: Replace all of the chocolate detail work with royal icing.

Yield: 30 pirate cookies

··· WHAT YOU WILL NEED ···

Cookie: **1 recipe Chocolate Sugar Cookies (page 88) for pirate hats and 1 recipe Sugar Cookies (page 48) for pirate faces**

Decoration: **1 cup dark wafer chocolate and 1 cup white wafer chocolate; an assortment of candy colors**

Miscellaneous: **2 half-sheet pans, pastry cones, pirate hat template (page 165), and 3-inch round cookie cutter**

1 Bake the pirate hat and face cookies and let them cool completely.

2 Melt the dark and white chocolates separately. Pour the chocolates into separate pastry bags. Cut small holes at the tip of each bag. Keep the chocolate warm on a heating pad or on a half-sheet pan over a barely simmering double boiler.

3 Pipe a ¼-inch dot of chocolate on the top of each round cookie. Before the chocolate sets, place the pirate hat on top so that it covers the top of the head. The chocolate, once set, acts as glue.

4 Using the white chocolate, pipe a skull and crossbones on each hat.

5 Using the dark chocolate, pipe hair coming out from under the hat, eyes, nose, smile, and stubble.

CHOCOLATE SUGAR COOKIES

Here is the chocolate cousin of our versatile and delicious Sugar Cookies (page 48). If making the pirate cookies, place half of the heads and half of the hats on the same baking sheet. Sometimes it is difficult to tell when chocolate cookies are baked, so this will help as they bake at the same time.

Yield: approximately 20 pirate hats

Line 2 cookie sheets with parchment paper. Preheat the oven to 350°F. Have all ingredients at room temperature.

In the bowl of an electric mixer at medium speed, cream:

4 ounces (1 stick) unsalted butter
¾ cup firmly packed light brown sugar

Add and thoroughly incorporate:

1 extra-large egg
½ teaspoon pure vanilla extract

On a piece of wax paper, sift together:

1½ cups all-purpose flour
⅓ cup cocoa powder
¼ teaspoon baking powder
½ teaspoon kosher salt

Add the dry ingredients to the butter mixture. Mix until the dough comes together.

Wrap the dough in plastic wrap and chill in the refrigerator for 30 minutes.

On a lightly floured board, roll the dough out ¼ inch thick. Slip parchment paper under the rolled dough and transfer it to a sheet pan. Chill the dough for 30 minutes.

Cut out the hats by tracing the pirate hat template (page 164) with the blade of a paring knife. Carefully slide a metal spatula under the cookies and transfer them to the prepared cookie sheets. Arrange the hats 1 inch apart. Bake for 10 to 15 minutes, or until set. Let the cookies cool in the pans for 5 minutes, then transfer the cookies to a wire rack to cool completely.

SOUR CREAM CHOCOLATE CAKE

While sour cream creates a wonderful moist consistency, it does not take away any of the chocolate flavor from this delicious dark cake.

Yield: one 9-inch round layer cake

Grease and flour two 9-inch round cake pans. Preheat the oven to 350°F. Have all ingredients at room temperature.

In the bowl of an electric mixer, beat at high speed until light and fluffy:

- **12 ounces (3 sticks) unsalted butter**
- **3 cups sugar**

Add slowly and beat on medium speed until well creamed:

- **4 extra-large eggs**
- **1 teaspoon pure vanilla extract**

On a piece of wax paper, sift together:

- **2½ cups all-purpose flour**
- **1 cup cocoa powder**
- **1 teaspoon baking soda**
- **½ teaspoon kosher salt**

At low speed, add the dry ingredients to the butter mixture alternately with:

- **1 cup sour cream**

Gradually mix in:

- **1 cup hot coffee**

Pour 3 cups of the batter into one pan and the remaining batter into the other pan. Bake the less full pan for 20 to 25 minutes and the fuller pan for 30 to 35 minutes, or until a cake tester inserted into the center of the cake comes out clean. Cool the cakes on a wire rack for 15 to 20 minutes before turning them out of their pans.

DINOSAUR CAKE

This dinosaur isn't too scary so it is perfect for budding paleontologists of all ages. Have fun and create your child's favorite dinosaur or create your own. My son helped me design this composite: the fierce smile of a T. rex, the plates of a stegosaurus, and the googly eyes of a kooky monster. —Liv

Serves approximately 18 people

WHAT YOU WILL NEED

Cake: 9-inch Sour Cream Chocolate Cake (page 89)

Icing: ½ recipe Kaye's Buttercream (page 11) or House Buttercream (page 13)

Filling: 4 cups Whipped Cream (page 17) or Whipped Milk Chocolate Ganache (page 19)

Decoration: ¼ cup dark wafer chocolate and 3 cups white wafer chocolate to make dinosaur plates, teeth, and eyes

Colors: Yellow and green candy colors and yellow, green, and red liquid gel colors

Tips: # 7, 8, or 9 round tip

Miscellaneous: two 9-inch round baking pans, cardboard round (start with a 9-inch round), pastry bag, coupler, pastry cones, half-sheet pan, dinosaur templates (page 160), parchment paper or cellophane, turntable, 12-inch (or larger) base

1 Bake the cake and let it cool completely. For best results, freeze for 1 hour or chill in the refrigerator for a few hours. Prepare the buttercream.

2 Cut out your cardboard base in the shape of the dinosaur by cutting a 3-inch pie slice from the round (see photo).

3 Trim the cake as directed on page 22, but DO NOT discard the dome. Place the cardboard template on top of the cake and, using a small serrated knife and the cardboard as a guideline, cut out the dinosaur shape. Invert so that the cardboard is now underneath the cake. Cut the cake into 3 layers. Place the dome back on top and carve to match the underlying shape. Using a small serrated paring knife, round the outer top edge of the cake.

4 Fill the cake as directed on page 23 using 3½ cups filling. Spread an additional ½ cup of whipped cream filling on the top of the filled cake and place the carved dome on top. Crumb coat the cake with buttercream (see page 26). Chill the filled cake for 30 minutes, or until the buttercream has set.

5 Melt the dark wafer and white wafer chocolates separately. Set aside 2 tablespoons white chocolate. Using the Color Mixing Chart on page 37, tint the remaining white chocolate: approximately ¾ cup lime green and ¾ cup dark green. Pour the chocolates into separate pastry cones. Using the templates on page 160, make googly eyes, approximately 5 lime green and 5 dark green plates, and teeth as illustrated in the Silhouette and Overpiping Chocolate Method (page 56, step 6). Vary the size of the plates and teeth, making some smaller and some larger.

PLAIN+SIMPLE Although our cake is carved (just a little), feel free to keep yours round. Pipe the teeth and eyes directly onto the cake, and use Hershey's Kisses for the spikes.

6 Prepare the colored buttercream: approximately ½ cup red and 2 cups lime green. Ice the inside of the dinosaur's mouth with red buttercream. Ice the rest of the cake with lime green buttercream (see page 26, Crumbing and Icing a Curved Cake).

7 Place the eyes on the face. Stick the teeth into the mouth, pressing them one-quarter of the way down into the cake. Arrange the plates into

the top and back side of the head, pressing them one-quarter of the way down into the cake. Overlap the colors in two rows.

8 Place the remaining green buttercream in a pastry bag with a coupler, and with a round tip, pipe a border around the edge of the mouth, an eyebrow, and, if desired, a border around the bottom edge of the cake.

SAND CASTLE CAKE

This cake is a great addition to any summer-inspired celebration. The carved fortress is encrusted with faux sand (graham cracker crumbs) and chocolate sea horses.

If you want to transform this into a castle fit for a princess, ice the cake with pink buttercream and pipe accents with purple and gold. To make it fit for a king, ice the cake with fudge icing and pipe accents with gray and silver.

Serves 15 to 18 people

WHAT YOU WILL NEED

Cake: 9 x 13-inch Peanut Butter Cake (page 95)

Icing: 1 recipe Kaye's Buttercream (page 11)

Filling: 1 recipe Matt's Fudge Icing (page 14)

Decoration: 1 cup dark wafer chocolate and ½ cup white wafer chocolate to make door, windows, and sea horses, plus 1¼ cups graham cracker crumbs

Colors: yellow and orange candy colors and yellow and brown liquid gel colors

Miscellaneous: 9 x 13-inch baking pan; cardboard cut to size of sand castle (start with a 9 x 13-inch cardboard, then use the template on page 169); pastry bag; coupler; pastry cones; door, window, and sea horse templates (page 166); half-sheet pan; parchment paper or cellophane; 12 x 20-inch (or larger) base

> **PLAIN+SIMPLE** Bake cupcakes and ice them half in sea-foam green buttercream and half in a sandy yellow buttercream. Add a dash of graham cracker crumbs for textural sand. Pipe seashells or starfish on top (see page 72, step 4).

1 Bake the cake and let it cool completely. For best results, freeze the cake for 1 hour or chill in the refrigerator for a few hours. Prepare the buttercream and the fudge icing.

2 Cut out your cardboard bases in the shapes of the sand castle and two walls (see page 169).

3 Trim the dome (if any) off of the cake. Place the cardboard castle template on top, lining up the bottom with one 13-inch edge, and trace the template with a small serrated knife to cut out the castle and walls. Try to keep the segments whole (don't cut off the small squares). Invert the cake so the cardboard is now underneath the main part of the castle and place the walls on their corresponding bases. Cut each cake in half horizontally with a serrated knife. Fill the main castle cake with the prepared fudge icing. Spread ½ cup of buttercream on the top of the filled cake and place one half of each wall segment on

CONTINUES

each side, leaving about a 3-inch gap in the middle (for the door). Crumb coat the castle and half walls (see page 28). Chill the filled cake for 30 minutes, or until the buttercream has set.

4 Melt the dark wafer and white wafer chocolates separately. Using the Color Mixing Chart on page 37, tint the white chocolate: approximately 2 tablespoons yellow and 2 tablespoons orange. Using the templates provided, make the sea horses as illustrated in the Multicolor Chocolate Appliqué Method (page 72, step 4). With the remaining chocolate, pipe the castle's door and windows. While the chocolate is still soft, sprinkle the graham cracker crumbs on top. Set aside to harden.

5 Prepare approximately 3 cups of sandy yellow buttercream and use it to ice the sand castle. Before the buttercream sets, sprinkle the graham cracker crumbs over the entire cake, pressing to adhere to the sides or where needed. Use a pastry brush to dust away any extra crumbs that may have accumulated between the turrets.

6 Adhere the cardboard base supporting the cakes to your base.

7 Pipe dabs of buttercream onto the underside of the doorway, windows, and sea horses. Invert them and set them carefully onto the castle (see photograph for placement).

Piping Sea Creatures

You will need a selection of round tips (#4, 8, 10, etc.) and/or pastry cones to create these underwater creatures. For more information on piping, see pages 28–30 and page 74.

* The fish starts with a large teardrop shape for its main body and is accented with smaller teardrops for the tail, fins, and mouth, and a dot for the eye.

* The starfish has five linear forms, each coming to a point at their outer edges, which radiate out from a center point. Pin-point dots, in a contrasting color, are overpiped to add texture.

* The seashell starts with a large teardrop form. Lines are over-piped, from the top edge of the main form, ending at a point at the bottom middle. Pipe a small figure-eight overlapping the bottom.

* For an octopus, pipe eight undulating lines, each tailing off at a point from a center point. Pipe an upside-down *U*, where the two sides connect to the body. Overpipe small dots on the tentacles and for eyes.

PEANUT BUTTER CAKE

Peanut butter adds a rich and warm earthy flavor that is irresistible. Pair this cake with chocolate or—for a twist on the classic PB&J—layer the cake with jam. Substitute almond butter or cashew butter for a lighter flavor.

Yield: one 9 x 13-inch cake

Grease and flour 9 x 13-inch pan. Preheat the oven to 350°F. Have all ingredients at room temperature.

On a piece of wax paper, sift together:
- **3 cups cake flour**
- **2 teaspoons baking soda**
- **¾ teaspoon kosher salt**

In the bowl of an electric mixer, beat at high speed until light and fluffy:
- **6 ounces (1½ sticks) unsalted butter**
- **2 cups packed light brown sugar**
- **½ cup peanut butter (chunky or smooth)**

Add slowly and beat on medium speed until well creamed:
- **2 extra-large eggs**
- **1 teaspoon pure vanilla extract**

At low speed, add the dry ingredients to the butter mixture alternately with:
- **2 cups buttermilk**

Scoop the batter into the prepared pan. Bake for 35 to 40 minutes, or until a cake tester inserted into the center comes out clean. Cool on a wire rack for 10 to 15 minutes before removing the cake from its pan.

START *your* ENGINES

From Fire Trucks to Rockets, Desserts That Get You Going

There is something about the sound of a motor that gets anyone's attention. Add some dazzling red lights, blaring sirens, bursts of fire, unimaginable speed—and you can keep our attention even longer. Does your little one LOVE things that go? Does he spend hours designing Lego space ships, hovercrafts, and fire trucks? If so, start your engines.

In honor of your little spitfire, host a party that's sure to get his wheels turning. If it's the summer, break out the hose and let the kids take turns putting out pretend "fires" (which are actually stacked cans). Fire helmets make perfect party favors.

And what will really make them happy? A fire truck cake and whoopie pie wheels.

For an out-of-this-world adventure, make cupcakes decorated like planets and extra-terrestrials, or create a three-dimensional rocket cake. Then let the kids make their own rockets out of paper towel rolls or cardboard tubes. Cut out tail fins for them to tape on the sides, and stuff red and yellow tissue paper in one end of the tube to look like blasting fire. Set out bowls of colored paper scraps and stick-on letters for decorating, beads for "riveting," and cone-shaped cups for toppers.

WHOOPIE PIE WHEELS

Is it a cookie? Is it a cake? Is it a pie? Whatever it is, I know it is DE-LI-CIOUS! This version is piped to look like wheels, sandwiched together with Kids' Buttercream, and topped with chocolate rivets.

Yield: approximately 16 wheels

Prepare a half recipe of:
>   **Kids' Buttercream (page 14).**

Line two cookie sheets with parchment paper. Preheat the oven to 350°F. Have all ingredients at room temperature.

On a piece of wax paper, sift together and set aside:
>   **2 cups all-purpose flour**
>   **1 cup cocoa powder**
>   **½ teaspoon baking soda**
>   **½ teaspoon kosher salt**

In the bowl of an electric mixer, beat at high speed until well blended:
>   **4 ounces (1 stick) unsalted butter**
>   **1 cup sugar**

Add at medium speed and beat until well blended:
>   **1 extra-large egg**
>   **1 teaspoon pure vanilla extract**

At low speed, add the dry ingredients to the butter mixture alternately with:
>   **1 cup plus 2 tablespoons buttermilk**

Place the batter in a pastry bag with a coupler. On one cookie sheet, pipe one-third of the batter into sixteen 2½-inch rings (with a hole in the center), approximately 2 inches apart. On the other cookie sheet, pipe the remaining batter into sixteen solid 2½-inch circles, starting in the center and spiraling out.

Bake for 10 minutes, or until the tops are slightly cracked. Cool the "pies" completely on the pan.

With a spatula, loosen all of the pies and turn over the solid circles. Using an offset spatula or a butter knife, spread a thin layer of Kids' Buttercream onto the flat side. Carefully sandwich the rings on top. For added effect, melt:
>   **¼ cup confectioners' chocolate**

Pour the chocolate into a pastry bag and cut a small hole at the tip. Pipe chocolate dots (rivets) in the middle (buttercream part) of each wheel.

MARBLE POUND CAKE

I love baking with confectioners' sugar; it makes cookies and cakes extra tender. I can still remember my mom's melt-in-your-mouth Christmas cookies. The taste and texture has stuck with me since childhood. More than thirty years ago, when I came across this recipe with my friend Wang, it had that magic ingredient and I knew I had to try it. We made it for a party and it was a big hit.

Here's a Bakehouse trick: The pound cake batter can be frozen in its prepared pan. Bring it to room temperature before baking.

Yield: one 12 x 16-inch sheet cake or approximately 7 cups batter

Grease the bottom of a half-sheet (12 x 16-inch rimmed) pan and line it with parchment paper. Grease and flour the parchment paper and the sides of the pan. Preheat the oven to 350° F. Have all ingredients at room temperature.

In the bowl of an electric mixer, beat at high speed until light and fluffy:
> **12 ounces (3 sticks) unsalted butter**

Add slowly and cream at high speed until light and fluffy:
> **4 cups (1 pound) confectioners' sugar, sifted**

Add one at a time, mixing well after each addition:
> **6 extra-large eggs**
> **1 teaspoon pure vanilla extract**

On a piece of wax paper, sift together:
> **2¼ cups cake flour**
> **½ teaspoon baking powder**

Add to the butter mixture and mix until combined.

Pour half of the batter into a medium bowl.

Add and stir to combine:
> **3 ounces unsweetened chocolate, melted and cooled to body temperature**

Using a tablespoon, scoop the two batters alternately into the prepared pan. Rap the pan on the counter to spread the batter evenly. Using a cake tester or a paring knife, make a circular pattern in the batter. This will create a pinwheel or swirled pattern. Bake the cake for 18 to 22 minutes (cover the cake with parchment paper if it browns too quickly), or until a cake tester inserted into the center of the cake comes out clean. Cool the cake on a wire rack for 15 to 20 minutes before turning it out of its pan.

Variation:

Bake the pound cake batter in a buttered and floured Bundt pan for 45 to 55 minutes (cover the cake with parchment paper if it browns too quickly), or until a cake tester inserted into the center of the cake comes out clean.

FIRE TRUCK CAKE

If your child loves to dress up in fire boots and helmets, if he is stunned silent whenever a fire truck drives by, or if she dreams of being a firefighter when she grows up, this is the perfect cake to make for a party. The cake is shaped, but there is not much carving involved; instead, the chocolate accents give the truck its three-dimensional feel.

Serves approximately 20 people

· ·
WHAT YOU WILL NEED
· ·

Cake: **12 x 16-inch Marble Pound Cake (page 99)**

Icing: **1 recipe Kaye's Buttercream (page 11) or House Buttercream (page 13) (you will have some buttercream left over)**

Filling: **1 recipe Whipped Cream (page 17) or ½ recipe Whipped Milk Chocolate Ganache (page 19)**

Decoration: **1½ cups dark wafer chocolate and 1½ cups white wafer chocolate to make fire truck wheels and accessories**

Colors: **red, yellow, orange, black, and sky blue candy colors and red, black, and yellow liquid gel colors**

Tips: **#10 round tip, #45 flat tip**

Miscellaneous: **2 half-sheet pans, cardboard (start with a 6 x 16-inch board), pastry bags, couplers, pastry cones, fire truck accessories templates (page 165), parchment paper or cellophane, 8 x 18-inch (or larger) base**

1 Bake the cake and let it cool completely. For best results, freeze for 1 hour or chill in the refrigerator for a few hours. Prepare the buttercream.

2 Cut the 6 x 16-inch cardboard into the shape of a fire truck: starting 4½ inches from the top front edge, cut a 3 (wide) x ¾-inch (deep) notch out of the top of the cake to create a separation between the truck's cab and storage compartment. Mark a point 4 inches up from the right-hand corner, and mark a point ¾ inch to the left from the upper right-hand corner. Using these points as a guideline, cut this small triangular segment off to create an angled windshield.

3 Cut the cake in half with a serrated knife so you have two 6 x 16-inch pieces. Stack the two pieces. Place the cardboard template on top and use a small serrated knife to cut out the fire

truck. Invert so that the cardboard is now underneath the cake.

4 Prepare the filling. Fill the cake with whipped cream and crumb coat the cake with buttercream as directed on pages 23 and 25. Chill the filled cake for 30 minutes, or until the buttercream has set.

5 Melt the dark wafer and white wafer chocolates separately. Set aside ¼ cup white chocolate. Using the Color Mixing Chart on page 37, tint the remaining white chocolate: approximately 2 tablespoons red, 2 tablespoons yellow, 2 tablespoons orange, 2 tablespoons sky blue, and 2 tablespoons gray. Using the templates provided, make a ladder, windows, 5 wheels, accessories, and lights, as described in the Multicolor Chocolate Method Appliqué technique

PLAIN+SIMPLE Bake the Marble Pound Cake (page 99) in a Bundt pan, ice with an old-fashioned finish (page 28) with Kids' Buttercream (page 14), and place chocolate spots (misshapen polka dots of various sizes) all over the cake—a Dalmatian-inspired treat your kids will beg for.

(page 72) and Silhouette and Overpiping Chocolate Method (page 56, step 6).

6   Prepare the colored buttercream: approximately 3 cups red, ½ cup tan, ¼ cup gray, and ¼ cup yellow.

7   Ice the truck with the red buttercream. Adhere the cardboard supporting the cake to your base.

8   Place the yellow, gray, and tan buttercream in separate pastry bags with couplers. With a flat tip, pipe a gray line across the bottom of the truck and a yellow line across the midline of the truck. With a round tip, pipe a hose coiling back and forth on the top rear of the truck. Continue the hose down to the bottom edge and pipe around the bottom edge to the front of the cake.

9   Place the 3 top wheels on the cake, so that half of the wheel overhangs the bottom edge. Cut the extra wheels in half, and place them on the bottom border directly beneath the top wheels. Place the ladder on the back end of the truck. Invert the remaining pieces and set them carefully onto the truck (see photograph for placement).

♥ Kids can ♥

The chocolate decorations on this cake don't have many details, so they are easier for a child to make. Have your child start with piping the dark chocolate wheels or the white chocolate ladder.

ROCKET CAKE

My son's friend Cooper was turning five and after much back-and-forth (rocket, robot, rocket, vampire, rocket, snowman . . .), he decided he wanted a rocket cake. I had made his birthday cake for the past three years and was glad for the inspiration. I carved his version out of a sheet cake, but this time around I decided to try using a sponge roll, and it worked perfectly!

For best results, in addition to the roll, bake a small cone-shaped cake for the rocket's tip (using, for example, Wilton's Mini Wonder Mold; see Suppliers on page 171); this way you will not have to carve the roll. If you opt to carve the cake, you may need to scrape out some of the filling on the carved portion in order for the buttercream icing to adhere to the cake.

Serves approximately 16 people

....

WHAT YOU WILL NEED

....

Cake: 12 x 16-inch Chocolate Sponge Roll (page 104); ½ recipe Milk Chocolate Cake (page 129) baked in a Wilton Mini Wonder Mold

Icing: ½ recipe Kaye's Buttercream (page 11)

Filling: 3 to 4 cups Whipped Milk Chocolate Ganache (page 19) or Whipped Cream (page 17)

Decoration: ¼ cup dark wafer chocolate and 2 cups white wafer chocolate to make rocket accessories and one small tube of sky blue or clear piping gel

Colors: red, orange, yellow, black, and blue candy colors and black and sky blue liquid gel color

Tips: #4 or 5 round tip, #44 or 45 flat tip

Miscellaneous: half-sheet pan, pastry bag, coupler, pastry cones, rocket templates (page 167), parchment paper or cellophane, 12 x 16-inch (or larger) base

1 Bake the sponge cake and let it cool. Bake a half-recipe of Milk Chocolate Cake in cone-shaped cake molds and let them cool completely (you will only need one; snack on the unused cones).

2 Prepare the Whipped Milk Chocolate Ganache and fill the chocolate sponge cake as directed on page 104. Wrap in plastic wrap and freeze for at least 1 hour. Prepare the buttercream.

3 Melt the dark wafer and white wafer chocolates separately. Set aside 2 tablespoons white chocolate. Using the Color Mixing Chart on page 37, tint the remaining white chocolate: approximately 2 tablespoons each of red, blue, orange, and yellow, and ¾ cup of sky blue. Pour the chocolates into separate pastry cones. Using the templates provided, make the rocket parts: window, flag, number (remember to reverse the templates of all numbers before piping), thrusters with flames, and wings (one with extensions, and one with the template reversed) as described in the Multicolor Chocolate Method Appliqué technique (page 72, step 4). Set aside to harden.

4   Adhere the roll to its base. Trim one-quarter of the cone off so it will lie flat, then adhere it to one end of the roll with a dab of buttercream. Crumb coat the cake with buttercream as directed on page 26. Chill the filled cake for 30 minutes, or until the buttercream has set.

5   Ice the sponge roll and cone together with the uncolored buttercream as directed on page 26.

6   Place some of the remaining white buttercream in a pastry bag with a coupler and, with a flat tip, pipe a border around the base. Pipe stripes, approximately 3 inches apart, across the rocket.

7   Prepare ½ cup gray buttercream. Place the gray buttercream in a pastry bag with a coupler, attach a small round tip, and pipe dots on all of the piped white stripes. Pipe vertical gray lines across the bottom of the rocket. Overpipe white lines to disguise the beginning and end of the gray lines.

8   Press the extended wing (press up to approximately where the dotted line was on the template) into the bottom of the roll. Line up the other two wings (flat side up) on the sides, placing them flush with the cake. Use a dot of buttercream to adhere them to the base. Place the flag, number, and window on the top of the rocket. Fill in the window with piping gel to give the effect of reflective glass. Press the flame thrusters into the bottom side of the rocket (press up to approximately where the dotted line was on the template).

CHOCOLATE SPONGE ROLL

Every Presidents' Day we transform this sponge roll into a "Lincoln Log" with chocolate-glaze bark, piped rings on both ends, and a chocolate ax embedded in the bark. Filled with whipped cream, it is light and delicious.

Yield: one 16-inch sponge roll

PLAIN+SIMPLE Fill with whipped cream, ice with Matt's Fudge Icing, and sprinkle candy stars or white nonpareils on top.

Grease the bottom of a half-sheet (12 x 16-inch rimmed) pan and line it with parchment paper. Preheat the oven to 400°F.

In a medium bowl, whisk lightly:
- **8 extra-large egg yolks**
- **1 teaspoon pure vanilla extract**

In the bowl of an electric mixer at high speed, use a whisk attachment to beat to soft peaks:
- **1 cup egg whites (6 to 7 extra-large egg whites)**

Slowly beat in and whip until stiff peaks form:
- **¾ cup sugar**

Sift over the yolks and add alternately with the whites:
- **¼ cup cake flour**
- **⅓ cup cocoa powder**
- **¾ teaspoon baking powder**

Pour the batter into the prepared pan and spread evenly with a spatula. Bake for 7 to 9 minutes, or until the cake begins to pull away from the sides of the pan. The top should spring back when lightly touched. Cool in the pan on a wire rack. When the cake has come to room temperature, run the blade of a metal spatula around the edge of the pan to loosen it. Invert the cake onto a piece of clean parchment paper or a slightly damp towel. Carefully peel away the parchment paper from the cake.

Prepare the filling of your choice. Using a rubber or metal spatula, spread the filling evenly over the entire surface of the cake. Beginning at one long edge, roll the cake over the filling, keeping the spiral as tight as possible. Wrap in plastic wrap. If you plan on icing and decorating the cake the same day it is baked, freeze for at least 1 hour, or until the filling has set completely. If storing the cake for a later date, you can freeze it for up to 2 weeks. If you ice cakes quickly, you can work with the cake frozen, otherwise, remove the roll from the freezer and let it defrost in the refrigerator overnight before icing. This will prevent the crumb coat from sweating, which would make it difficult for the final coat of icing to adhere.

Helpful Hint: **Always separate egg yolks and whites while the eggs are cold. It makes the task easier.**

HYBRID CUPCAKES

One bite of these cupcakes reveals an added bonus: chocolaty cheesecake. They look like the surface of the moon when they bake, but the wonderful taste makes up for the craters.

Yield: 24 cupcakes

Grease the top of two standard 12-cup muffin pans and line them with paper liners. Preheat the oven to 350°F. Have all ingredients at room temperature.

Chocolate Cupcakes

Sift into the bowl of an electric mixer:

- 1 cup all-purpose flour
- ½ cup cocoa powder
- 1 teaspoon baking soda
- ½ teaspoon baking powder
- ½ teaspoon kosher salt

Add and mix to combine:

- 1 cup sugar

In a medium bowl, whisk together:

- ½ cup sour cream
- 1 extra-large egg
- ¼ cup unsalted butter, melted and cooled
- ½ cup hot tap water
- ½ teaspoon pure vanilla extract

Add to the dry ingredients, and mix at low speed for 2 minutes, scraping down the bowl halfway through.

Divide the batter evenly among the prepared cupcake molds.

Chocolate Cheesecake Filling

In a small saucepan over medium heat, mix to combine:

- ½ cup heavy cream
- ½ cup plus 2 tablespoons sugar

Bring to a boil, reduce heat to a simmer, and cook without stirring until the mixture is caramel colored (about 10 minutes). Remove from the heat and stir in:

- 5½ ounces semisweet chocolate, chopped

Stir until the chocolate is melted.

Add and stir to combine:

- ⅓ cup sour cream

In the bowl of an electric mixer, beat until smooth and creamy:

- 1 pound cream cheese (two 8-ounce packages)

Add the chocolate mixture to the cream cheese and beat on low speed just to combine, scraping down the bowl halfway through.

Still on low speed, mix in:

- 2 extra-large eggs, lightly beaten
- 1 teaspoon pure vanilla extract

Scrape down the bowl again. Mix the batter until smooth. Divide the cheesecake batter evenly over the cake batter. Each liner should be approximately three-quarters full. Bake for 20 to 25 minutes, or until the cheesecake looks set and the cupcake batter rises through the cheesecake. Cool the cupcakes on a wire rack for 15 minutes before turning them out of their pans.

OUT OF THIS WORLD CUPCAKES

Does your child reenact scenes from a galaxy far away? Does she love visiting the planetarium? Do glow-in-the-dark stars cover his bedroom ceiling? If you answered yes to any of these questions, here are the cupcakes for your next party. The enormous wonders of outer space are brought down to our size: Cupcakes are transformed into the planets in our solar system, into aliens, and even into UFOs.

Yield: 24 cupcakes

·· WHAT YOU WILL NEED ··

Cake: **24 Hybrid Cupcakes (page 105)**

Icing: **1 recipe Kids' Buttercream (page 14) and/or Matt's Fudge Icing (page 14)**

Decoration: ½ cup dark wafer chocolate and 2½ cups white wafer chocolate to make planet sections, 1 small jar of white nonpareils

Colors: black, blue, red, yellow, and green candy colors and blue, orange, and yellow liquid gel colors

Miscellaneous: two standard 12-mold muffin pans; pastry cones; planet, alien, and spacecraft templates (page 164); half-sheet pan; parchment paper or cellophane

1 Bake the cupcakes and let them cool completely. For best results, freeze for at least 1 hour.

2 Prepare the icing(s) of your choice.

3 Melt the dark wafer and white wafer chocolates separately. Set aside 2 tablespoons white chocolate. Using the Color Mixing Chart on page 37, tint the remaining white chocolate: approximately 2 tablespoons light green, 2 tablespoons green, 2 tablespoons red, 2 tablespoons orange, 2 tablespoons yellow, 2 tablespoons blue, and 2 tablespoons gray. Using the templates provided, make 24 designs as illustrated in the Assembled Chocolate Method on pages 130 and 132, step 3.

4 Prepare the colored buttercream(s) of your choice. You will need approximately 2 table-spoons to cover one cupcake. To make 2 of each of the cupcakes pictured, mix approximately ¼ cup red and ½ cup each of orange, yellow, light blue, and sky blue. Also, have ¾ cup Matt's Fudge Icing on hand.

5 Ice the cupcakes (4 light blue, 4 sky blue, 4 yellow, 4 orange, 2 red, and 6 with fudge) as directed on page 28. Ice Earth and Jupiter with their dominant color, and then use your offset spatula to spread, and lightly blend, the accent color on top.

6 Place the designs on the cupcakes (see photograph for guidance), pressing to set when needed. If the icing has set already, put a dollop of icing on the underside of each design and place it right side up on the cupcake.

STEP right UP

A One-Ring Circus Filled with Yummy Attractions

What fun, what magic, what thrills! A trip to the circus is a trip into a dream world, where almost anything is possible. You can fly on a trapeze, balance in midair, play with wild beasts, and captivate an audience with magic and laughter.

Charm your guests with a one-ring circus of your own. Everyone gets a cookie balloon, a faux ice cream cone, and funnel cake (my childhood favorite). The main attraction—a three-tiered circus cake with a big-top tent and chocolate trapeze artists, clowns, and animals— will inspire many oohs and aahs.

The entertainment can be the guests themselves: Let the children perform their own circus or magic acts. Have plenty of props to choose from, such as hats, clown makeup, dress-up clothes, balls, hoops, cards, scarves, boxes, and stuffed animals. If your child is a budding prestidigitator, let him perform his own magic show to entertain the crowd. Or hire a real magician to create illusions for all ages to enjoy.

In keeping with the illusionist theme, you (The Amazing *your name here*), might perform a little magic of your own, making chocolate rabbits hop out of a hat-shaped cake. And the audience goes wild . . . HOORAY!

CIRCUS CAKE

I love the circus, whether it is a little traveling circus like the one I saw when I was ten, the festive Big Apple Circus, or the awe-inspiring Cirque du Soleil, where my husband got taped to a pole by one of the clowns because we arrived a little late. I had too many ideas to fit on one cake, so this one is tiered. The bottom tier is the center ring, where the animals and clowns perform. The second tier is where the acrobats, trapeze artists, and tightrope walkers strut their stuff, and the big top, on the uppermost tier, rises above them all.

Serves approximately 25 people

WHAT YOU WILL NEED

Cake: 8-inch, 6-inch, and 4-inch round White Chocolate Cake (page 113)

Icing: 1 recipe Kaye's Buttercream (page 11) or House Buttercream (page 13)

Filling: 1 recipe Whipped White Chocolate Ganache (page 19)

Decoration: ½ cup dark wafer chocolate and 3 cups white wafer chocolate to make circus figures, details, and tent top, plus one small jar of colored sprinkles or nonpareils

Colors: pink, red, orange, yellow, purple, blue, and green candy colors and yellow, red, and blue liquid gel colors

Tips: #4 or 5 round tip, #44 or 45 flat tip

Miscellaneous: 8-, 6-, and 4-inch round pans, one 8-inch cardboard round, two 6-inch cardboard rounds, two 4-inch cardboard rounds, pastry bags, couplers, pastry cones, circus templates (page 167), half-sheet pan, parchment paper or cellophane, ⅛-inch- to ¼-inch-diameter wooden dowels (drinking straws can substitute), clean pruning shears (or kitchen scissors), 12-inch (or larger) wood or other sturdy base

1 Bake the cakes and let them cool completely. For best results, freeze for 1 hour or chill in the refrigerator for a few hours. Prepare the buttercream.

2 Prepare the filling. Fill and crumb coat each individual cake as described on pages 23 and 25. Chill the filled cakes for 30 minutes, or until the buttercream has set.

3 Melt the dark and white wafer chocolates in separate bowls. Set aside 2 tablespoons white chocolate. Using the Color Mixing Chart on page 37, tint the remaining white chocolate: approximately 2 tablespoons each of pink, red, orange, light peach, yellow, royal blue, light blue, lavender, lime green, and light to medium brown. Pour the chocolates into separate pastry cones. Using the templates provided, make the circus characters, two tent roofs, balloons, polka dots, popcorn, pretzels, and tent ruffles as directed in the Multicolor Chocolate Method Appliqué technique (page 72, step 4). Extend the bottom of the tent tops into a 1-inch triangle with chocolate, as noted on the template. Set aside to harden.

To lift and transfer a cake:
Slide an offset spatula under the cardboard supporting the cake and use it to lift the cake on one side. Slide your hand under the cake, moving the spatula to the opposite side. Carefully lift the cake, making sure it is balanced, and line it up with the center of the bottom tier, using the line you drew as a guide for placement. Let part of the edge (not held by your hand or spatula) rest on the guideline, and then slowly remove your hand. When the cake is almost completely resting on the bottom tier, slowly remove the spatula, pulling it up at a slight angle so as not to disturb the icing of the bottom tier.

4 Set aside ½ cup of uncolored buttercream. Prepare the colored buttercream: approximately 2 cups yellow, 1 cup blue, and ½ cup red.

5 Ice the 8-inch cake with yellow buttercream. Glue the cardboard round supporting this bottom tier to the center of your base.

6 Lightly place a 6-inch cardboard cake round in the center of the bottom tier (or hold the round slightly above the tier), and mark the circumference of the cake round with a toothpick. Carefully remove the cake round without disturbing the buttercream. Press a dowel all the way into the center of the cake. (Ideally the cake is level

CONTINUES

and all points are the same height.) Mark the dowel at the buttercream line with a pencil or hold it with your finger. Remove the dowel and cut it 1/16 inch shorter than that line, using clean pruning shears. Using this dowel as a guide, cut 4 more dowels to the same length. Insert the dowels into the cake, placing 1 dowel in the center and the remaining dowels in a circle around it, all within the demarcation.

7 Ice the 6-inch tier with blue buttercream and center it on top of the bottom tier, using the line you drew as a guide for placement. Cut and insert 3 dowels (as in step 6), arranged in a triangle, to support the top tier.

8 On the 4-inch cake, freehand pipe a tent opening in melted chocolate (see photograph). Starting at the point, fill in the tent opening with the melted chocolate. Once the area is filled, scrape the excess chocolate off of the bottom edge before it sets. Place the remaining uncolored buttercream and the red buttercream in separate pastry bags with couplers. With a flat tip, pipe alternating red and white vertical stripes around the sides of the 4-inch cake, keeping the chocolate area clear. Pipe alternating red and white stripes on the top of the cake. Pipe a red sash around the tent opening to disguise where the stripes and chocolate meet. Center the cake on top of the middle tier.

9 Place the remaining blue buttercream in a pastry bag with a coupler, and with a #44 tip, pipe a flat border around the base of the cake. Pipe a flat red border on top of the blue, followed by another blue on top of the red. Adhere the animals and clowns randomly around the bottom tier. Some can overlap. Fill in with polka dots.

10 Place approximately 2 tablespoons of yellow buttercream in a pastry cone and freehand pipe ropes (slightly curved parallel lines for the trapeze artists and single lines for the tightrope walkers) around the middle tier. Adhere the trapeze artists and tightrope walkers to the ropes. Place chocolate balloons around the base of the middle tier.

11 Place the tent ruffles around the top and bottom borders of the 4-inch cake. Change the tip on the red bag to a round tip and pipe a loopy border on top of the ruffles. Lightly mark the position of the tent roofs on the top tier with their points. They should be centered with their backs facing each other. Stick a thin knife into the cake at these points. Carefully press the tent roofs into the slits until their bottoms are resting on the icing. Fill in the empty spaces between them with piped confetti using the leftover tinted buttercream. Lean the ringmaster against the tent.

WHITE CHOCOLATE CAKE

White chocolate has a very distinctive yet subtle flavor. To enhance the cake's flavor we add flecks of white chocolate and fill it with white chocolate mousse.

Yield: one 3-tiered layer cake (4-inch, 6-inch, and 8-inch layered rounds)

PLAIN+SIMPLE Bake this cake in fun cupcake liners and place dollops of white chocolate mousse on top with chocolate balloons.

Grease and flour two 8-inch round pans, two 6-inch round pans, and two 4-inch round pans. Preheat the oven to 350°F. Have all ingredients at room temperature.

In the bowl of an electric mixer, beat at high speed until light and fluffy:

- 8 ounces (2 sticks) unsalted butter
- 2⅔ cups sugar
- 2 teaspoons kosher salt

Add and mix well:

- 8 ounces melted white chocolate, cooled but still in a liquid state

On a piece of wax paper, sift together:

- 4½ cups cake flour
- 1 tablespoon baking powder
- 1 teaspoon cream of tartar

Add the dry ingredients to the butter mixture alternately with:

- 1½ cups milk
- 1 teaspoon pure vanilla extract

Mix in:

- 2 cups (6 ounces) grated white chocolate

In a clean bowl of the electric mixer, with a whisk attachment, whip to stiff peaks:

- 6 extra-large egg whites (1 cup)

Continue beating and slowly add:

- ¼ cup sugar

Gently fold the egg whites into the batter.

Fill one 4-inch pan with 1 cup batter and the other with ½ cup batter. Fill one 6-inch pan with 2½ cups batter and the other with 1 cup batter. Fill one 8-inch pan with 4 cups batter and the other with 2⅓ cups batter. Bake the low 4-inch for 23 to 25 minutes and the high 4-inch for 30 to 33 minutes. Bake the low 6-inch for 25 to 28 minutes and the high 6-inch for 36 to 40 minutes. Bake the low 8-inch for 27 to 30 minutes and the high 8-inch for 42 to 45 minutes, or until a cake tester inserted into the center comes out clean. Cool on a wire rack for 5 to 10 minutes before removing the cakes from their pans.

BALLOON COOKIES

I found my balloon cookie cutter online (see Suppliers, pages 171 to 172), but if you can't find a "party balloon" cutter, an egg, snow globe, or diamond ring cookie cutter will also work.

Yield: approximately 24 cookies

WHAT YOU WILL NEED

Cookies: **24 Lemon Butter Cookies (page 116)**

Icing: **1 recipe (or 1 cup) Simple Lemon Glaze (page 116)**

Decoration: **twenty-four 6- or 8-inch lollipop sticks**

Colors: **red, yellow, green, blue, and pink liquid gel colors (or choose one color)**

Miscellaneous: **half-sheet baking pan, 3-inch balloon cookie cutter, pastry cones**

1 Bake the cookies and let them cool completely. Prepare the Simple Lemon Glaze.

2 Place 1 tablespoon of glaze in a pastry cone and cut a small hole at the tip. Prepare the colored icing using the remaining glaze: approximately 3 tablespoons each of red, yellow, green, blue, and pink.

3 Spread a thin layer of the colored icing over each cookie. Do not hold the cookies by the lollipop stick while spreading; instead, hold the cookie or keep the cookie on the sheet pan. Use the uncolored glaze to pipe a "white" highlight on the upper right side of each balloon. Let the cookies dry overnight.

Note: The lemon glaze reacts with the colors; purple turns immediately gray when mixed in, and what is initially a vibrant red (or yellow, green, or blue) may frost over as it dries—but they are still quite pretty. If you want pure colors, use Royal Icing (page 15).

♥ *Kids can* ♥

Have your child help cut out the balloon-shaped cookies and arrange them on the half-sheet pan. Teach them to press firmly into the dough so the cookie cutter cuts all the way through, and then give the cookie cutter a little shake, which will release the cookie. Then show them how to scoop up the cookies with a spatula and slide them onto the sheet pan.

LEMON BUTTER COOKIES

The addition of cream cheese to the dough gives these cookies a slight tang that you don't get from a plain butter cookie. I added lemon zest to give it some extra zing, and I was quite pleased with the flavor and texture.

Yield: approximately 24 cookies

Line 2 cookie sheets with parchment paper. Preheat the oven to 350°F. Have all ingredients at room temperature.

In the bowl of an electric mixer at medium speed, mix 1 minute to combine:
  4 ounces (1 stick) unsalted butter
  3 ounces cream cheese

Add and mix to combine:
  1½ cups confectioners' sugar

Add and thoroughly incorporate:
  1 extra-large egg
  ½ teaspoon pure vanilla extract
  1 tablespoon finely grated lemon zest

On a piece of wax paper, sift together:
  2¼ cups all-purpose flour
  ¼ teaspoon baking powder

Add the dry ingredients to the butter mixture. Mix until the dough comes together.

Wrap in plastic wrap and chill for 30 minutes.

On a lightly floured board, roll the dough out ¼ inch thick. Cut out with balloon cookie cutters.

Arrange the cookies 1 inch apart along the long sides of the cookie sheets. Carefully insert 6- or 8-inch lollipop sticks about ½ inch into the bottom of the balloons.

Bake for 8 to 10 minutes, or until lightly colored. Let the cookies cool in the pans for 5 minutes, then transfer the cookies to a wire rack to cool completely.

SIMPLE LEMON GLAZE

Sift into a bowl: 1 cup confectioners' sugar, plus additional if needed. Slowly whisk in: 1 tablespoon strained fresh lemon juice, plus additional if needed. If the icing is too thin, whisk in more confectioners' sugar by the table-spoonful. To tint the glaze, add food coloring drop by drop until you have the desired color. Use the glaze immediately or place plastic wrap directly on the surface of the glaze. It can be stored in the refrigerator for 1 week.

FUNNEL CAKES

When I was growing up my mom would take me to the Paramus Park mall to buy new school clothes, and while we were there, I would make her take me to the food court, where they had a funnel cake stand. The funnel cakes were made to order and were then drenched in confectioners' sugar as soon as they left the hot oil—a true deep-fried heaven. And I am very happy to say my mom has successfully created a recipe worthy of my fondest memories. —Liv

Yield: 3 to 4 funnel cakes

In a large bowl, whisk together:
- 1 extra-large egg
- 1 cup milk
- ¼ teaspoon pure vanilla extract

On a piece of wax paper, sift together:
- 1⅓ cups all-purpose flour
- 2 tablespoons sugar
- ¼ teaspoon kosher salt
- ½ teaspoon baking powder
- 1 teaspoon baking soda

Whisk the dry ingredients into the wet ingredients just to combine.

The batter should easily pour from a cup measure with a lip. If it is too thick, stir in more milk 1 tablespoon at a time. Cover with plastic wrap and let the batter rest at room temperature for 1 hour.

Have on hand:
- ¼ cup confectioners' sugar

In a large, heavy pot, heat to 375°F:
- 48 fluid ounces (or 2 inches) vegetable oil

Pour the batter into a squeeze bottle or a cup measure with a lid. Carefully squeeze or pour the batter randomly around the pan, overlapping on itself a few times. Cook for 1 to 2 minutes, then,

using tongs, carefully flip the funnel cake and cook for another minute. Remove from the oil and place on a brown paper bag or a half-sheet pan lined with paper towels. Dust with the confectioners' sugar. Serve immediately.

PLAIN+SIMPLE Remove the cupcake liners, cut the cupcakes in half, place them in glass bowls, and top with scoops of vanilla ice cream.

♥ Kids can ♥

Lay out bowls of buttercream and sprinkles, along with chocolate cones. Let the kids design their dream ice cream cone—maybe five scoops high topped with colored sprinkles?

ICE CREAM CONE CUPCAKES

These playful renditions of ice cream cones will delight your guests and have your kids screaming for ice cream.

Yield: 20 cupcakes

WHAT YOU WILL NEED

Cake: **20 Root Beer Cupcakes (page 120)**

Icing: **1 recipe Kids' Buttercream (page 14) and/or Kids' Chocolate Buttercream (page 14), according to your design**

Decoration: **1 cup dark wafer chocolate and 2½ cups white wafer chocolate to make cones, plus 1 jar of rainbow or chocolate sprinkles**

Colors: **yellow and red (if making cherries) candy colors and green liquid gel color**

Miscellaneous: **three 6-cup muffin pans, pastry cones or bags (with coupler and #8 tip), ice cream cone templates (page 166), half-sheet pan, parchment paper or cellophane**

1 Bake the cupcakes and let them cool completely. For best results, freeze for at least 1 hour. Prepare the buttercream(s).

2 Melt the dark wafer and white wafer chocolates separately. Set aside 2 tablespoons dark chocolate. To make 10 sugar cones and 10 wafer cones, using the Color Mixing Chart on page 37, tint the white chocolate: approximately ½ cup light-medium brown, ¼ cup dark brown, ¼ cup tan, and 2 tablespoons red (if making cherries). Pour the tinted chocolates into separate pastry cones. Using the templates provided, make the ice cream cones, as illustrated in the Multicolor Chocolate Method Appliqué technique (page 72, step 4).

3 For mint chocolate chip ice cream cupcakes, prepare the light green buttercream. You will need approximately 3 tablespoons of buttercream for each cupcake (two tablespoons to spread, one to pipe). Spread the reserved dark chocolate in

an even layer onto parchment paper, let set, and then break into small chips.

4 Ice the cupcakes with the prepared buttercream. Press the cones horizontally into the buttercream, up to where the dotted line is on the template. If needed, add a bit more icing to stabilize the cone. Place the remaining buttercream(s) in a pastry cone. Cut a large hole at the tip of the cone and pipe a crazy border overlapping the cone. Sprinkle the buttercream with colored sprinkles or the chips of chocolate.

ROOT BEER CAKE

Nothing beats a root beer float on a hot summer's day. Fill our Root Beer Cake with whipped cream (which acts as the ice cream in a root beer float), and your mind will play tricks on you—with each bite, you have the sensation of tiny carbonated bubbles exploding on your tongue.

The root beer extract we used can be found at www.zatarains.com.

Yield: 4 low 7-inch cakes or 16 to 18 cupcakes

To make Ice Cream Cone Cupcakes (page 118): Grease the top of three standard 6-cup muffin pans and line them with paper liners.

To make the Abracadabra! cake (page 122): Grease and flour four 7-inch round pans.

Preheat the oven to 350°F. Have all ingredients at room temperature.

In the bowl of an electric mixer, beat at high speed until light and fluffy:
  8 ounces (2 sticks) unsalted butter
  1 cup granulated sugar
  ½ cup firmly packed light brown sugar

Add, one at a time, and creaming well after each addition:
  4 extra-large eggs

On a piece of wax paper, sift together:
  2½ cups cake flour
  2½ teaspoons baking powder
  1 teaspoon kosher salt

In a small bowl, combine:
  ½ cup root beer
  ½ cup heavy cream
  2 teaspoons root beer extract

Add the dry ingredients to the butter mixture alternately with the root beer mixture, beating at low speed until combined.

If making cakes: Pour 1½ cups of the batter into each of the four prepared pans. Bake for 23 to 25 minutes, or until a cake tester inserted into the center of the cake comes out clean. Cool the cakes on a wire rack for 15 to 20 minutes before turning them out of their pans.

If making cupcakes: Scoop the batter into the prepared molds, filling each three-quarters full. Bake for 18 to 20 minutes, or until a cake tester inserted into the center of a cupcake comes out clean. Cool the cupcakes on a wire rack for 5 to 10 minutes before removing them from the pans.

Piping Animals

With these techniques, you can decorate treats with your child's favorite creature using piping instead of chocolate. You will need a selection of round tips (#4, 8, 10, etc.) and/or pastry cones. For more information on piping, see pages 28–30 and 74.

The body of many animals (elephant, lion, zebra, and giraffe) starts with the same basic form. Place a round tip on a pastry bag with a coupler (the larger the tip, the larger the animal will be). Hold the bag nearly perpendicular to the cake surface and lightly touch the pastry tip to the surface of the cake where you want to start piping the lower left foot. Lift up the tip slightly as you begin to apply pressure and move the bag straight up until the leg is the desired length, and then change direction. Make a rather abrupt right turn and increase pressure to form the body (stomach area). When the body is the desired length, make another abrupt turn downward. Make the second leg the same length as the first and then tail off. For other animals, such as the monkey, pipe a large oval for the main form of the body.

Using an assortment of colors, pastry cones, and round tips, pipe on details as illustrated in these step-by-step photographs.

ABRACADABRA!

One of the first three-dimensional cakes I ever made was a magic hat, and to this day it remains one of my favorites. Because it involves very little sculpting it is a great starter cake for a novice decorator.

Serves approximately 15 people

WHAT YOU WILL NEED

Cake: four 7-inch rounds of Root Beer Cake (page 121)

Icing: ½ recipe Kaye's Buttercream (page 11) or House Buttercream (page 13)

Filling: 1 recipe Whipped Cream (page 17)

Decoration: ¼ cup dark wafer chocolate and 4¼ cups white wafer chocolate to make rabbits and hat brim, plus 1 small container of candy confetti

Colors: pink and purple candy colors and purple, green, yellow, and pink liquid gel color

Tips: #44 or 45 flat tip; #16, 17, or 18 star tip; #6, 7, or 8 round tip

Miscellaneous: four 7-inch round baking pans, 6-inch and 7-inch cardboard rounds, pastry bags, couplers, pastry cones, rabbit template (page 166), half-sheet pan, parchment paper or cellophane, 12-inch (or larger) base

1 Bake the cakes and let them cool completely. For best results, freeze for 1 hour or chill in the refrigerator for a few hours. Prepare the buttercream.

2 Trim the domes off of the cakes and discard. Stack the cakes on a 7-inch cardboard round. Place a 6-inch cardboard circle on top. Using this circle and the bottom cardboard as a guide, carve the cake at an angle, starting at the 6-inch circle and ending at the 7-inch circle. Continue around the entire circumference of the cake. The cake should now look like an upside-down flowerpot. Prepare the filling. Fill and crumb coat the cake (see pages 23 and 26). Chill the filled cake for 30 minutes, or until the buttercream has set.

3 Make the templates. To make the brim, draw a 9-inch circle onto parchment paper and draw a 5-inch circle in the center of the 9-inch circle. Trace two rabbit templates onto parchment

paper. Turn one upside down and one right side up. Place another sheet of parchment paper (or cellophane) over them. Melt the dark wafer and white wafer chocolates separately. Set aside 1 cup of the white chocolate. Using the Color Mixing Chart on page 37, tint the remaining white chocolate: approximately 1 cup purple and 2 tablespoons pink. Pour the chocolates into separate pastry cones. Make one purple brim and two white mirror-image rabbits as illustrated in the Shading and Portraiture Chocolate Method (page 76). Set aside to harden.

4 Prepare the colored buttercream: approximately 2 cups purple, ¼ cup pink, ¼ cup lime green, and ¼ cup yellow. Place ¼ cup of each color (including purple) in a separate pastry bag with a coupler. Place a #45 tip on the green bag and random tips on each of the other colors.

The free-form and carefree buttercream confetti piped on this cake does not need a controlled hand, so it is fun for kids to make. Fill the pastry bags with colored buttercream, let your child choose a pastry tip, and then let him or her squeeze the buttercream randomly around the chocolate rabbit. Kids will also enjoy sprinkling candy confetti on top.

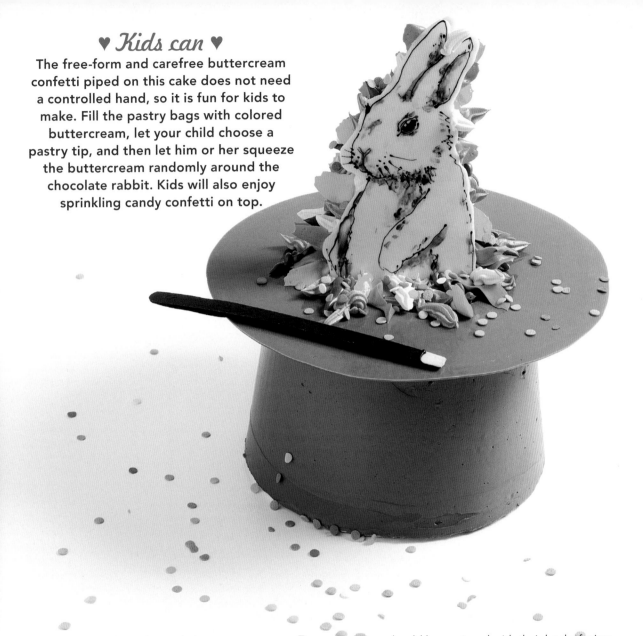

5 Ice the cake with purple buttercream as described in Crumbing and Icing a Curved Cake on page 26. Adhere the cardboard round supporting the cake to its base. Pipe a flat green band around the top edge of the cake. Center the purple chocolate brim on top.

6 In the hole created by the brim, lightly mark the position of the rabbits on the center of the cake.

They should be centered with their backs facing each other. Stick a thin knife into the cake at these points, and carefully press the rabbits into the slits until their front paws are resting near the icing. Fill in the empty spaces between and around the rabbits with piped confetti, using the pastry bags of colored buttercream. Sprinkle with candy confetti.

IT'S A *Zoo in* THERE

Wild Creatures Inspire Wild Creations

On the farm or at the zoo, animals are always popular with kids. My friend Sayantani recently hosted a "wild" birthday party for her daughter, Sunaya; everyone was invited to make a donation to the World Wildlife Fund in lieu of a gift. The party favors were personalized with stickers and toy animals to match each child's favorite creatures. Sunaya, who loves butterflies, wore wings all day and had a butterfly piñata for all of the kids to hit and scavenge; and, of course, I made her a cake with a giant chocolate butterfly on top.

If your child has a favorite animal, design the party around it. Make animal cupcakes—wolves, sharks, bears, tigers, cows, parrots—the possibilities are endless. Maybe some child out there is a fan of donkeys, but if not, mix it up a little and play "Velcro the snout on the pig" or "tape the tail on the monkey." For our last Halloween party we played "pin the face on the vampire bat." My son helped me draw a

bat on poster board and he colored it in with crayons. I scanned the face we drew into the computer, printed out twelve copies, cut them out, and placed double-stick tape on the back. I think you know the rest: blindfold, spin, spin, spin, and watch as the children veer off course and stick a bat face on the wall.

After a visit to a working farm or a petting zoo with your children, wash hands thoroughly and then head home for a farm party. Go hog wild and set the table with a gingham tablecloth, serve corn on the cob and sliced cucumbers and tomatoes, and finish off the meal with fresh Apple Pie (page 159). Or just wow them with our Barn Cake (page 126).

For the child who loves visiting the aquarium or adores Karlos K. Krinklebine (the fish from *The Cat in the Hat*), we have an unexpected treat, and it isn't cake; it's a fishbowl filled with fruit juice gelatin and edible chocolate decorations.

BARN CAKE

When I was three I lived on a farm (a spinning and weaving school in Canada) with my mom, and the image of the barn remains etched in my memory—definitely a classic. Complete with a cow, a pig, a sheep, and a hen, this Barn Cake, modeled after the barn in Canada, is perfect for the animal lover in your home.

Here's a fun alternative: Instead of carving a barn out of cake, a young student of mine suggested baking a round cake, icing it with green buttercream, piping a fence around the sides, and inserting standing chocolate farm animals and a barn on top.

The barn template can be transformed into a haunted house replete with chocolate ghosts, bats, and mummies or even a gingerbread house for Christmas, iced with chocolate buttercream and decorated with a real candy roof and candy decorations. —Liv

Serves 15 to 18 people

··
WHAT YOU WILL NEED
··

Cake: 9 x 13-inch Milk Chocolate Cake (page 129)

Icing: approximately ½ recipe Kaye's Buttercream (page 11) or House Buttercream (page 13)

Filling: 1 recipe Matt's Fudge Icing (page 14)

Decoration: ¼ cup dark wafer chocolate and 1½ cups white wafer chocolate to make animals

Colors: pink, red, and yellow candy colors and red, yellow, and green liquid gel colors

Tips: #44 or 45 flat tip

Miscellaneous: 9 x 13-inch baking pan, cardboard cut to size of barn and silo (start with a 9 x 13-inch piece and see page 168 for template), pastry bags, couplers, pastry cones, farm animal templates (page 164), half-sheet pan, parchment paper or cellophane, 12 x 16-inch (or larger) base

1 Bake the cake and let it cool completely. For best results, freeze for 1 hour or chill in the refrigerator for a few hours. Prepare the buttercream and the fudge icing. Reserve 1 cup of fudge icing for decorating.

2 Cut out your cardboard base in the shapes of the barn and silo (see page 168).

3 Trim the dome (if any) off of the cake. Place the cardboard templates on top, lining up the bottom of the barn template with one 9-inch edge, and run a small serrated knife around the edge of the template to cut out the barn. Invert so that the cardboard is now underneath the cake. Cut the extra pieces so that you have two small right triangles and two quadrangles (see the template for where to cut). Arrange the extra

CONTINUES

pieces on the silo template. The two larger pieces will fit together to form a rectangle. Carve the smaller triangular pieces to fit on the roof.

4 Using a serrated knife, cut the barn cake in half horizontally. Fill the cake with the prepared fudge icing and crumb coat it with the buttercream (see pages 23 and 25). Chill the filled cake for 30 minutes, or until the buttercream has set.

5 Stick the silo pieces to each other with dabs of buttercream and crumb coat.

6 Melt the dark wafer and white wafer chocolates separately. Set aside ¼ cup white chocolate. Using the Color Mixing Chart on page 37, tint the remaining white chocolate: approximately 2 tablespoons yellow, 2 tablespoons red, 2 tablespoons light brown, 2 tablespoons light pink, and 2 tablespoons pink. Pour the chocolates into separate pastry cones. Using the templates provided, make one of each farm animal and one fence as illustrated in the Multi-color Chocolate Method Appliqué technique (page 72, step 4). Set aside to harden.

7 Set aside ½ cup uncolored buttercream. Prepare the colored buttercream: approximately 2 cups red, 2 tablespoons yellow, and 2 tablespoons green.

8 Place the reserved fudge icing in a pastry bag with a coupler, and with a flat tip, starting at the bottom edge on each side of the cake, pipe overlapping slats on the barn roof. Spread the extra fudge icing on the round roof of the silo.

9 Place the red buttercream in a pastry bag with a coupler and, with a flat tip, pipe vertical slats on the sides and top of the barn and silo.

10 Adhere the cardboard base supporting the cakes to your base.

11 Using melted dark chocolate, pipe random vertical lines to enhance the vertical slats, and pipe random horizontal lines to represent the ends of the wood slats. Pipe dots for nail holes. Pipe, and fill in, a square window on the top center of the barn. Outline where the barn door will be and pipe door handles.

12 Place the remaining white buttercream in a pastry bag with a coupler and, with a flat tip, pipe decorative slats across the barn, around the window and door, and on the roof edge (see photo for placement).

13 Place the yellow and green buttercream in separate pastry cones and pipe hay (blades of grass, see below) randomly around the base of the barn and poking out of the hayloft window.

14 Invert the animals and set them carefully along the bottom edge of the barn and silo. Place the chicken in the hayloft window.

GRASS

Tips—any small round tip (such as #3, 4, or 5), pastry cones, or any multi-holed tip (#233, 89)

Grass combines linear piping with the flourish of a teardrop. Hold the bag at a 45-degree angle and lightly touch the pastry tip to the surface of the cake where you want to start piping. Lift up the tip slightly as you begin to apply pressure and move the bag upward, at a 45-degree angle. Continue in this direction until the blade of grass is the desired length, then to tail off, gradually release pressure to form a point.

MILK CHOCOLATE CAKE

When we were experimenting with cake recipes for this book, this cake was a wild success with the staff. It has since become a great addition to our stock cake collection at the bakery. Lighter in flavor than its dark chocolate cousin, but equally satisfying, our Milk Chocolate Cake is sure to please the kids.

Yield: one 9 x 13-inch cake

Grease and flour a 9 x 13-inch pan. Preheat the oven to 350°F. Have all ingredients at room temperature.

In the bowl of an electric mixer, beat at high speed until light and fluffy:
   6 ounces (1½ sticks) unsalted butter
   ⅔ cup granulated sugar
   ⅔up packed brown sugar

Add, one at a time, creaming well after each addition:
   3 extra-large eggs
   1½ teaspoon pure vanilla extract

Add:
   8 ounces melted milk chocolate, cooled

At low speed, add:
   1⅓ cup buttermilk

The mixture may look separated.

On a piece of wax paper, sift together:
   2⅓ cups cake flour
   1½ teaspoons baking powder
   1 teaspoon baking soda
   ½ teaspoon kosher salt

Add the dry ingredients to the butter mixture, mixing until just incorporated.

Pour 2½ cups of the batter into one pan and the remaining batter into the other. Bake for 35 to 40 minutes, or until a cake tester inserted into the center of the cake comes out clean. Cool the cakes on a wire rack for 15 to 20 minutes before turning them out of their pans.

ANIMAL CUPCAKES

Transform a plain cupcake into a wild animal with chocolate appliqué eyes, snouts, and ears—the possibilities are seemingly endless. The first animal cupcake I ever made was a cartoonish lion, but now I make monkeys, zebras, sharks, elephants, and more.

The animal designs shown here are made with assembled pieces, a variation of the Chocolate Method. The faces are made in segments and assembled after hardening to add a sense of depth. For example, the chimpanzee's ears and face are made separately and then attached to an iced cupcake.

Yield: 16 cupcakes

Cake: **16 Cookie Cupcakes (page 133)**

Icing: **1 recipe Kids' Buttercream (page 14), Kids' Chocolate Buttercream (page 14), and/or Matt's Fudge Icing (page 14), according to your desired design**

Decoration: **The amounts of chocolate may differ depending on your chosen design. To be on the safe side, have approximately 1 cup dark wafer chocolate and 2 cups white wafer chocolate on hand to make animal segments.**

Colors: **Red, pink, yellow, orange, black, blue, and/or green candy**

colors and red, pink, yellow, orange, blue, black, and/or green liquid gel colors. Choose colors according to your intended design.

Miscellaneous: **two standard 12-cup muffin pans, pastry cones, animal face templates (pages 162–163), half-sheet pan, parchment paper or cellophane**

1 Bake the cupcakes and let them cool completely. For best results, freeze for at least 1 hour. Prepare the icing(s) of your choice.

2 Melt the dark wafer and white wafer chocolates separately. Using the templates provided, make 16 animal designs (see step 3 for an example you can follow), and for more information, see the Chocolate Method on pages 131–35.

3 To make chimpanzees, set aside 1 tablespoon of white chocolate for the twinkle in the eyes. Using the Color Mixing Chart on page 37, tint the remaining white chocolate a light peach color. Pour the dark chocolate, white chocolate, and

colored chocolate into 3 separate pastry cones. Keep the chocolates warm on a sheet pan over a barely simmering double boiler or on a heating pad. Cut a very small hole (1/32 inch) in the dark chocolate pastry cone. With a fine line, trace the contour of the ears, the eyes, and the interior lines on the chimp's face; there is no need to pipe an outline around the face. Cut a medium hole (1/32 to 1/16 inch) in the peach pastry cone. Fill in the face and fill in the ears up to the dotted line. The chocolate should be approximately 1/8 inch thick, but it can be thicker. Set aside to harden. When hardened, carefully flip both

CONTINUES

designs and gently peel off the parchment paper. Cut a small hole (¹⁄₃₂ inch) in the white pastry cone and pipe a small dot on each eye.

4 Here are some other sample chocolate amounts: To make 16 pigs, melt 1¼ cups of white wafer chocolate and ⅛ cup of dark wafer chocolate. Set aside 2 tablespoons of the white chocolate. Using the Color Mixing Chart on page 37, tint the remaining white chocolate: approximately ¼ cup dark pink and ¼ cup light pink. To make 16 koalas, melt 2 cups of white wafer chocolate and ¼ cup of dark wafer chocolate. Set aside 2 tablespoons of the white chocolate. Using the Color Mixing Chart, tint the remaining white chocolate: approximately 2 tablespoons pink and ¾ cup gray. To make 16 lions, melt ¼ cup of dark wafer chocolate and 2 cups of white wafer chocolate. Set aside 2 tablespoons of the white chocolate. Using the Color Mixing Chart, tint the remaining white chocolate: approximately 2 tablespoons pink, ¼ cup orange, and ¼ cup yellow-orange. Set aside the completed designs to harden. For all other designs, use the photograph as a color guide and melt and tint the chocolate accordingly. The predominant colors will need the most chocolate, while the details will need less.

5 If needed, prepare the colored buttercream. Each cupcake will need approximately 2 tablespoons of buttercream. The lion will need an additional tablespoon of orange for the piped mane. The shark will need 1 tablespoon each of white and blue buttercream. Ice the cupcakes with an old-fashioned icing as directed on page 28.

6 Invert the designs and place on the cupcakes, pressing to set when needed. For some designs, like the chimp, press the ears one-quarter of the way into the icing. If the icing has set already, adhere a dot of icing to the underside of each design and place it right side up on the cupcake.

PLAIN+SIMPLE Frost the cupcakes with colored frosting and pipe on leopard or cow spots, or zebra or tiger stripes.

COOKIE CUPCAKES

Why not have the best of both worlds: cookies and cake. Here we added crushed Oreos to the cake batter, but you can substitute your favorite hard cookie in equal measure.

Yield: 16 to 18 cupcakes

Grease the top of two standard 12-cup muffin pans and line them with paper liners. Preheat the oven to 350°F. Have all ingredients at room temperature.

In the bowl of an electric mixer, beat at high speed until light and fluffy:

- **4 ounces (1 stick) unsalted butter**
- **1 cup sugar**

Add, one at a time:

- **3 extra-large eggs**
- **1 teaspoon pure vanilla extract**

On a piece of wax paper, sift together:

- **2¼ cups cake flour**
- **1 teaspoon baking powder**
- **¼ teaspoon baking soda**
- **¼ teaspoon kosher salt**

Add the dry ingredients to the butter mixture alternately with:

- **1 cup buttermilk**

Stir in:

- **¾ cup chopped chocolate sandwich cookies (approximately 6 Oreos)**

Scoop the batter into the prepared pans, filling each three-quarters full. Bake for 15 to 18 minutes, or until golden. The tops should spring back when lightly pressed. Cool on a wire rack for 5 to 10 minutes before removing the cupcakes from the pan.

3-D FISHBOWL

This is as close as I get to constructing a sailboat inside a bottle. Yes, it's made in a real fishbowl, but the rest is edible: green-tinted fruit juice gelatin, a candy seabed, and chocolate seaweed. The chocolate goldfish happily swims around in its little underwater home.

Serves approximately 8 people

WHAT YOU WILL NEED

Filling: **1 recipe Fruit Juice Gelatin (opposite)**

Decoration: **½ cup dark wafer chocolate and 2 cups white wafer chocolate to make fish, seaweed, and coral, plus small round candies (such** as round SweeTart Minis) to use as gravel

Colors: **green, orange, yellow, and pink candy colors and teal or sky blue liquid gel colors**

Miscellaneous: **small glass fishbowl (approximately 4-cup capacity), pastry cones, fish and coral template (page 166), half-sheet pan, parchment paper or cellophane**

1 Melt the dark wafer and white wafer chocolates separately. Set aside 2 tablespoons of the white chocolate. Using the Color Mixing Chart on page 37, tint the remaining white chocolate: approximately ¼ cup yellow, 2 tablespoons light orange, 2 tablespoons dark orange, 2 tablespoons coral, 2 tablespoons lime green, and 2 tablespoons green. Pour the chocolates into separate pastry cones. Using the templates provided, make a goldfish and assorted coral and seaweed as illustrated in the Shading and Portraiture Chocolate Method (page 76). Set aside to harden.

2 Pipe dark chocolate onto the bottom of the fishbowl. Cover with a layer of candy. Pipe additional yellow chocolate on top. Before the chocolate has completely set, carefully insert the coral and seaweed. Hold in place until set. If needed, pipe additional chocolate for support around the chocolate decorations. Pipe a dot of chocolate on the back of the goldfish. Adhere it to one of the seaweed strands. Hold in place until set.

3 Prepare the fruit gelatin. Pour 1 cup of the gelatin into a bowl and add teal or sky blue food coloring one drop at a time until you have the desired tint. Be careful not to add too much color or the chocolate fish and seaweed will be hard to see. Stir in the remaining gelatin. Let the gelatin cool, but do not let it set. When the gelatin reaches room temperature, carefully pour it into the fishbowl.

4 Place in the refrigerator until completely set, about 3 hours.

FRUIT JUICE GELATIN

Wobbly, wiggly, yummy, and fun—ordinary gelatin is transformed into an extraordinary underwater home.

Yield: approximately 3 cups gelatin

In a small saucepan, bring to a boil:
> **3 cups clear or lightly colored juice (white cranberry, apple, or white grape)**

Pour into a large bowl:
> **1 cup clear or lightly colored juice (white cranberry, apple, or white grape), chilled**

Over the top of the cold juice, sprinkle:
> **1 ounce powdered unflavored gelatin (4 packages Knox gelatin)**

Set aside for 1 minute.

Add the hot juice to the bowl and stir until the gelatin completely dissolves (about 5 minutes). Add food coloring if desired.

Let the gelatin come to room temperature, but do not let it set. Follow the directions opposite.

TRICK *and* TREAT

Spooky and Sugary Surprises

When I was a preteen, I cohosted a Halloween party with my best friend, Amy. Everyone came in costume. I was Medusa and Amy was the Statue of Liberty. We bobbed for apples. We played memory: A tray filled with about twenty different objects (a skeleton key, lipstick, a twig, a Swedish Fish, and other Halloween-y objects) was placed in front of us for about thirty seconds. It was then removed and we had to write down all of the objects we could remember in one minute. Next, my favorite game, the doughnut-eating contest: Doughnuts were tied with string and hung at eye level from the porch. With our hands tied behind our backs, we had to eat our doughnuts as fast as possible without letting them drop. We all roared with

laughter as doughnuts bounced off our cheeks, dusting our faces with sugar.

Although kids love a good trick, isn't this holiday really about the treats? Halloween can be a time to prepare seasonal sweets—such as chocolate rice cereal Bone Crunchers or Pumpkin Spice Cake. Since Halloween is such a visual holiday, have fun decorating the treats, too. Make the Pumpkin Spice Cake into a mummy head, create a 3-D cauldron filled with chocolate pudding, or if you are having a masquerade party, make edible cookie masks. Have them ready for guests to wear and eat or let the kids decorate their own with royal icing, sanding sugar, and sprinkles. The masks can be Mardi Gras style or spooky with scars and spikes.

special party project

MAD SCIENTIST

Using ingredients found in your kitchen cabinet, set up a mad scientist table at the party. This is amusing for younger kids, who are still fascinated by pouring and stirring, and for older children, who are actually fascinated with the science behind the reaction. To contain the mess, place all of the ingredients and receptacles on rimmed sheet pans.

The first concoction: vinegar and baking soda explosions. Mix white vinegar with the food coloring of your choice and pour into measuring cups or any container that is easy to pour from. Fill a bowl with baking soda. Set the baking soda, vinegar, bottles, spoons, funnels, and medicine squeezers on the table and let the kids mix and experiment. When you mix the baking soda and vinegar you get a foaming reaction that is endlessly entertaining to four-year-olds.

The second concoction: cornstarch ooze. Although young ones don't quite grasp the oddity of a non-Newtonian substance (basically a substance that is neither liquid nor solid), they fully enjoy the tactile experience of playing with this ooze. Add a couple of drops of food coloring to water. In a medium bowl, mix the water, tablespoon by tablespoon, into ¼ cup of cornstarch. Eventually it will become difficult to stir. As you add more water, the cornstarch will feel like it is solidifying, but at the same time, it will appear to be in the liquid state . . . a weird thing to witness indeed.

MUMMY CAKE

We have a slew of egg-shaped pans at the bakery, and at Halloween, these mummy faces are a hit.

2 mummy heads serve approximately 16 people

....
WHAT YOU WILL NEED
....

Cake: **2 egg-shaped Pumpkin Spice Cakes (page 140)**

Icing: **½ recipe Kaye's Buttercream (page 11)**

Filling: **1 recipe Caramel Whipped Cream (page 20) or Whipped Cream (page 17)**

Decoration: **½ cup dark wafer chocolate**

Tips: **#103 or 104 petal tip**

Miscellaneous: **egg-shaped baking pans, pastry bag, coupler, 11-inch (or larger) base**

1 Bake the cakes and let them cool completely. For best results, chill the cakes for 1 hour. Prepare the buttercream and the filling.

2 Cut the domes off of the bottom of the cakes. Cut the cakes in half horizontally. Fill the cakes with the whipped cream as directed on page 23. Using a small paring knife, cut out two oval eye holes (½ inch to ¾ inch deep at the center) along the center line of each head. Place a dot of buttercream between and slightly below the eyes. Adhere one cutout eye piece to the buttercream and gently mold into a nose shape. Place a dot of buttercream slightly below the nose. Repeat for the other mummy head. Crumb coat the cakes (page 26). Chill the filled cakes for 30 minutes, or until the buttercream has set.

3 Melt the dark chocolate. Pour the chocolate into a pastry cone. Pipe a thin layer of chocolate into the eye sockets.

4 Place the prepared buttercream in a pastry bag with a coupler and a petal tip. Starting at the top of the head, pipe overlapping horizontal (sometimes irregular) lines to represent the wrappings. With the exception of exposing a small slit of chocolate where the eyes are, cover all of both cakes with piped buttercream.

PUMPKIN SPICE CAKE

The inspiration for this recipe came from a Rosh Hashanah cake we used to make at the bakery, which I have since adapted for other uses. Liv describes it as pumpkin pie in cake form—so why not bake one for your next Thanksgiving?

See Suppliers on page 171 for where to purchase egg-shaped pans.

Yield: two 8-inch-long egg-shaped cakes

PLAIN+SIMPLE Bake the Pumpkin Spice Cake in a pumpkin-shaped pan. Pipe green vines and leaves.

Grease and flour 2 egg-shaped pans (approximately 8 inches long). Preheat the oven to 350°F. Have all ingredients at room temperature.

In the bowl of an electric mixer, beat at high speed until light and fluffy:
- 6 ounces (1½ sticks) unsalted butter
- 1 cup sugar

Add one at time, and beat on medium speed until fluffy:
- 3 extra-large eggs

On a piece of wax paper, sift together:
- 2¼ cups cake flour
- 2½ teaspoons baking powder
- 2½ teaspoons ground cinnamon
- ¼ teaspoon ground ginger
- ¼ teaspoon ground cloves
- ¾ teaspoon kosher salt

In a medium bowl, whisk together:
- ¾ cup pumpkin puree
- ½ cup buttermilk
- ⅓ cup honey
- 1 teaspoon pure vanilla extract

At low speed, add the dry and liquid ingredients alternately to the butter mixture. Mix until combined.

Divide the batter evenly between the pans. Bake for 40 to 45 minutes, or until a cake tester inserted into the center of the cake comes out clean. Cool the cakes on a wire rack for 15 to 20 minutes before turning them out of their pans.

CAULDRON BUBBLES

"Double, double toil and trouble; fire burn and cauldron bubble." More fun than toil, our chocolate cauldron is magical to make. These chocolate shells filled with chocolate pudding will delight every witch and warlock that makes an appearance on Halloween.

2 cauldrons serve approximately 10 people

WHAT YOU WILL NEED

Filling: **1 recipe Chocolate Pudding (page 19) and 2 cups Whipped Cream (page 17)**

Decoration: **6 cups dark wafer chocolate and ½ cup white wafer chocolate to make cauldrons and flames, 2 balloons (small helium-grade balloons work best), mini pretzel sticks, 1 jar confetti sprinkles**

Colors: **red, orange, and yellow candy colors**

Tips: **#20, 21, or 22, or any larger open star tip**

Miscellaneous: **pastry bag, coupler; pastry cones; cauldron handle template (page 165); half-sheet pan; parchment paper; tall, narrow plastic or glass container or measuring cup for dipping the balloons (5 to 6 inches in diameter and height); two 6-inch (or larger) bases**

CONTINUES

♥ *Kids can* ♥

Bring the kids into the kitchen to help with
this magical creation. They can do almost all
of the decorating, starting with blowing up
and dipping the balloons. When the cauldrons are ready, the kids can fill them with
the chocolate pudding and whipped cream,
then sprinkle confetti on top. They can even
pipe the chocolate fire at the base.

Note: You will need a lot of chocolate for this recipe, and there will be chocolate left over. Just remember to store the leftover chocolate in a cool, dry place.

1 Prepare the chocolate pudding and let it cool completely in the refrigerator.

2 Blow up 2 balloons so they are each 3 to 4 inches in diameter. Tie the balloons closed. Line a half-sheet pan with parchment paper.

3 Melt the dark wafer and white wafer chocolates separately. Pour the dark chocolate into a tall, narrow container. The container should be wide enough to accommodate the balloon but narrow enough so that the chocolate is at least 3 inches deep.

4 Holding a balloon securely by the tied end, submerge it halfway to three-quarters of the way into the melted dark chocolate; you will have to apply even pressure to dip the balloon. Then pull the balloon straight up and place it on the sheet pan to set. Hold it in place until it balances. A small chocolate base should form as the chocolate settles. Repeat with the remaining balloon. When the chocolate has hardened, redip each balloon in the melted chocolate (remelt the chocolate if needed). This will thicken and reinforce the sides. Again, pull the balloon straight up out of the chocolate, allowing some of the chocolate to drip off before setting it back on the sheet pan to set.

5 Dip 2 pretzel sticks halfway into the chocolate. Transfer them to parchment paper and let the chocolate set. When the chocolate has hardened, dip the opposite side. Set aside on the parchment paper to harden completely.

6 Tint the white chocolate: approximately 2 tablespoons each of red, orange, and yellow. Pour the colored chocolates and 2 tablespoons of the dark chocolate into separate pastry cones.

7 Pipe out the dark chocolate cauldron handles as described in the Silhouette and Overpiping Chocolate Method on page 56, step 6.

8 Once the second layer of chocolate on the balloon has set, place the tray in the freezer for 1 to 2 minutes (just a flash-freeze). Remove the tray from the freezer and pop each balloon with a sharp knife. Carefully remove the balloon from the cauldron. The helium balloons tend to peel away easily, but if you experience any difficulty, a quick blast from a crème brûlée torch will help remove the balloon skin.

9 Adhere each cauldron to its base with a drop of chocolate.

10 Fill each cauldron with 2 to 2½ cups chocolate pudding. Prepare the whipped cream. Place the whipped cream in a pastry bag with a coupler and, with a star tip, fill in the rest of the cauldron (½ cup to 1 cup per cauldron). Sprinkle the top of the cauldron with candy confetti. Stick one chocolate-covered pretzel halfway into each cauldron.

11 Adhere the handles to the sides of the cauldron with dots of melted chocolate, gently holding them in place until the chocolate has set.

12 Pipe red, orange, and yellow flames coming up the sides of the cauldron. Do not squeeze too hard; excess chocolate has a tendency to drip back down, pooling at the base of the cauldron. Spread and blend the chocolates randomly with a small offset spatula.

MASQUERADE COOKIES

Whether you are hosting a fabulous Mardi Gras celebration or a Halloween party for your kids, these cookies will be a playful addition to the festivities. You can decorate the cookies one of two ways: If you want the icing to dry faster, spread a thin layer of royal icing on the cookie, dip it in sanding sugar, and overpipe with contrasting colors. Otherwise, thin the royal icing with water and pour, pipe, or spread it on the cookie for a smoother finish. You will need to make these a day ahead so the icing has time to set.

WHAT YOU WILL NEED

Cookie: **12 sugar cookie masks (see page 48)**

Icing: **1 recipe Royal Icing (page 15)**

Decoration: **white sanding sugar, 12 wooden Popsicle sticks**

Colors: **purple, yellow, green, and teal liquid gel colors, or choose colors according to your party's theme**

Miscellaneous: **half-sheet baking pan, pastry cones, mask template (page 164)**

1 Bake the cookies and let them cool completely. Prepare the icing. Keep the icing covered with a damp cloth.

2 Using the Color Mixing Chart on page 37, prepare the colored royal icing: approximately 1½ cups lavender, 2 tablespoons purple, 2 tablespoons yellow, 2 tablespoons lime green, and 2 tablespoons teal.

3 Choose between the following 3 decorating techniques: icing with sanding sugar, flooded icing with a reservoir, or flooded icing without a reservoir.

A Icing with Sanding Sugar (for faster drying): Place 2 tablespoons of each color in separate pastry cones. Cut a small hole at the tip of each cone. Spread a thin layer of lavender royal icing over the entire cookie. Immediately sprinkle white sanding sugar over the top or dip the cookie into a plate of sanding sugar, pressing gently to adhere. Shake or dust off any excess sugar. Pipe dots, stripes, or a pattern of your choice onto each cookie, using the other colors. Let the cookies dry overnight.

B Flooded Icing with a Reservoir: Reserve ½ cup lavender icing. Add water teaspoon by teaspoon to the remaining lavender icing until it is the consistency of Elmer's glue. Place the icings in separate pastry cones. Cut a small hole at the tip of each cone. Pipe a line around the edge of the mask and the eye holes with the firmer icing. Flood this "reservoir" with the thinned icing. Nudge the thinned icing up to the firm icing wall with

the tip of the cone. If desired, thin out the remaining colors and overpipe wet-on-wet details, or let the lavender base set for at least an hour and overpipe details with firm icing. Let the cookies set overnight.

C Flooded Icing without a Reservoir: Add water teaspoon by teaspoon to the lavender icing until it is the consistency of Elmer's glue. Place the icing in a pastry cone and cut a small hole at the tip of the cone. Pipe the icing to within ¼ inch of all edges of the cookie, then nudge the icing up to the edges of the cookie with the tip of the cone (without squeezing). Let the cookies set overnight before overpiping any details. Let the cookies set overnight, once again, after adding piping details.

BONE CRUNCHERS

These coffin-shaped treats are dipped in chocolate and decorated with white chocolate skeletons. Each time you bite into one you hear the cracking and crunching of "bones."

Use the same technique to make shaped trees for Christmas, eggs for Easter, or hearts for Valentine's Day.

Yield: 10 coffins

Butter a 9 x 13-inch pan. Cut out a cardboard coffin template (see page 161).

Butter a medium bowl.

Pour in:
6 cups rice cereal

In a large glass bowl, microwave for 1 to 2 minutes, stirring every 30 seconds, until melted:
3 tablespoons unsalted butter
5 cups (10.5 ounce package) mini marshmallows

Add and stir in:
2 ounces unsweetened chocolate, finely chopped
2 ounces semisweet chocolate, finely chopped

Pour the marshmallow-chocolate mixture over the rice cereal. Stir to combine. Spread the mixture in the prepared pan, pressing evenly to flatten. Let sit and come to room temperature. Using a paring knife and the template, cut the treats into coffin shapes.

Freeze the cut treats for 1 hour.

Meanwhile, in the microwave, melt:
3 cups dark confectioners' chocolate

Dip half of each coffin shape into the melted chocolate and place on a pan lined with parchment paper. Freeze just until the chocolate has set (about 2 minutes). Dip the other half of the coffin in the chocolate and let set.

Melt:
½ cup white confectioners' chocolate

Place the melted white chocolate in a pastry cone. Pipe freehand skeletons on the coffins. Let the treats set.

♥ *Kids can* ♥

Kids can help mold the rice cereal treats into the pan—then they get to eat whatever sticks to their fingers. When it comes time to decorate the coffins, let the kids pipe on their own goofy skeletons.

WHAT, no CAKE?

Alternative Sweet Endings

*C*ake may be the obvious choice for most kids' parties, but in this chapter it's all about other sweet endings. You see, I was a picky kid; I didn't like chocolate and could always do without cake. My dream birthday cake, oddly enough, was made of flan. Nowadays I whip up my own crème caramel, or I'll have my mom bake me a delicious fruit pie. To make the pie more festive, cut out holes in the top crust and insert tall, thin candles. When all of the candles are lit, it looks like the Fourth of July. These kinds of fireworks are sure to bring a smile to your face, whether it's your big day or Independence Day.

So, whether you and your child prefer brownies, cookies, or pies, don't feel unfestive. Make these treats special and personalized. Design a colorful chocolate inscription, buy fun candles, or place the dessert on a fancy cake pedestal. Perk up your table setting, too. Break out the fine china. On my tenth birthday, my friend and I had dinner at a fancy restaurant where my mom was a waitress—she served us sparkling apple cider in champagne glasses and we felt oh-so-important and mature. Spread out a bright tablecloth, scatter some confetti, and don't forget balloons. These little touches will turn your get-together into a party.

COOKIE CARD

Instead of sending a paper card in the mail, make a sugar cookie card (see page 48 for cutting and baking directions) to celebrate a loved one's birthday. After the card has baked and cooled, decorate it and write an inscription on the inside with Royal Icing (see page 15). Let dry overnight. Cut two ¼-inch-wide ribbons 8 inches long. Thread the ribbons through the holes in the cookie card and tie them in a loose bow, so you can open the card. Place a piece of 4 x 6-inch parchment paper between the cookies to protect the inscription.

HAPPY BIRTHDAY TO YOU! BROWNIE

This rich and super-chocolaty brownie is decorated with fun chocolate stand-up letters. Spell out HAPPY BIRTHDAY to your birthday boy or girl, I LOVE YOU for Valentine's Day, or CONGRATULATIONS for Graduation Day.

Serves approximately 48 people (cut into 2-inch squares)

WHAT YOU WILL NEED

Brownie: **1 recipe Super Fudge Brownies (page 153)**

Icing: **1 recipe Matt's Fudge Icing (page 14)**

Decoration: **1½ cups white wafer chocolate to make letters**

Colors: **red, yellow, and blue candy colors, or choose colors according to what's appropriate for your child**

Miscellaneous: **half-sheet pan, pastry cones, parchment paper or cellophane, 13 x 17-inch (or larger) base**

1   Bake the brownie and let it cool completely. Prepare Matt's Fudge Icing.

2   Run a paring knife around the edge of the brownie. Center the base on top of the brownie pan. Invert the base and pan, so the brownie is upside down on its base. Peel off the parchment paper.

3   Ice the brownie with the fudge icing, and then run the tip of an offset spatula diagonally back and forth across the brownie. Drag a small paring knife (or the thin blade edge of the spatula) across the fudge perpendicular to the first pattern. Make these marks, approximately ¾ inch apart, across the entire top of the brownie. The crossing of the two patterns will create a wavy texture.

4   Melt the wafer chocolate. Using the Color Mixing Chart on page 37, tint the white chocolate: approximately ¼ cup each of red, yellow, and blue. Pour the colored chocolates into separate pastry cones. Draw the letters you need to spell out your inscription on parchment paper and flip the paper so the letters are backwards/mirror image. Feel free to choose a font (approximately 50-point size) from a word-processing program, and print out a homemade template, but still trace the letters on parchment paper and invert them. Make sure the letters are small enough to fit across the brownie (some overlapping is okay). Using your template, pipe out the letters in different colors as directed in the Silhouette and Overpiping Chocolate Method (page 56, step 6). Extend the bottom of each letter 1 inch with chocolate. Set the letters aside to harden. When set, overpipe designs on the letters in the 2 contrasting colors.

5   Lightly mark the position of each letter with their extensions on the iced brownie. Stick a thin knife into the brownie at these points. Carefully press the letters vertically into these slits.

PLAIN+SIMPLE Instead of stand-up letters, keep them flat, or pipe a colorful inscription directly on the brownie.

SUPER FUDGE BROWNIES

This is one of the best brownies I have ever eaten—it packs a punch! The potent chocolate flavor means a little bit goes a long way. One half-sheet of brownies will feed more people than you think!

These brownies also freeze like a dream after baking; you can wrap the slices individually so that whenever the urge hits, you are good to go. Just nuke the brownies for 10 seconds to satisfy any chocolate craving.

Yield: 48 brownies (cut into 2-inch squares)

Grease and line a half-sheet (12 x 16 x 2-inch rimmed) pan with parchment paper. Preheat the oven to 350°F. Have all ingredients at room temperature.

In a small heat-proof glass bowl, melt in the microwave:

12 ounces unsweetened chocolate, chopped
2 ounces semisweet chocolate, chopped

In the large bowl of an electric mixer at medium speed, cream until light:

¾ pound (3 sticks) unsalted butter
2 cups granulated sugar
1 cup packed light brown sugar
1 teaspoon kosher salt

Slowly add and cream:

6 extra-large eggs
1 teaspoon pure vanilla extract

Add the melted, slightly cooled, chocolate and mix to combine.

On a piece of wax paper, sift together, then add to the butter mixture:

2 cups all-purpose flour
¼ cup cocoa powder

Add and stir in:

1½ cups chocolate chips
1½ cups toasted chopped pecans (see Note)

Spread the batter evenly onto the prepared pan. Bake for 20 to 25 minutes, or until a cake tester inserted into the center comes out with moist crumbs attached. Let the brownie cool completely in the pan.

Note: To toast pecans, place the nuts on an ungreased half-sheet pan. Bake at 350°F for 12 to 15 minutes, or until fragrant. Let cool.

FLAN

Flan has to be my favorite dessert, but I am partial to my mom's recipe. I've tried other versions at restaurants, but none compares to the caramel flavor and smooth delicacy of hers. Perhaps it is the addition of evaporated milk that makes it so unique. Perfection. I ask for it on my birthday, for Cinco de Mayo, and as a simple dessert to end any meal. —Liv

Serves approximately 10 people

Have on hand a 10-inch round cake pan or pie dish or a ring pan. Preheat the oven to 325°F.

In a medium bowl, combine thoroughly:
- **4 extra-large eggs**
- **½ cup sugar**
- **⅛ teaspoon kosher salt**
- **½ teaspoon pure vanilla extract**
- **¼ teaspoon pure almond extract**

In a small saucepan, scald:
- **1¼ cups evaporated milk (10-ounce can)**
- **1¼ cups whole milk**

Add the milk mixture to the egg mixture. Whisk just to combine. Strain the mixture through a sieve into a clean bowl, preferably one with a spout.

Meanwhile, in a small saucepan, cook until caramel colored:
- **¾ cup sugar**
- **2 tablespoons water**

Do not stir the sugar mixture (you can gently shake the pan if necessary). As it cooks, lightly brush the sides of the saucepan with a pastry brush dipped in water to prevent crystallization. Pour the caramelized sugar into the 10-inch cake pan. Let the mixture harden. Pour the egg and milk mixture on top of the caramelized sugar.

Place in the oven a rimmed sheet pan or roasting pan large enough to hold the 10-inch cake pan. Place the flan pan on top of the sheet pan. Carefully pour hot water into the sheet pan to a depth of approximately ½ inch.

Bake for 45 to 55 minutes, or until the flan has set. Remove the flan pan from the water bath and set the flan pan on a wire rack to cool to room temperature. Remove the sheet pan from the oven, being careful not to splatter yourself with hot water. Refrigerate the flan in the pan for 2 hours or overnight.

To unmold, run a knife around the edge of the flan. Place a plate at least 2 inches larger than the flan pan on top. Hold the plate and pan firmly in both hands and invert. The flan should slip right out with the caramel sauce pooling around the edges. Scoop or slice and serve with some of the caramelized sugar spooned on top.

OLD-FASHIONED FRUIT PIE

I've often had birthday pie instead of birthday cake, sticking candles into the pie's crust, but I knew there had to be better way. So, to add a touch of whimsy to an otherwise commonplace dessert, I cut polka dots out of the top crust; the holes make the perfect candle holders. If you have alphabet cookie cutters (or can freehand-cut the letters), cut out the name of the birthday boy or girl to personalize the pie.

Choose from old-fashioned apple, peach blueberry, or strawberry rhubarb filling; the recipes follow.

Serves 10 to 12 people

PIE DOUGH

I've been using this pie dough recipe for more than thirty years. It is rich and buttery, with a touch of flakiness—the perfect shell for our classic fruit pies and for chocolate cream pie (filled with our Chocolate Pudding, page 19, and topped with fresh whipped cream).

Yield: top and bottom crust for a 9- or 10-inch pie

Have on hand a 9- or 10-inch pie pan.

In a food processor, pulse, just to combine:
- 3 cups all-purpose flour
- 2 tablespoons sugar
- 1 teaspoon kosher salt

Add:
- 6 ounces (1½ sticks) cold unsalted butter, cubed
- ¼ cup vegetable shortening

Pulse until the butter is the size of peas in the mixture.

Transfer the mixture to a medium bowl.

Have on hand:
- 1 cup ice water

Add 8 tablespoons of the ice water to the butter and flour mixture, distributing evenly. Mix and gather the dough into a ball. If the dough is still dry or crumbly, add more water 1 tablespoon at a time until you are able to form the dough into a ball.

Divide the dough evenly and form it into 2 balls. Flatten the balls and wrap each in parchment paper or plastic wrap and refrigerate for 30 minutes (or overnight).

On a lightly floured board, roll the dough out to a ⅛-inch thickness and approximately 12 inches in diameter. To get a circular shape, turn the dough a quarter turn after each couple of passes with the rolling pin. Once you have the desired size and shape, fold one of the circles of dough in half and then in quarters. Fit the dough into the pie pan, with the point in the center of the pan, and unfold. Lift the edges of the dough to allow it to naturally fit the contour of the pan. Pressing gently, if needed, shape the dough to the sides and bottom of the pan. About 1 inch of dough should hang over the edge. Set aside.

Cut circles out of the top crust using a small round cookie cutter or the wide end of a piping tip (leaving at least a 1½-inch edge around the pie dough uncut). Alternatively, cut out the name of the birthday girl or boy with alphabet cookie cutters (leaving at least a 1½-inch edge around the pie dough uncut). Fold the dough in half and then in quarters.

Fill the prepared pie dough with the fruit filling of your choice. Top with the second dough, with the point in the center of the pan, and unfold. Press gently around the edges to form the dough to the fruit and the pan.

CONTINUES

Crimp the dough around the edge of the pan: Roll the dough over onto itself so that it rests on (or over) the lip of the pan. Press the thumb and index finger of one hand into the dough's inner edge and press the index finger and thumb of the other hand into the dough's outer edge, so that the thumb of one finger lines up between the thumb and index finger of the other. Continue around the entire edge of the piecrust. Alternatively, simply press a fork into the dough to flatten it and leave a decorative indentation.

FRUIT FILLINGS

Prepare a pie shell, as directed on page 157. Preheat the oven to 350°F with a half-sheet pan placed on the middle rack.

In a large bowl, combine:

as directed on page 157

FOR PEACH BLUEBERRY:

3 cups blueberries (fresh or frozen)
3 cups sliced peaches (fresh or frozen), approximately 5 fresh peaches
1 cup sugar
3 tablespoons instant tapioca
¼ teaspoon kosher salt
2 tablespoons fresh lemon juice

FOR APPLE:

8 Granny Smith apples, peeled, cored, and sliced
⅔ cup sugar (or up to ¾ cup if you like it sweeter)
2 tablespoons all-purpose flour
¾ teaspoon ground cinnamon
¼ teaspoon ground nutmeg
⅛ teaspoon kosher salt
2 tablespoons fresh lemon juice

FOR STRAWBERRY RHUBARB:

1 pound rhubarb, cut into ½-inch pieces
2 pints fresh strawberries, hulled
1½ teaspoons grated orange zest
1 cup sugar
¼ cup plus 1 tablespoon all-purpose flour
3 tablespoons instant tapioca

Pour the fruit mixture into the prepared pie shell.

Evenly distribute over the top:
1 tablespoon unsalted butter, cut into ½-inch cubes

Place the folded top pie dough on top of the filling and unfold. Crimp the pie dough as directed opposite. Place the pie on the hot half-sheet pan and bake for 1 hour, or until the juices are bubbling and the crust is lightly browned. Cool on a wire rack.

♥ *Kids can* ♥

Kids can help with so many steps of making a pie, from peeling apples and measuring spices to pulsing pie dough in a food processor and "playing" with the rolling pin. My mom taught me at a young age to crimp a pie shell; for a simpler technique, let the kids press a fork around the crust edge for a decorative finish. —Liv

Templates

The collection of templates we used to create the cookies and Chocolate Method decorations in this book are on the following pages. To achieve the correct size for the templates, each template should be increased. The percentage needed to enlarge is listed below the template image. This can be done on a photocopy machine or by scanning and increasing the size in a photo or drawing program, then printing.

Woodland Fairies
Pages 42–44
Enlarge 200%

Miss Pink Accessories
Pages 70–72
Enlarge 200%

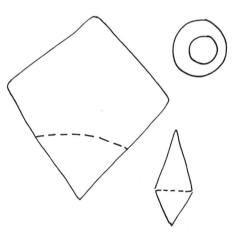

Dinosaur Tooth, Plate, and Eye
Pages 90–91
Enlarge 150%

Coffin
Pages 146–147
Shown at 100%

Teacups and Teapots
Pages 46–47
Enlarge 150%

Bed Headboard
Pages 54–56
Enlarge 200%

Bed Footboard
Pages 54–56
Enlarge 200%

Animals
Pages 130–132
Enlarge 200%

Out of This World Cupcake Segments
Pages 106–107
Enlarge 200%

Farm Animals
Pages 126–128
Enlarge 200%

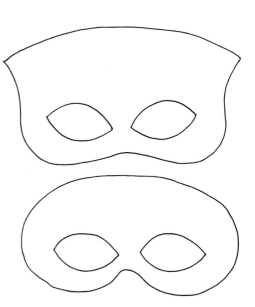

Masquerade Cookies
Pages 144–145
Enlarge 200%

Fire Truck Cake Accessories
Pages 100–101
Enlarge 150%

Cauldron Handle
Pages 141–143
Shown at 100%

Treasure Chest Lock
Pages 84–85
Shown at 100%

Pirate Hat for Cookies
Page 87
Enlarge 150%

3-D Fishbowl
Page 134
Enlarge 200%

Rabbit for Abracadabra! Cake
Pages 122–123
Enlarge 200%

Sand Castle Cake Sea Horse, Door, and Window
Pages 92–94
Enlarge 200%

Ice Cream Cone Cupcakes
Pages 118–119
Enlarge 200%

Rocket Cake Accessories
Pages 102–103
Enlarge 200%

Circus Characters and Accessories
Pages 110–112
Enlarge 200%

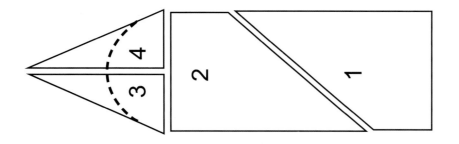

Silo for Barn
Pages 126–128
Enlarge 200%

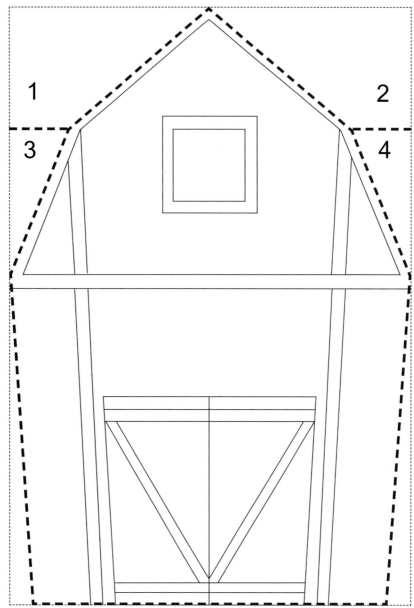

Barn
Pages 126–128
Enlarge 200%

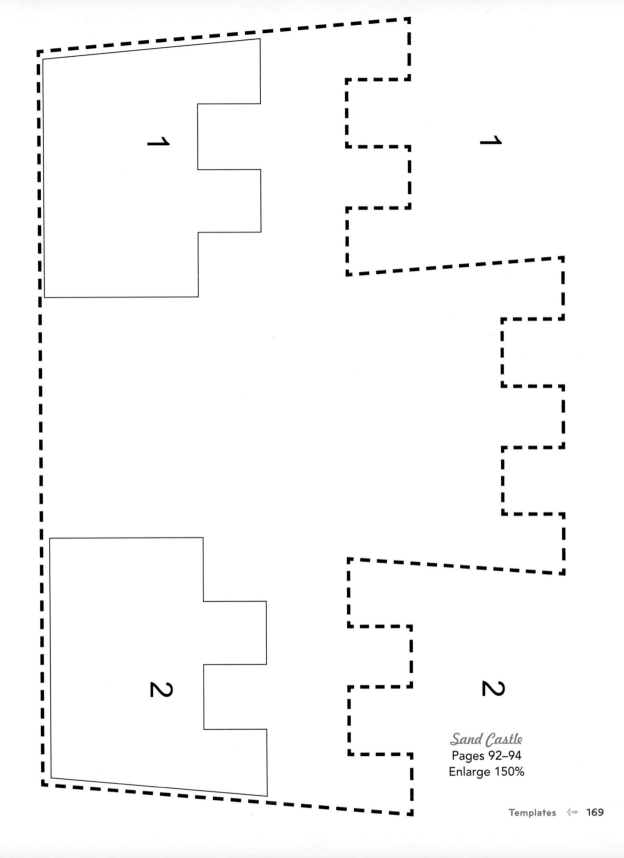

1

1

2

2

Sand Castle
Pages 92–94
Enlarge 150%

Measurement Conversions

At the bakery we weigh all of our ingredients, but we broke down all of our recipes into cup measurements for the book and the home cook. For those of you who like to weigh your ingredients, here are some basic conversions from cups to ounces and grams. Weigh or measure the dry ingredients before sifting.

	CUPS	WEIGHT IN OUNCES	WEIGHT IN GRAMS
all-purpose flour	1 cup	5 ounces	141.747 g
cake flour	1 cup	3.5 ounces	99.2233 g
cocoa powder	1 cup	4 ounces	113.398 g
granulated sugar	1 cup	7 ounces	113.398 g
brown sugar	1 cup	8 ounces	226.796 g
confectioners' sugar	1 cup	4 ounces	113.398 g
butter	1 cup	8 ounces	226.796 g
1 large egg	scant ¼ cup	1.67 ounces	47.34 g
1 extra-large egg	¼ cup	2 ounces	56.7 g
12 large egg whites	1 cup		
	CUPS	LIQUID OUNCES	LIQUID MEASUREMENTS
milk	1 cup	8 ounces	.2366g Liter

Suppliers

The suppliers listed below stock baking and decorating tools and ingredients that are not readily available in supermarkets.

Williams-Sonoma

Retail locations throughout the United States
877-812-6235
www.williams-sonoma.com
In addition to carrying a wide range of bakeware (including many of the pans used in this book) and specialty baking ingredients, this national chain also carries great decorating starter kits.

Wilton Industries, Inc.

2240 West 75th Street
Woodridge, IL 60517
800-794-5866
www.wilton.com
Decorating tools, bakeware (Mini Wonder Mold and egg-shaped pan), display equipment, wafer chocolate, and food coloring (candy colors and gel colors).

New York Cake and Baking Distributors, Inc.

56 West 22nd Street
New York, NY 10010
800-942-2539 or 212-675-7953
www.nycake.com
Decorating supplies including food coloring, pastry bags, and tips.

King Arthur Flour Baker's Catalogue

P.O. Box 876
Norwich, VT 05055-0876
800-827-6836
Flagship Store:
135 Route 5 South
Norwich, VT 05055-0876
802-649-3361
www.kingarthurflour.com
Everything from cake pans to electric mixers, specialty ingredients to chocolate, decorating tools, and display equipment.

The Foodcrafter's Supply Catalog

P.O. Box 442
Waukon, IA 52172-0442
800-776-0575
www.kitchenkrafts.com
A wide range of baking and decorating tools from candy making equipment to bakeware and display.

Pfeil and Holing

58-15 Northern Boulevard
Woodside, NY 11377
800-247-7955
www.cakedeco.com
This is where the Bakehouse purchases the majority of our decorating tools and colors (Chefmaster candy colors and liquid gel colors).

The following craft stores have retail locations throughout the United States. They carry cake decorating and candy making supplies including bakeware, confectioners' chocolate, food coloring, and piping and icing tools. Store locators are available on their Web sites.

Michaels
800-642-4235
www.michaels.com

A.C. Moore
888-226-6673
www.acmoore.com

Jo-Ann Fabric and Craft Stores
888-739-4120
www.joann.com

Miscellaneous online retailers

www.foosecookiecutters.com
Great selection of cookie cutters.

www.thecookiecuttershop.com
Where we found our 3-inch birthday balloon cookie cutter.

www.zatarains.com
Our source for root beer extract.

www.countrykitchensa.com
Sells a variety of candy and cake decorating supplies, as well as high-ratio shortening.

www.cookscakeandcandy.com
Sells a variety of candy and cake decorating supplies, as well as high-ratio shortening.

www.cellodepot.com
Sells precut squares of cellophane.

Index

Chocolate Sponge Roll filled with
Whipped Cream

Cheesecake

Citrus Sponge Roll filled with
Whipped Milk Chocolate Ganache

Sour Cream Chocolate Cake
filled with Cookies and Cream

Pumpkin Spice Cake filled with
Caramel Pudding Cream

Freckled Orange Cake

Raspberry Swirl Cake

Marble Pound Cake

Peanut Butter Cake filled with
Whipped Milk Chocolate Ganache

Milk Chocolate Cake filled with
Chocolate Pudding Cream

White Chocolate Cake filled
with Whipped White Chocolate
Ganache

Banana Chocolate–Chocolate
Chip Cake filled with Sliced
Bananas and Whipped Cream